THE WANTON JESUIT AND THE WAYWARD SAINT

A Tale of Sex, Religion,
and Politics in Eighteenth-Century France

The WANTON JESUIT

and THE

WAYWARD SAINT

MITA CHOUDHURY

THE PENNSYLVANIA STATE UNIVERSITY PRESS
UNIVERSITY PARK, PENNSYLVANIA

Earlier versions of portions of this book have appeared in "A Betrayal of Trust: The Jesuits and Quietism in Eighteenth-Century France," *Common Knowledge* 15, no. 2 (2009): 164–80, © 2009 Duke University Press, all rights reserved; "'Carnal Quietism': Embodying Anti-Jesuit Polemics in the Catherine Cadière Affair, 1731," *Eighteenth-Century Studies* 39, no. 2 (2006): 173–86; and "Female Mysticism and the Public Sphere in Eighteenth-Century France," in *Under the Veil*, ed. Katherine Quinsey (Newcastle: Cambridge Scholars Press, 2012), 145–71, published with the permission of Cambridge Scholars Publishing.

Library of Congress
Cataloging-in-Publication Data

Choudhury, Mita, 1964– , author.
The wanton Jesuit and the wayward saint : a tale of sex, religion, and politics in eighteenth-century France / Mita Choudhury.
 pages cm
Summary: "Investigates the scandalous 1731 trial in which a young woman in the south of France accused her Jesuit confessor of seduction, heresy, abortion, and bewitchment. Examines this trial in the context of growing public disenchantment with the church and the monarchy"—Provided by publisher.
Includes bibliographical references and index.
ISBN 978-0-271-07081-0 (cloth : alk. paper)
1. Girard, Jean-Baptiste, 1680–1733—Trials, litigation, etc.
2. Cadière, Marie-Catherine, 1709– —Trials, litigation, etc.
3. Trials (Seduction)—France—Aix-en-Provence—History—18th century.
4. Jesuits—France—History—18th century.
5. Sexual misconduct by clergy—France—History—18th century.
6. Jansenists—France—History—18th century.
I. Title.

KJV135.G57C48 2015
345.44'0253—dc23
2015022780

The Pennsylvania State University Press is a member of the Association of American University Presses.

It is the policy of The Pennsylvania State University Press to use acid-free paper. Publications on uncoated stock satisfy the minimum requirements of American National Standard for Information Sciences—Permanence of Paper for Printed Library Material, ANSI Z39.48–1992.

This book is printed on paper that contains 30% post-consumer waste.

Additional credits: Details on pages iii, 1 (fig. 6), 11, 13, 33, 47 (fig. 6), 69, 89, 107 (fig. 9), 125, 127, 153 (fig. 11), and 171 (fig. 12) are from *Historische print- en dicht-tafereelen van Jan Baptist Girard, en juffrou Maria Catharina Cadiere*. Courtesy of Bibliothèque Méjanes, Aix-en-Provence.

Printed and bound by SHERIDAN BOOKS
Composed in MINION PRO
Printed on NATURES NATURAL
Bound in ARRESTOX

For

SUHAS CHOUDHURY (1935–2011)

and

DOLLY CHOUDHURY

Contents

Illustrations

Acknowledgments

The inspiration for this book came from two sources that have enriched my career as an historian and a teacher. I became aware of the Girard/Cadière affair while doing research on convents and nuns; Sarah Maza, mentor *par excellence*, told me about this "great story" from Provence in the early eighteenth century. I filed it away, not fully appreciating the complexity of the affair. I returned to the Cadière scandal when I began teaching at Vassar College. Ever curious and fearless, Vassar students surprised me with a bombardment of questions on Jansenism and religious politics, topics I introduced apologetically. I soon realized that this trial was the perfect vehicle to carry students and readers into the world of eighteenth-century religious dissent and politics, to understand the connections between gender, sexuality, and religion, and to appreciate how a public was formed in the Old Regime.

The research and writing of *The Wanton Jesuit and the Wayward Saint* was made possible thanks to the following sources. Vassar College has generously funded this project via the Mellon Faculty Enhancement grant, the Gabrielle Beck fund, the Olin College Fund, and the Anne McNiff Tatlock '61 Endowment for Strategic Faculty Support. I also wish to thank the following at Vassar College for helping me procure these funds: the Dean of Faculty's office, the Committee on Research, Pinar Batur, Anne Pike-Tay, and Amanda Thornton. I am grateful to the National Endowment for the Humanities for a fellowship that allowed me to give my full attention to the writing. I owe special thanks to Judith Dollenmayer of the Vassar Grants Office for her enthusiasm for the project and for her willingness to go above and beyond any reasonable request for help!

No historian can undertake a project without the generous assistance of librarians and archivists. Monsieur Philippe Ferrand provided such assistance during my visits to the Bibliothèque Méjanes in Aix-en-Provence. I would also like to thank the staffs at the Bibliothèque nationale de France and the Bibliothèque de l'Arsenal in Paris, the Bibliothèque municipale d'Avignon (Médiathèque Ceccano), the Archives départementales in Aix, the Archives départementales and the Bibliothèque municipale in Toulon, and the Bibliothèque municipale in Dijon. Special thanks also go to Madame Gaëlle Neuser at the Musée Paul Arbaud in Aix. I remain especially grateful to Valérie Guittienne-Mürger and Fabien Vandermarq, who always give me a warm welcome and access to the many treasures at the Bibliothèque de la Société de Port-Royal on the rue Saint-Jacques in Paris. In the United States, Vassar College's interlibrary loan staff has almost never said "no." And thanks go to Ron Patkus, head of Vassar's Special Collections, for his patience and support.

The community of French historians and scholars has been essential to the development of this book. Conversations with Dale Van Kley, Thomas Kaiser, Bob Kreiser, and Jeffrey Merrick have been enormously fruitful for considering eighteenth-century French politics. Comments on conference papers from Joan Landes, Dan Smail, and Chuck Walton gave me much food for thought. Yet again, Sarah Maza deserves special thanks for her comments on a paper I delivered more than a decade ago on first starting the Cadière project; she also gave me invaluable feedback during the final throes of manuscript completion. Throughout this project, Daniella Kostroun has been a wonderful colleague and friend, willing to provide advice at a moment's notice. At different times, Linda Lierheimer, Lynn Mollenauer, and Leslie Tuttle have asked hard questions and provided great insight. Although we have never met, Stéphane Lamotte generously shared his dissertation with me, and I remain in awe of his research.

My experience teaching at Vassar was the impetus for this book, and Vassar has offered friendships that have made this book possible. Heartfelt thanks go to Lydia Murdoch, who provided unwavering support and caring through every stage of this book. Susan Hiner also read portions of the manuscript and helped me with various translations. Karen Robertson enthusiastically listened to my ideas about women and mysticism after I gave a talk at a Women's Studies First Friday event before a group of generous feminist scholars from different disciplines across campus. Tom Hill and Brian Lukacher helped locate information on satyrs, a quest that came out of an "offhand," yet insightful, comment. My accountability group, which included Curtis Dozier, Laura Kasson-Fiss, Julie

Park, and Susan Trumbetta, gave me the courage to write. Both Jim Merrell and Jim Olsen provided incisive and insightful feedback during the early stages of the project. I cannot thank Barbara Monaco enough for her support during some difficult times. And Michelle Whalen deserves a standing ovation for her cheerful willingness to help whenever asked. Over the years, various student research assistants—Alyssa Aquino, Peter Chesney, Elizabeth Cole, and Henk Isom—helped gather and organize information.

I extend deep thanks to Eleanor Goodman at Penn State University Press, who enthusiastically supported this project from the moment she read my proposal. No one could ask for a better editor. Charlee Redman showed amazing patience during the final stages of the book. Thanks to Laura Reed-Morrisson for her meticulous editing. I would also like to thank the anonymous readers for thoughtful, thorough comments that strengthened the book.

The writing of a book is inextricably interwoven with one's life. My family has given me support that cannot be sufficiently acknowledged in words. John Reisbord has been the model husband, father, editor, and historian. His belief in me and his generous willingness to be a single parent at times made this book possible. Sophie and Nicky Reisbord grew up with this book; the labor I experienced with Nicky coincided with the completion of "'Carnal Quietism': Embodying Anti-Jesuit Polemics in the Catherine Cadière Affair, 1731," published by *Eighteenth-Century Studies*. My children bring a richness to my life that cannot be measured. My love and thanks for their humor and proud acceptance that their mother is a "French historian."

Sadly, this project has been shaped by death as well as birth, a reminder that life must have both. My father, Suhas Choudhury, became ill and passed away during the writing. While there is now a gap that cannot be filled, I will always be grateful for the love and support he and my mother, Dolly Choudhury, have given me. Both, in their individual ways, showed me the vitality of faith, which helped me appreciate the complexity of religious culture in the eighteenth century. They believed, and continue to believe, that an intellectual life matters and instilled in me the importance of being open to different people, places, and ideas. Growing up, I lived in and traveled to countries throughout Asia, Africa, Europe, and North America. This experience enabled me to be a South Asian woman who, of all things, studies early modern France! For all this, I dedicate this book to my parents.

INTRODUCTION

In June 1749, lawyer Édmond Barbier noted the arrest of Denis Diderot, a "man of wit and *belles-lettres*," who would later make key contributions to the French Enlightenment.[1] He believed that the Paris police had incarcerated the *philosophe* because they thought he had written a lewd novel, *Thérèse philosophe ou mémoires pour servir à l'histoire du P. Dirrag, et de Mademoiselle Éradice*. After five months in the Château de Vincennes, Diderot was released, despite the police's conviction that he was "dangerous, talking about holy Mysteries with contempt."[2] Authorities suspected that he had composed a number of sacrilegious texts but, in fact, did not connect him with *Thérèse philosophe*.[3] The real author remained shadowy, but the book became the century's best-selling pornographic novel. Mixing sizzling sex with impious philosophy, the heroine, Thérèse, chronicles how various mentors—a libertine noblewoman, a cleric, and a courtesan—gave her a well-rounded sexual and intellectual education.

Barbier was less concerned with the novel's blasphemous content and more excited by the fact that it included "the history of Father Girard, Jesuit, and the demoiselle Cadière in Aix-en-Provence, which created such a stir."[4] This "history" appears in Thérèse's account of the affair between her friend Mademoiselle Éradice, who "loved God like one loves her lover," and the famous confessor Father Dirrag.[5] While "all of Europe" knew their story, Thérèse is privy to a more intimate episode.[6] At Éradice's invitation, she hides in a closet to observe Father Dirrag's spiritual "instructions." Éradice promises, "You'll see . . . the power of my spiritual exercises and the stages of repentance through which the good father is leading me to sainthood. And you'll no longer be able to doubt the ecstasies and the raptures which these exercises produce."[7]

Through a crack, Thérèse watches Dirrag teach his enthusiastic young penitent the mystical principle of "oubliez-vous, laissez-faire"—"forget yourself and let yourself go." Éradice kneels in prayer, buttocks exposed, as he whips her while quoting the Bible and then declares, "You should now be . . . in a state of the most perfect contemplation; your soul should be detached from your senses. If my child does not disappoint my holy expectations, she sees nothing, hears nothing, and feels nothing."[8] Having urged her to ignore all physical sensations, the confessor penetrates her from behind, telling Éradice that what she feels is a segment of the original cord St. Francis of Assisi wore around his waist. Thérèse observes "His Holiness" during orgasm: "He was like a satyr, his lips frothing, his mouth ajar, grinding his teeth and snorting like a bull."[9] After Dirrag leaves the room, the ecstatic Éradice exclaims, "Yes, I have seen Paradise unveiled; I've experienced angelic bliss. . . . By virtue of the holy cord my soul was almost freed from matter."[10] Clearly, the distinction between mystic and sexual union was blurred at best.

This seduction scene juxtaposed blind faith and clerical hypocrisy. According to historian Robert Darnton, the 1748 publication of *Thérèse philosophe* belonged to a transformative moment in French intellectual culture. Diderot, Montesquieu, Voltaire, and Rousseau all published substantial works at midcentury. Just three years after *Thérèse philosophe*, the first two volumes of the monumental *Encyclopédie* appeared.[11] Erotic fiction and a massive compendium of knowledge may seem to have little in common. However, Darnton locates *Thérèse philosophe* in "the bawdy, naughty, cheeky world of the early Enlightenment, where everything was held up to question and nothing was sacred."[12] The novel belonged to a distinctive Enlightenment genre, the *livre philosophique*, which fused frenzied sexual activity with philosophical deliberations on the soul, morality, and individual happiness—the same weighty topics scrutinized by the *Encyclopédie*.[13]

Pairing *Thérèse philosophe* with an Enlightenment classic suggests that the novel's secular outlook reflects the beginning of a new, more "modern" mindset. There is much to support this claim. For example, the abbé T . . . , one of Thérèse's mentors, pontificates on the incompatibility between Christian teachings and nature: "To be the perfect Christian, one must be ignorant, to believe blindly, to renounce all pleasures . . . , to abandon one's relatives, friends, to maintain one's virginity, in a word do everything that is contrary to nature."[14]

However, returning to Édmond Barbier, we see that *his* first impulse was not to connect the novel with Enlightenment philosophy but to recall the story of Jean-Baptiste Girard (Dirrag) and Catherine Cadière (Éradice), central figures in a trial that had rocked France seventeen years earlier. This scandal began in late 1730 when Catherine Cadière, the twenty-year-old daughter of an olive oil merchant in Toulon, accused the fifty-year-old Jesuit Jean-Baptiste Girard of shocking crimes in the confessional. Their relationship—one of confessor and penitent—began quietly enough in 1728. Within a year, however, the young woman's body had become a battleground between demonic possession and divine ecstasy. Friends and neighbors believed that Catherine was on the brink of sainthood, destined to be another Teresa of Avila or Catherine of Siena. But the story of Catherine the saint and Father Girard the saint-maker turned sour. In November 1730, Catherine denounced Father Girard for sexual misconduct. A few months later, the torrid scandal became a fraught judicial conflict.

Although the trial took place in Aix-en-Provence, four hundred miles from Paris, all France followed the sensational case. Private correspondence, official exchanges, and police records from 1731 indicate that everyone in the realm had an opinion on it. Elites updated each other on the voluminous legal briefs, or *mémoires judiciaires*, in which lawyers made inflammatory claims about evil Jesuits and false mystics, sexual misdeeds and conspiracies. English and German translations quickly appeared, suggesting that much of Europe was equally fascinated. Periodicals, pamphlets, songs, and other polemics circulated in cafés and taverns, taking aim at everyone from Father Girard to the judges.

The story's salacious details may explain this fervid interest. Catherine claimed that Father Girard had urged her "to accept a state of [demonic] possession," to embrace indecent visions, and, finally, to embrace him.[15] Catherine soon found herself yet more compromised in a pregnancy that Father Girard then terminated with an abortifacient. Soon after her revelations to her new confessor (and possible lover), Father Nicolas Girieux, Catherine went to authorities in Toulon to seek justice.

Clumsy official handling of the case aggravated the scandal. By January 1731, matters in Toulon were stalemated. Louis XV then commanded the region's royal judicial courts, the parlement of Provence, to try the case. Meanwhile, Cardinal André-Hercule de Fleury, then prime minister, and Chancellor Henri d'Aguesseau corresponded with powerful individuals in Toulon and Aix, hoping to quash the affair quickly and quietly. It was too late. The presiding judges were at each other's throats, and the trial dragged on into the fall. Moreover, the affair divided the public, whose interpretations of the trial read like a "he said/she said" melodrama. Indeed, the marquis d'Argens observed how the affair created rifts everywhere—within families, between lovers.[16]

We, too, are drawn to the details of Catherine and Girard's relationship. What really happened behind closed doors? The truth is lost to us, buried under layers of accusations and the passage of time. Instead, I would draw readers' attention to how men and women of the eighteenth century reacted to the scandal. Intervention by the realm's most powerful individuals and the public's passionate responses show that this trial was not simply about a sexual liaison between an aging cleric and his young penitent. Jean-Baptiste Girard conjured up images of Urbain Grandier and Louis Gaufridy, seventeenth-century priests burned at the stake for witchcraft. The Girard/Cadière affair may have started as the last witchcraft trial in French history, but, at bottom, it was a political affair.[17] For readers today, the trial sheds light on two intersecting phenomena: growing uncertainties about the role of the sacred in buttressing the power of traditional figures of authority in French society, and the compelling presence of the public in eighteenth-century politics and religion. While *Thérèse philosophe* used the Girard/Cadière scandal as a vehicle to denounce Christian teachings, this book examines how the affair was firmly rooted in the world of faith as well as political and religious dissent.

Over the past three decades, historians have shown that religious disillusionment emerged not out of the Enlightenment but out of the divisions erupting around Jansenism, a contentious French Catholic sect with origins in the early seventeenth century.[18] Even as the Catholic Church vigorously supported free will, Jansenists (as their detractors called them) steadfastly believed in predestination, the notion that only God—not human choices or actions—determined salvation. Jansenists seemed to undermine the hierarchy that elevated clergy over laity. In defense of individual conscience, Jansenists sometimes defied ordained priests, challenging the notion that a priest must mediate between God and the lay individual.

4

To modern readers, such theological issues are arcane, but for early mod-ern men and women, questions about eternal salvation and religious conformity were intensely relevant to their souls and their community. Thus, the clergy occupied a central place in the lives of the laity. For many devout persons, relationships between confessors and penitents rested on trust and reverence. The Cadière trial exposed the fragile negotiation between the private world of confession and the public authority of the clergy.

The case also gained political urgency as the conflict over Jansenism intensified after the anti-Jansenist bull *Unigenitus* appeared in 1713. For the aged Louis XIV, Jansenism undermined the absolutist principle of *un roi, une loi, une foi*—"one king, one law, one faith." On the grounds of conscience, Jansenists resisted the king's authority as well as the Church's chain of command. Jansenists also espoused a more "republican" Church in which bishops and church officials were not appointed by the king but elected by the clergy.[19] Jansenism threatened Louis XIV's vision of a well-ordered body politic that prized authority and tolerated no religious dissent. By persuading Pope Clement XI to publish *Unigenitus*, Louis XIV sought to stamp out the "heresy" of Jansenism. But immediately after his death in 1715, large numbers of clergy lodged official appeals against *Unigenitus*, supported by prestigious institutions such as the Sorbonne and the parlement of Paris. Outside Paris, Provence became an important node of resistance to the bull.

This conflict had reached a flash point on the eve of the Girard/Cadière affair. During the late 1720s, Cardinal Fleury relaunched a campaign to cleanse the clergy of Jansenism. Ultramontane, or pro-papal, bishops now tirelessly pursued suspected Jansenists, who were often imprisoned or exiled. On March 24, 1730, Louis XV declared that *Unigenitus* was "the law of church and state," which outraged the parlements and further politicized the Jansenist movement. Then, in July 1731, Jansenist devotees, known as the *convulsionnaires*, writhed and screamed in the Paris cemetery of Saint-Médard. For some, their behavior was miraculous; for others, an embarrassment.[20] With their backs against the wall, Jansenists found a godsend in the Girard/Cadière affair, especially since they held the Jesuits responsible for all their woes.

For Catherine Cadière's supporters, Jansenist and non-Jansenist alike, the trial was not just about one wanton priest but the pernicious influence of France's most powerful religious order—the Jesuits, known formally as the Society of Jesus. Jesuit priests acted as royal confessors, spiritual directors, and educators, positions with privileged access to the king and to elite

French families. Many contemporaries, including ecclesiastics and men of law, regarded the Society as too influential and too independent, beyond the power of the Crown and leaders of the French Church. The Jesuits were widely seen as foreign interlopers seeking to usurp the king's authority and control his subjects.[21] Jansenists loathed the Jesuits, who were the Catholic Church's fiercest gatekeepers of free will and clerical superiority. The Jesuits saw Jansenists as heretics whose beliefs verged on Calvinism. This mutual antipathy only worsened with the arrival of *Unigenitus*, a document the Jansenists claimed that the Jesuits had orchestrated.

Despite the Society's power, anti-Jesuit sentiment seemed to gain traction. In the years before the Cadière trial, anonymous pamphlets spread anti-Jesuit messages to "expose" Jesuit immorality and the Society's threat to political and social order. Now, the Girard affair dealt a serious blow to the Jesuits' reputation and added another layer to the black legend of the "wily Jesuit."[22]

In the long run, far more was at stake than individual reputations. The public disputes over Jansenism destabilized the sacred underpinnings of authority in early modern French society. Divine-right kingship was at the core of Bourbon absolutism. The king's authority was legitimate and incontestable because it was God-given; in turn, the most Catholic king was expected to uphold Catholic doctrine. Furthermore, the power invested in the realm's institutions and leaders, like the parlements and their magistrates, was also sacred because the king sanctioned it.

But like the acrimonious debates over *Unigenitus*, the Cadière scandal precipitated intense, often hostile scrutiny of such authority. No evidence exists that Catherine herself had Jansenist sympathies, although there is evidence that both her brother Étienne-Thomas and Father Nicolas did. More importantly, certain men of law, such as attorney general Jacques-Joseph Gaufridy and the lawyer François Gastaud, as well as satirists in Provence and Paris, hated the Jesuits and relentlessly criticized *Unigenitus*. Their efforts on behalf of Catherine Cadière or, more accurately, against Father Girard transformed the trial from a local sex scandal into a referendum on religious authority. Their strategy? They appealed to the public through inflammatory arguments intrinsically tied to the campaign against *Unigenitus* and the Jesuits. The Cadière affair highlighted the dangers of clerical overreach to the spiritual and, indeed, physical welfare of French men and women.[23]

During the summer of 1731, these claims hardly seemed exaggerated. The Jesuits' efforts to protect Father Girard at all costs prompted popular fear that the order violated the rights of the king's subjects. Moreover, magistrates who supported Father Girard were accused of blind devotion and corruption. Ultimately, this animosity rebounded on the Crown: Cardinal Fleury was believed to be in league with the Jesuits and, at the very least, Louis XV appeared unable to control either faction. Religious quarrels, unrestrained clerical powers, and repressive Crown measures contributed to the "desacralization" of the French monarchy—the gradual erosion of divine-right ideology and royal prestige. A cameo of the larger conflicts around *Unigenitus* and the Jesuits, the notorious Cadière affair played an important role in this process.

Lawyers' and polemicists' efforts to involve the public during the trial dovetailed with an important shift in Jansenism in the early 1730s: its expanding support among men of law, the bourgeoisie, and the *menu peuple* of Paris. By 1733 and well into the 1750s, men of law actively intervened on behalf of the appellant clergy; they more or less replaced theologians and bishops as opponents of *Unigenitus*. Barbier repeatedly noted that the "people" of Paris were avid Jansenists whose zeal had been "ignited by a number of priests who have been removed" from their parishes.[24] Similarly, the Girard/Cadière trial shows how the disputes over clerical abuse occurred not only in ecclesiastical councils and judicial chambers but also in homes and in the streets. Contemporary accounts detail how, in the summer of 1731, crowds comprising elites and nonelites gathered at Catherine's prison in Aix and around the courthouse where the Provençal magistrates were deliberating. In the days following the October 10 verdict, riots and celebrations in Toulon caused property damage and led some to fear for their lives.

Despite these violent episodes, the public did not simply represent a mob, nor was it a passive audience. Lawyers and polemicists consistently presented their arguments before "public opinion" and asked the public to identify with Catherine: *her* cause was the cause of *all* believers and *all* French subjects. Verses vilifying Girard painted Catherine as the victim of a Jesuit seducer who had also violated her spiritual and civic rights. Catherine's lawyer, Jean-Baptiste Chaudon, described the public as "so enlightened, so rightly the adjudicator of virtue and of merit, Sovereign Arbitrator of men's reputations, the true Judge of their innocence."[25] He thus endowed the public with an authoritative, potentially decisive position.

Over the past few decades, historians have emphasized how the process of desacralization and the emergence of public opinion became key features in French politics during the 1750s. According to Keith Baker, "French politics broke out of the absolutist mold. The reign of silence imposed by an absolute monarch could no longer contain debates and contestations that made increasingly explicit appeal to a world of public opinion beyond the traditional circle of institutional actors."[26] The Crown was besieged from all sides. In the summer of 1750, the marquis d'Argenson remarked in his journal how the people of Paris called their king "Herod," referring to the notorious Jewish king responsible for the Massacre of the Innocents.[27] Instead of toeing the line, the princes and the parlement of Paris challenged the Crown's policies. At the same time, the Jansenist conflict was reignited, thanks to ultramontane bishops and priests who refused to administer the sacraments to suspected Jansenists.

These events of the mid-eighteenth century signified a "moment" in French political history, much as the publication of *Thérèse philosophe* was a "moment" in the same period's intellectual history.[28] They marked the emergence of a public, an abstract entity signifying a secular community of reasoning individuals. This public possessed a more "modern" sensibility in which the norm was not to obey but to question rationally. This perspective of a "public" and its challenges to authority points toward the French Revolution. Yet just two years after the Girard/Cadière trial, Voltaire published the *Philosophical Letters*, which one critic described as "the first bomb dropped on the Old Regime."[29]

Readers may ask what difference twenty years makes in identifying a public that can express seditious statements. The Girard/Cadière trial represented a watershed event that allows us to think beyond a "prerevolutionary" moment and more about the eighteenth century as a long sequence of turmoil and transition. As Thomas Kaiser states, "it is undoubtedly true that after 1750 rhetorical appeals to the public increased and the authority of public opinion grew. But by then, the monarchy and the public had been tangled in a tumultuous embrace for a long time."[30] Even in the decades before the 1730s, political reformers and financiers appealed to "enlightened" public opinion. Skepticism and irreverence punctuated popular songs and poems that drifted around the cafés frequented by ordinary people—people whose lives were deeply intertwined with Catholic practice and belief.[31]

The Girard/Cadière trial illuminates how disaffection and dissent grew within the complex world of French Catholicism. It illustrates what Dale Van Kley has argued for decades—that religious conflict was pivotal in bringing about the demise of the Old Regime.[32] The affair coincided with a time when the Catholic community was unstable and contested as a result of the Jansenist controversies. In the weeks after the trial, ultramontane bishops and royal officials believed that the Catholic faith was threatened and that support for Catherine equaled sedition and disorder. Through the Cadière affair, we also see the "politics of contestation" evolving outside legal institutions and the rhetoric of constitutionalism. Public opinion coalesced around a scandal that began as a private affair, originating in a world inhabited by most French subjects. Although the Jesuits were often cast as foreign, an imaginary Other, in reality they were integral to people's lives as priests and advisors, making the Cadière affair much more traumatic.

We might think of eighteenth-century French society as a fabric woven of strong, sustaining threads of the sacred, of authority, of obedience. The Girard/Cadière affair tore fiercely at this fabric. In time, the strain would cause eighteenth-century French men and women to grow disenchanted with their church, with their authorities, and at last with their king.

The GIRARD/CADIÈRE RELATIONSHIP

A COMMUNITY OF FAITH

The enduring fascination with Catherine Cadière and Jean-Baptiste Girard rests on their supposedly illicit relationship and the sensational accusations they made against one another. Legal briefs, poems, gossip, and rumor, circulating through France and Europe, kept the scandal alive and fresh. For over two centuries, narratives of the case have resurfaced in fictional forms, religious treatises, and scholarly discussions. But we should not forget that this *cause célèbre* began in Toulon, where people and events were shaped from the start by the town's particular social, political, and cultural dynamics.[1]

Located in southern France on the Mediterranean coast, Toulon, to many eighteenth-century observers, seemed a world away from France's cultural capital, Paris, and its political center, Versailles, seat of the Bourbon monarchy. Nonetheless, it would be a mistake to overstate Toulon's social and economic isolation. Its harbor was home to important components of France's royal navy, which drew a constant flow of newcomers, including naval officers and royal officials who competed for status with

MAP 1

France in the 1760s. From *Atlas moderne, ou Collection de cartes sur toutes les parties du globe terrestre* (Paris: Lattré, [1762–1773]). Courtesy of Special Collections, Vassar College Library.

Toulon's native elite. The city's politics were characterized, first and foremost, by the occasionally contentious relationship between locals and outsiders who came to this remote town on the king's business.[2]

Interaction between locals and non-natives also influenced Toulon's religious life and was an undercurrent of the relationship between Catherine and Father Girard. Catherine's religious sensibilities directly reflected the "baroque" Catholicism of Provence, where visual, visceral faith was often central to neighborhoods and friendships. Striving to improve her inner life, the sheltered Catherine sought spiritual guidance. Ultimately, she found it not in a local priest but in Father Girard from the eastern province of Franche-Comté. Significantly, Girard was a member of the Society of Jesus. As a Jesuit, he embodied all the authority of France's most powerful clerical order, which enjoyed the patronage of the king and the Church's top officials.

CATHERINE CADIÈRE'S TOULON

In the modern imagination, Provence has special resonance: sun-bleached farmhouses, endless fields of lavender and sunflowers, mountains on one side and breathtaking sea views on the other. This vision, perhaps best captured by Impressionist painters, has drawn millions of visitors. But in the eighteenth century, Provence was largely a transit stop. Voyagers, particularly wealthy English ones on the "grand tour," regarded Provence as an alternative route to Italy via Lyons, the second most popular destination in France after Paris. According to Tobias Smollett, "travelers, bound to the southern parts of France, generally embark in the *diligence* at Lyon, and glide down [the Rhône] with great velocity."[3] After three days, passengers took carriages from Avignon, and if they preferred sea travel, they chose the "pleasantest, but longest," road to Marseille, then east to Toulon, where they could take a ship from either city.[4]

Situated on the sea and surrounded by three mountains, Mont Faron, Mont Caume, and Mont Coudon, Toulon was the ideal Mediterranean town, blessed with palm trees and sunshine. Journeying through France during the summer of 1789, the agriculturalist Arthur Young described the route to Toulon in mixed terms: "The country to Toulon is more interesting [than Marseille]; the mountains are bolder; the sea adds to the view; and there is one passage among the rocks, where are sublime features. Nine tenths are waste mountain, and a wretched country of pines, box, and miserable aromatics, in spite of the climate."[5] But even the climate could betray. Like most of Provence, Toulon faced high winds—especially the mistral, known as the *mestral* in Provençal, which Smollett noted as "the severest that ever I felt."[6]

Thus, the world in which Catherine Cadière was raised offered contrasts between sunshine and harsh wind, great natural beauty and stark peaks—disparities mirrored in social and cultural contrasts. The city's location and its importance to the French navy guaranteed a steady flow of visitors from the outside world. On the other hand, its remoteness allowed Toulon to develop a distinct society, fortified by a distinctive religious culture.

The youngest of four children, Catherine was the only daughter of Joseph Cadière and Elisabeth Pomet. Originally from a tiny village, or *bourgade*, outside Toulon, Joseph had worked in the city for an olive oil merchant, Pomet, marrying his daughter Elisabeth in 1689.[7] It appears that at Pomet's death, Joseph took over the business.[8] In many respects, this marriage and Joseph's subsequent "promotion" suggest common themes pervasive in eighteenth-century marriage and private life. Yet unusual elements distinguished the Cadières from other members of the lower bourgeoisie of Provence.

Marriage in the early eighteenth century was not simply an institution shaped by love and attraction. While compatibility was thought necessary for a stable union, marriage was about community.[9] At stake were alliances, acquisition of property and goods, and potential social advancement. Some Provençal families adopted a more "noble" pattern, in which the single heir, generally the eldest son, acquired most of the family's property and financial assets; others chose a more equitable approach that divided family wealth based on age, need, and other factors.

No matter which pattern a family embraced, one principle remained fairly consistent. Inheritance laws in Provence, the Statuts de Provence, deliberately disadvantaged women. According to a 1778 commentary, these laws expressed the "common wish by the fathers to preserve the family name and dignity. And that can be done through male children. Girls are the ultimate term and the end of the paternal family."[10] Indeed, upon marriage, women generally relocated to their husbands' households, identifying themselves with a new family. Though they kept their maiden names, their community referred to them as "wife of. . . ."[11]

The Cadières' marriage went against the grain. For Joseph a rural man like Cadière, marrying the boss's daughter and inheriting the business was a clear step up. Conversely, Elisabeth's marriage to a man who had once worked for her father might be regarded as a step down. But unlike merchants from Nantes and Bordeaux, who prospered from an expanding and lucrative Atlantic economy, Toulon's merchants faced a stagnant economy made more difficult by slow, sometimes hazardous travel through the mountainous Massif Central to the north. Marriage as a path to upward mobility was not necessarily viable for small-scale merchants like the Pomets. Elisabeth Pomet's father seems not to have had the option of bequeathing his shop to male heirs. However, the marriage between Elisabeth and Joseph Cadière kept Pomet's olive oil trade in the hands of someone familiar with its workings.

The paramount importance of preserving the business was also reflected in arrangements after Joseph's death. The Cadières would go on to have four surviving children, with the last, Catherine, born in 1709. Catherine's father died when she was still a child, and it appears that Elisabeth took over the family business, soon to be joined by her oldest son, Laurent, whose installation as proprietor reestablished traditional patterns of inheritance. At the same time, efforts to maintain the Cadière/Pomet family business superseded *his* desire to renounce the world and become a Carthusian monk.

Where did the business of selling olive oil place this family in the local society of eighteenth-century Toulon? The Cadières lived in the western part of town on the tiny rue de l'Hôpital, off the larger rue Royale (now the rue Jean Jaurès), in the parish of Sainte-Marie.[12] Like many of Toulon's streets in this era, the rue de l'Hôpital was narrow, damp, and often dark, thanks to shadows cast by buildings. Closed sewers and regular garbage collection did not exist. We can only imagine the odor emanating from homes and businesses on the street, especially on hot days when buildings blocked the wind.[13]

The location of the Cadière residence in this part of town meant that the family inhabited a gray area between elites and working people. As small-time merchants, the family did not rank among the long-established municipal elites such as the Martinis d'Orves, the Marins, or the Gavoty or d'Antrechaux families. But as owners of their store, however small, the Cadières stood apart from the world of artisans—tanners, butchers, and workers toiling in Toulon's military arsenal. Cadière *père* may have been a simple olive oil merchant, but the family was hardly marginal. By marriage, Joseph Cadière had established himself as a respected proprietor of a stable business. Moreover, the Cadières lived in some comfort. Catherine's lawyer, Jean-Baptiste Chaudon, described the family as being left with an ample portion "appropriate to their station" when Joseph Cadière died.[14] Above the store, they lived in modest apartments where Catherine had her own bedroom, and they also owned a small country home, or *bastide*.

Despite their relative security, the Cadière family was shaped by tragic events that may be seen as markers of Catherine's life. She was born on November 12,

1709, the year of the Great Frost or Grand Hiver, the coldest winter in Europe in five hundred years. It began on the night of January 5 as icy winds blew through northern France. Destroying harvests, the weather halted agricultural and commercial activity; ice-choked rivers made travel treacherous or impossible.[15] In Marseille, Toulon's maritime neighbor and rival, nearly two thousand women attacked bakers on April 7, pillaging stores and accusing officials of grain speculation; a few days later, women in Aix-en-Provence also protested.[16]

For some, the fact that this miserable winter began on the eve of the Epiphany, the Day of Kings, represented a divine indictment of Louis XIV (1643–1715) and the disastrous War of the Spanish Succession (1701–13). A song circulating in this period shows popular discontent:

> Our father, who art in Versailles,
> Your Name is no longer glorious,
> Your kingdom is no longer great,
> Your will is no longer done on earth and on sea.
> Give us our bread that we all lack.[17]

However much municipal officials tried to assist the starving poor and the Crown denounced grain speculation, one policy persisted: relentlessly high taxes were extracted to fund the war against the Grand Alliance of Britain, the Dutch Republic, and the Holy Roman Empire.

When Catherine Cadière entered the world, Toulon's population hung on by a thread. Even before the severe winter, Toulon was desperate, especially during the siege of summer 1707. Attempting to block Louis XIV's grandson Philip from assuming the Spanish throne, France's enemies unsuccessfully tried to invade Toulon from the south. But for Toulon, the routing of the Grand Alliance on August 15 was a Pyrrhic victory.[18] Three thousand fell sick on the *rade*, while the town was forced to melt ammunition to pay personnel. A year and a half later, on January 6, 1709, the Grand Hiver descended, followed on February 1 by the notorious mistral and glacial conditions. Olive trees, oaks, and orchards perished, as did game. The ensuing famine was intensified by English admiral George Byng's blockade of the harbor, which lasted until January 1710.

For Elisabeth Pomet, carrying her last child in 1709, the birth and survival of this child would require a miracle. Jules Michelet's account of the Cadière family suggests that Elisabeth sought precisely that, spending her pregnancy in constant prayer and surviving on rye bread. In mid-November, two months before Toulon's reprieve, she delivered a sickly infant whose health remained fragile for years. According to Michelet (1798–1874), both Catherine and her older brothers suffered from glandular swellings that sometimes opened up.[19] Soon after her birth, Catherine contracted smallpox, which contributed to her frail health but left no noticeable marks on her face. The marquis d'Argens would describe her as having "beautiful eyes, white skin, a virginal air, and being well proportioned."[20]

Against all odds, Catherine survived. Even without the added traumas of frost and famine, life expectancy for infants was tenuous; the Cadières' first-born, another Catherine, had died. Joseph also appears to have died suddenly in August 1710 when his youngest and only surviving daughter was barely ten months old.[21] Did Joseph die when smallpox attacked the house?[22] Whatever the cause, Elisabeth Pomet was left on her own to run a business and raise four children. Illness and a father's death, plus natural and man-made catastrophes, must have shaped a melancholy childhood.

How did Catherine and her family cope with loss and crisis? The primary image we have of the Cadières is that of a family sustaining itself through Christian ideals, which they valued more than financial prosperity. In Catherine's brief description of her father during the trial, she ignored his profession and her family's social status. Instead, she underscored that Joseph Cadière had been a devout Christian who "had lived in a very Christian manner, and he died in the same way; God had blessed his business, because he shared it with the poor."[23]

The person most responsible for this Christian upbringing was Catherine's mother, who "carefully raised her children à la vertu," to be virtuous.[24] The eldest, Laurent, gave up entering religious orders, but the second son, François, often characterized as an "innocent" and simple soul, studied theology under the Jesuits; "his piety and his exactitude in completing his duties soon led to his promotion to religious orders." While the Jesuits wanted him to begin his novitiate with them, he chose instead to become a priest.[25] The youngest son, Étienne-Thomas, was the family scholar. After receiving a degree at the Sorbonne, he joined the Dominican order, or the Order of Preachers.[26]

Catherine conformed to the pious model established by her parents and brothers. She might have been raised in "obscurity," but she was a cherished child, and her mother gave her the education to be expected from a woman "as Christian as she [Elisabeth Pomet] was."[27] The Cadières were relatively prosperous, so it is unlikely that Catherine attended schools like the free parish schools for poor girls run by the Sisters of Charity.[28] By the end of the 1720s, she was "partially" literate—like many women of her status, she could read, but not write. It appears that her reading was almost exclusively restricted to devotional literature, notably the writings of the famous St. Teresa of Avila (1515–1582). Until she met Jean-Baptiste Girard in 1728, Catherine placed her spiritual life under the direction of local clergy—Father Giraud, the curé of Toulon's cathedral of Sainte-Marie, Father Alexis from the order of Carmelites, and Monsieur Dolonne, the vicar of the parish of Saint-Louis: "Under their direction this girl was an example of virtue, and she had such a taste for devotion and piety that she had refused on several occasions proposals that were honorable and advantageous."[29]

In the months before the trial, the images circulating across France all suggest that Catherine's intense faith was exceptional. But was it? Not really. Catherine's faith reflected the Catholic Reformation's impact on Toulon and Provence. Historian Michel Vovelle has characterized the region's spiritual devotion as a "baroque piety" emerging in the wake of the Catholic Reformation (1545–1648). Baroque piety was defined by passion and emotion, its manifestations sensuous and theatrical. Many Catholic churches built in the late seventeenth century deliberately sought to awe and inspire believers by inundating their senses. As incense and aromatic candles burned, the faithful heard organ music and angelic choirs praising the grandeur of God. Churches under Louis XIV commissioned paintings, sculptures, and altarpieces depicting Biblical scenes filled with characters wrought with emotion.

Catherine's spiritual life evolved in such supercharged religious spaces. Minutes from her home was the cathedral of Notre-Dame-de-la-Sède, more often known as Sainte-Marie, which contained an ornate marble and stucco retable, a framed altarpiece holding the Holy Sacrament.[30] Elevated above the congregation, the altarpiece designed by Pierre Puget (1620–1694) gave the upraised eyes of Toulon's worshippers a dramatic image of God, robes flowing, arms raised, flanked by angels and saints.

The intense drama such sculptures radiated spilled into the streets. Toulon was a city of public spirituality, a community where frequent religious processions captured the flamboyant theatricality of the baroque by displaying ornate crucifixes, relics, and uniformed clergy. These staged processions, initiated by elites, were not the only defining hallmarks of Catholic Renewal. Wealthy and poor alike asked processions to accompany them to their graves. However humble the coffin, it was followed by monks and nuns, and the caskets of influential notables might be attended by upward of a thousand people.[31]

Catherine's piety appears also to have been shaped by another element that characterized Catholic Renewal: the proliferation of lay religious associations.

The most common form of religious sociability available to laymen was the confraternity, "a group organized by the laity with a religious character" whose goal was to infuse the sacred into everyday life.[32] By the beginning of the eighteenth century, confraternities had begun to disappear in most of France. Provence, however, was an exception. During Catherine's childhood, Toulon had confraternities, specifically the *confréries des pénitents*, whose members were distinguished by white, black, gray, or red outer garments. Their purpose was to nurture religious devotion through charitable works and participation in town festivals; they also represented a form of sociability, reflecting a desire "to come together for the sake of coming together."[33]

Although the recognized confraternities of Toulon were homosocial worlds that excluded females, the town's women embraced aspects of this social life designed for men. While the core of Catherine's spiritual life was located in her family, her friendships with Marie-Anne Laugier and other devout women indicate that her social circle was composed of *dévotes*. These were women "imbued with the sense of a mission to influence and change the world in which they lived in accordance with their understanding of Christian religious and moral principles."[34] Other women in Catherine's *dévote* coterie included Anne-Marie Chauvet (known as Madame Guiol), Anne Batarelle, Anne-Rose Reboul, and Claire Gravier. They eventually became the core of Jean-Baptiste Girard's circle of penitents. Catherine also participated in charitable activities, working in hospitals and workhouses. At thirteen, she and her friend Marie-Anne Laugier, a seamstress two years her senior, intended to join the third order of Saint Teresa, a subsidiary female order of the Carmelites. These plans never came to fruition, perhaps because of Catherine's fragile health or her family's resistance to losing their only daughter.[35] Did Catherine's devoutness lead her to seek likeminded people? Or did these organic friendships, which developed in neighborhoods and parishes, mold the religious convictions of a sheltered, impressionable young girl?

In late 1720, Catherine would see her community and its faith tested by the beginning of the Marseille plague, sometimes known as the plague of Provence. First erupting in Europe in 1348, plague continued to recur regularly in France and Europe between 1500 and 1700, though demographic statistics show that pandemic episodes were waning significantly.[36] The 1720 plague in Provence was the last large-scale episode of its kind in France. Humans contracted plague through contact with rodents, whose presence on ships spread the disease along trade routes. It is, therefore, not surprising that Marseille, France's major commercial port on the Mediterranean, was the first to be hit in the summer of

1720. News of Marseille's predicament spread fast, but hope remained that the disease could be contained. In the meantime, Toulon's municipal leaders sent Marseille condolences and offers of assistance.[37] Indeed, they initially extended shelter to inhabitants of Marseille who provided a *billet de santé*, a certificate of health, clearing them of contamination.

A detailed record of these efforts survives thanks to Jean d'Antrechaux, first consul of Toulon, who thirty-five years later published an account of actions taken against the seemingly unstoppable plague. Officials faced many challenges in trying to prevent or contain the epidemic. Toulon's streets, like the rue de l'Hôpital, were narrow and dark, and clean water was not easily accessible. The town's inhabitants had developed a notorious habit of throwing their garbage, including human waste, into the streets. Pamphlets ordered the public to keep the streets clean; guards were placed at the city gates, and an isolation area was created for potential patients.

Despite careful measures by the municipal government, Toulon was overrun by plague in the autumn of 1720. D'Antrechaux and his fellow consuls took on the herculean task of quarantining not just townspeople but material goods as well. But greed superseded fear. On October 5, 1720, a Toulonnais merchant, Cancelin, journeying west from Bandol, obtained some silk that had been imported into France via Marseille. The unfortunate Cancelin died five days later, and his daughter died on October 17. D'Antrechaux attributed a second wave of plague to yet another episode characterized by avarice and ignorance. When an old widow named Tassy, "with modest property," passed away, her three heirs raided her house to lay their hands on her goods. One of them, Bonnet, died suddenly on December 6, and a second, Michel, became ill three days later. He, his wife, and his son were taken to the hospital of Saint Roch and died within ten days of one another.[38] Although the town issued quarantine laws on February 18, the worst was yet to come. By April, reported deaths averaged 200 per day, the crisis compounded by a scarcity of bread and meat. When the epidemic subsided in the summer of 1721, Toulon had lost nearly half its population. D'Antrechaux put the total at 13,283 out of 26,276 residents but also argued that if "foreigners," or non-residents, were taken into account, the number would be closer to 16,000.[39] The twenty-seven-year-old consul himself was not immune from tragedy—he lost three brothers, two uncles, and a sister. By June, the young d'Antrechaux was Toulon's only surviving consul.

D'Antrechaux's painstaking account describes the scale of the devastation, but it offers less insight into people's emotional response to the crisis. His was not a personal memoir but an official account, addressed to the secretary of the

FIGURE I

"Veue du Cours de Marseille, dessiné sur le Lieu pendant la peste arrivée en 1720." Bibliothèque nationale de France, Paris.

navy, Jean-Baptiste Machault (1701–1794), comte d'Arnouville. Nevertheless, we glimpse what the people of Toulon experienced. According to d'Antrechaux, "fear [had] spread everywhere," so that "when the suppression of quarantine arrived, everyone made a point of using the freedom to go out with reserve."[40] Looking out their windows, people likely observed scenes such as those in an illustration of Marseille during the same months: empty streets in which one only saw corpses and individuals responsible for disposing bodies (fig. 1). Grief went hand in hand with fear. A family rarely suffered the loss of only one member.

As the death toll mounted, the plague ended public life as the Toulonnais knew it. Festivals around religious observances, commemorations of military victories, and the greeting of dignitaries were the heart of Toulon's civic identity. But during the second bout of plague in December 1720, the bishop of Toulon closed down Christmas festivities, and "there was neither midnight Mass nor sermons in any Church, and since that day Toulon was like a closed town in which the Plague had closed all passages."[41] Undoubtedly, the absence

Henri-Xavier de BELZUNCE de CASTELMORON,
Né en Périgord en 1671; Vicaire-Général d'Agen;
Sacré EVÊQUE de MARSEILLE en 1710;
Abbé Commendataire de N.D. des Chambons,
et de s.^t Arnould de Metz;
refusa l'Eveché-Pairie de Laon en 1723, et l'Archevêché de Bordeaux en 1729; fut
honoré du Pallium par Clément XII en 1731, et mourut en 1755, âgé de 84 ans.

Pestis valde gravis! (Exod. ch.9 ¥.29.)

SE VOVET HOSTIA. (Sentel.)

FIGURE 2
Henri-Xavier de Belsunce
de Castelmoron (1671–1755),
bishop of Marseille (1710–
1755). Bibliothèque nationale
de France, Paris.

of celebrations like midnight mass on Christmas Eve contributed to the feeling
that the town itself was on the brink of death. Père Maurice, a Capuchin monk,
wrote that no one could hide because the "plague will follow you there [the
'inaccessible' hiding place] and will end your sensual and irresponsible life in a
few hours."[42]

Despite moments of apocalyptic despair, the plague in Toulon and
Marseille fostered an ethos of Christian self-sacrifice. Henri-François-Xavier
de Belsunce de Castelmoron (1671–1755), archbishop of Marseille, became
emblematic of the self-sacrificing cleric (fig. 2): "In the midst of this Boschian
horror strode the saintly figure of Belsunce, his cassock sleeves rolled high, a
sponge of aromatic herbs under his nose to keep the stench of putrescent flesh
at bay, offering alms, comfort and confession to the sick and dying."[43] A somewhat more indolent figure than Belsunce, the bishop of Toulon, Louis-Pierre
de La Tour du Pin-Montauban (1679–1737), did not approach his apostolic duties with quite the same fervor. He did administer last rites to the infected and

dying and quickly ordained young seminarians to offer spiritual consolation to the needy. The Dominicans gave up their convent to house the ordinary sick, allowing hospitals to focus on the plague-infected. Other members of Toulon's religious community risked infection and death in order to care for the sick and provide spiritual solace to the afflicted.[44]

In the end, what united these distraught communities and gave them hope was worship of the Sacred Heart. The cult gained popularity during the late seventeenth century, when it became a sanctioned religious office or authorized service. Led by the Oratorian priest Jean Eudes (1601–1680), devotional practices focused on Christ's physical heart, symbolizing His boundless love of humanity. However, it was a nun, Marguerite-Marie Alacoque (1647–1690), who became the iconic symbol of Sacred Heart devotion. Alacoque belonged to the order of the Visitation of Mary, which emphasized intense meditation and prayer. In her convent in Paray-le-Monial in Burgundy, the Visitandine nun experienced a series of profound mystical visions in which Christ had revealed His heart, wounded by all the sins of humanity. Alacoque ultimately gained a notable following when the Jesuits celebrated her visions as part of a larger effort to expand devotion to the Sacred Heart throughout France.

Nearly a half century later, the cult took center stage in Provence thanks to another Visitandine nun in Marseille, Anne-Madeleine Rémuzat (1696–1730), who wielded tremendous influence over Bishop Henri Belsunce.[45] According to Belsunce, in the years before the plague, Rémuzat had warned that "God had made it known to her that He was angered by Marseille, and that if this town did not repent, he was going to bring his vengeful arm down on her, in a manner so terrible that the Universe, for which it was an example, would be terrified." At the nun's urging, Belsunce used the plague as leverage and on October 22, 1720, received a civic ordinance that established in perpetuity a citywide festival dedicated to the Sacred Heart.[46] The bishop of Toulon followed suit and initiated a similar celebration. On October 30, the Te Deum was sung, offering thanks to God, a service in which Toulon's entire population participated.[47] These spectacular observances highlighting Christ's suffering heart, complete with religious regalia, relics, and music, must have provided emotional catharsis to the bereft population and inspired hope that God would "return" to Toulon. Significantly, the Sacred Heart featured heavily in Catherine Cadière's spiritual journey to perfection, giving her both a spiritual blueprint and female religious role models in Alacoque and Rémuzat.

In Jules Michelet's view, the fragility of Catherine Cadière's post-plague childhood left her weak and impressionable, an easy target for seduction and domination by the predatory Jean-Baptiste Girard. The Cadières may not have lost immediate family, but in a town deprived of half its population, it is highly unlikely that they did not experience bereavement and grief when they returned to Toulon, now "a deserted and unrecognizable town."[48] Thus, we cannot completely ignore Michelet's character study, if for no other reason than we know that Catherine grew up in a community scarred by death and deprivation. We must also remember that before the plague, the working world of Toulon was already defined by piety. Indeed, this piety influenced Catherine to seek Father Girard's spiritual guidance.

JEAN-BAPTISTE GIRARD, AN OUTSIDER IN TOULON

When Jean-Baptiste Girard arrived in Toulon in 1728, he was an outsider. A native of the Franche-Comté, Father Girard was a member of the Jesuits, who had arrived in Toulon less than fifty years earlier. The presence of the Jesuits, like the naval officers and other officials who came to the city on the king's business, reflected how Toulon, despite its remoteness, was very much influenced by outsiders. As we shall see, Jean-Baptiste Girard became a controversial, polarizing figure in part because of his affiliation with a religious order whose wealth and power provoked hostility in Toulon's local community. Girard's relationship with Catherine developed in this divided world, and it would exacerbate existing rifts between locals and outsiders.

In many respects, tensions in Toulon society were the product of the French state's active presence in the town. Toulon's large natural harbor and its strategic location on the Mediterranean gave it military importance. Louis XIV and his minister Jean-Baptiste Colbert (1619–1683) took a strong interest in this *port royal*; under the direction of Sébastien Vauban (1633–1707), *maréchal* of France, the town expanded its military arsenal and fortifications. Artists and builders from outside came to work in the dockyards and on the town's fortifications. Arriving in Toulon from the Alps to the northeast, the Englishman Philip Playstowe paid tribute to these workers as he gushed about entering "through a most magnificent gate, ornamented with trophies and inscriptions in honour of Louis XIV."[49]

The crown's interest in Toulon as a strategic stronghold introduced new elements into the local population, from social outcasts to elites with significant power. Although the British penal system of the eighteenth century was hardly benign, Playstowe was distressed at the sight of galley slaves in Toulon's dockyard: "those poor unhappy men called galley-slaves, chained by the leg together

. . . many of whom have been guilty of no other crime than smuggling three or four pounds of tobacco, or salt, or perhaps killed a partridge, pheasant, or hen (to hinder their families from starving)."[50]

Atop the social spectrum were high-ranking royal naval officers appointed by the king, who lived in an opulence befitting their station.[51] If the Cadière family did encounter such important personages as the Beaussiers or the Thomases, it may have been through business. Some notables were considered "foreign" to Toulon, as they came from Bordeaux or other French regions. Despite familial connections by marriage, these "outsiders" remained distinct from Toulon's municipal leaders, like the consul d'Antrechaux, for whom navy elites were interlopers with no real ties to the community.

Crises such as the plague brought these resentments to the surface. Although d'Antrechaux paid homage to the naval officers who offered assistance to the pestilence-ridden town, he tersely noted that others were not so generous: "the rich only thought of taking shelter right away, and the poor only had tears and powerless wishes to offer us."[52] The consul's comments may have been cast in terms of rich and poor, but it is more likely that he was thinking of nobles like the marquis de La Valette, who owed his title to the Crown and promptly retreated to his country estates at the plague's onset, not returning to Toulon until the fall of 1721. Indeed, a decade later, no one mentioned the Cadières' probable flight from Toulon during those desperate months. D'Antrechaux's comment arguably revealed resentment and jealousies among elites—those who benefitted from royal approbation and those who did not.

The long arm of the monarchy also created rifts among local clergy. Toulon's clerical community comprised only 1.5 to 2 percent of the town's inhabitants. It was nevertheless essential to the management of charities, implementation of the religious calendar, and community education. Clerics may have shared a goal of ensuring that their flock led Christian lives, but they competed for wealth, power, and influence.[53] Fault lines divided the secular clergy, generally parish priests under the bishop's authority, from the regular clergy, who followed monastic rules specific to their orders. Rivalries festered between those with long-standing ties to local society and those who were relative outsiders, like the Jesuits, whom the king had recently installed in Toulon. For Father Girard, perhaps the most dangerous conflict arose from the theological ferment of Augustinian Jansenism, which pitted the Jesuits against the Oratorian community.

Tension between the secular clergy, especially priests, and the regular monastic clergy was unsurprising, given that regular clergy were more numerous and far wealthier. The bishop of Toulon, La Tour du Pin-Montauban, earned a relatively modest income, somewhere between 10,000 and 13,000 livres; in comparison, the bishop of Marseille enjoyed 30,000 livres, supplemented by 35,000 earned from nearby abbeys.[54] Unlike Paris, which at the time of the Revolution had fifty-two parishes, Toulon's diocese was relatively poor, containing only two parishes. In the first half of the eighteenth century, at any time, roughly 40 members of the secular clergy served these parishes. By contrast, the city's nine male religious communities had 231 members, while its four female orders enrolled 187 sisters and female pensioners.[55] The oldest monastery belonged to the Dominicans, but most of the town's monasteries and convents were products of the Catholic Renewal and Counter-Reformation. Male orders, such as the Oratorians and Capuchins, and female communities, such as the Ursulines and Visitandines, established houses in Toulon in the early seventeenth century. Their convents and monasteries took up prime real estate in the town as well as holdings in the surrounding countryside or *terroirs*. In the decades before the French Revolution, this visible wealth excited the resentment of both secular clergy and laity.[56]

In the eighteenth century, three religious orders dominated Toulon: the Capuchins, the Oratorians, and the Jesuits. Established in 1588, the Capuchins, a mendicant order, were deeply enmeshed in Toulon's civic and religious life. According to one historian, the friars practically "confessed the entire town."[57] During the plague, twenty-one of thirty friars perished due to their unwavering care of the sick. It is likely that Capuchin friars also served as chaplains on warships in or near Toulon.[58]

While Toulon's people loved the Capuchin friars for their dedication to the community, the other two orders attracted more attention, in part because of their mutual antipathy.[59] The Oratorians were dedicated to education; in 1625 they founded a *collège* that became the primary source of secondary education for the sons of Toulon's governing elite. But they encountered a formidable rival in 1686 when Louis XIV established Toulon's royal marine seminary, to be run by the Jesuits, who were renowned for their pedagogical methods. The king also envisioned the Jesuits opening their own *collège* to educate not just naval personnel but Toulon's male youth, reflecting a pattern found in most of the realm. But here, the Sun King's will was checked. Municipal leaders opposed the project, and the Jesuits turned their attention to training navy chaplains.

The rivalry between the two orders was exemplified in an architectural showdown between the Oratorians and Toulon's town leaders, on one side, and the Jesuits and the king, on the other. Each side used the construction of new facilities as a vehicle for expressing power and status in the town.[60] Pooling their financial resources, Toulon's elites and the Oratorians built a new four-building *collège*, complete with portal, church and sacristy, and refectories. The project, however, was hampered by financial difficulties. The Oratorians and their municipal supporters must have watched with bitter envy as the Jesuits' new seminary moved forward swiftly, thanks to the king's largesse. Adding fuel to the fire, Louis XIV endowed the completed seminary with an annual revenue of 10,500 livres, augmenting the Jesuits' sizeable holdings and making it the wealthiest religious order in Toulon.[61] This display of wealth and power may have reinforced the Jesuit presence in Toulon, but it did not make them part of the community. Instead, their ties to the king marked them as outsiders, a pressure group to advance the interests of king and navy.

The fraught relationship between the Jesuits and the Oratorians was not unique to Toulon. How was it that the Jesuits, who only numbered 3,000 when they were expelled from France in 1764, became the most hated religious order in France? The reasons were many and complex, but "anti-Jesuitism" began almost as soon as Jesuits arrived in France in the mid-sixteenth century.[62] While the Oratorians were French, founded by Cardinal Pierre de Bérulle (1575–1629) in 1611, the Jesuits were a foreign order whose Spanish origins were never forgotten. During the 1530s, former Spanish soldier Ignatius of Loyola (1491–1556) had established the Society of Jesus to serve as shock troops in the war against Protestant heresy. These origins, the order's relative autonomy, and its ability to insinuate its members into influential positions fed widespread suspicion throughout French society.

In his memoirs of the last decades of Louis XIV's reign, the duc de Saint-Simon (1675–1755) described how many contemporaries believed that the Jesuits held sway by "being the confessor of nearly all the kings and Catholic sovereigns and of almost the whole public through their instruction of youth, and by their talent and their arts."[63] Indeed, from the reign of Louis XIV until the Jesuits' expulsion, with one exception, all royal confessors were Jesuits.[64] Saint-Simon's anxieties about their dominance partly explain why Toulon's municipal authorities, along with the Oratorians, resisted the establishment of a Jesuit *collège*.

Rivalry between Oratorians and Jesuits was grounded not simply in envy but also in doctrinal conflicts surrounding Jansenism. The structure of the Catholic Church has always suggested a monolith, a perception that reflects both design on the part of the institution and suspicion from non-Catholics. By the early eighteenth century, the Catholic Church had regrouped from the devastating setbacks of the Protestant Reformation. However, it would be a mistake to assume uniformity in doctrine. In the early seventeenth century, a small group of French theologians began embracing a series of theological directives grounded in the teachings of Saint Augustine, the same Church father who influenced Protestant leaders such as Martin Luther and John Calvin. This movement, named after Cornelius Jansen (1585–1638), bishop of Ypres, revolved around Augustine's ideas of efficacious grace and predestination.[65] Jansen and his followers firmly believed that God alone determined salvation and vehemently rejected the role of human free will in gaining salvation. In their view, humanity was corrupt and weak-willed, depending completely on God's justice and mercy.[66] The antithesis of baroque piety, "Jansenists," as opponents derisively labeled the sect, adopted an austere faith and lifestyle that emphasized rigorous contemplation of one's sinful nature and God's greatness.

These beliefs created an unbridgeable chasm between Jansenists and Jesuits.[67] Jansenist adherents dissented with the Catholic establishment through their firm belief in predestination. In contrast, the Jesuits were the Church's vanguard in defending free will, which admitted human effort and responsibility into the quest for salvation.[68] Errors and flaws could be forgiven if one's intentions were good. Through such teachings, the Society acquired a reputation among its detractors for a Machiavellian willingness to cut spiritual and theological corners to attract powerful allies. One of the most persuasive voices spreading this idea was the mathematician Blaise Pascal (1623–1662), whose *Provincial Letters* remained one of the most popular Jansenist critiques of Jesuits. Conversely, the Jesuits thought Jansenism a "heresy," and individual Jesuits such as Louis XIV's confessor François Annat (1590–1670) denounced the Jansenist indictment of Jesuit morality as "venom."[69]

Such theological disputes sharpened when Louis XIV introduced the anti-Jansenist papal bull *Unigenitus* in 1713. For Louis XIV, Jansenists were perpetual dissenters threatening his absolutist vision of state and society, and as a result, he pressured Pope Clement XI (1700–1720) to issue *Unigenitus*.[70] In large measure, this edict condemned the Jansenist theologian and Oratorian Pasquier Quesnel's *Réflexions morales* (1671), which captured the central Jansenist principles Louis XIV abhorred.[71] In particular, Quesnel (1634–1719) advocated a more egalitarian definition of the Church that essentially repudiated the hierarchical relationships between bishops and priests and between laity and clergy. For a monarch whose reign was an endless display of patriarchal hierarchy, such notions directly challenged his authority.[72]

Toulon and Provence were caught between these opposing understandings of Christian belief and *Unigenitus*. Outside the Paris basin, the southern province was a Jansenist stronghold. The Oratorians, the Dominicans—the order Catherine's brother Étienne-Thomas joined—and the Carmelite monks harbored Jansenist beliefs. Key clerical figures such as the Jansenist Jean Soanen (1647–1740), bishop of Senez in the alpine region of Provence, fiercely refused to accept *Unigenitus*.[73] Soanen battled powerful opponents such as Henri Belsunce, the bishop of Marseille, who saw the plague as divine retribution against Jansenism. And in Toulon, La Tour du Pin-Montauban issued decrees against clerics who refused to accept *Unigenitus*; these actions put him in conflict with the Oratorians as well as the parlement of Provence and the Sorbonne in Paris.[74] But there were also individuals like the Toulonnais priest Father Giraud, who identified with the Jansenist movement perhaps because he was "a Catholic who does not like Jesuits."[75]

Thus, Jean-Baptiste Girard could hardly be described as a neutral party when he came to Toulon in April 1728. He belonged to the wealthiest order, one that many distrusted or despised. Furthermore, the forty-seven-year-old Jesuit occupied a position of authority and prominence when he became rector of the Jesuit royal seminary. An outsider, Girard arrived confidently, staunchly supported by his order and the anti-Jansenist bishop of Marseille. Not surprisingly, then, in this atmosphere his unorthodox methods of spiritual direction had the potential to create an explosion.

Who was this priest who three years later would incite such passions? Contemporary descriptions suggest a man simultaneously repulsive and compelling. In his memoirs, the marquis d'Argens characterized the Jesuit as "excessively ugly," and nearly a decade later, he elaborated further in *Thérèse philosophe*: "His [Girard's] face was the kind that our painters give to satyrs. Although excessively ugly, there was something spiritual in his physiognomy." Father Girard seems to have been a charismatic figure who "appeared to be occupied only with the affairs of heaven."[76] Even Catherine's lawyer, Jean-Baptiste Chaudon, who churned out hundreds of pages eviscerating Father Girard, acknowledged the "air of modesty, of austerity and mortification [that] permeated his face and all his mannerisms."[77]

Girard's early history remains somewhat obscure. He was born in Dôle around 1681 in the eastern province of Franche-Comté, almost 350 miles directly north of Toulon and about 25 miles southeast of Dijon in the Jura Mountains just north of the Alps. Where Toulon was identified by its Mediterranean harbor and northern ring of mountains, Dôle was a city of canals on the edge of the

Chaux forest to the east. Despite their stark geographical differences, Franche-Comté and Provence shared one characteristic. Both were border territories whose people tended to see the French monarchy as a distant, outside power. Indeed, once possessed by the Spanish Habsburgs and the dukes of Burgundy, Franche-Comté had become a part of France only in 1678, at the end of the Franco-Dutch wars (1672–78). The region was known for its independent spirit; well into the eighteenth century, its inhabitants deeply hated the French who had annexed them.

Perhaps his native land's insistence on its uniqueness rebounded on Father Girard, who seemed determined to stand out. Girard was known as a scholarly man, having taught theology at one point. But his real fame rested on his gifts as a confessor and spiritual director. Ten years before his installation in the royal seminary of Toulon, the Jesuit had resided in Aix-en-Provence, principally confessing nuns and other devout women. During this time, Girard maintained a correspondence with "the saint of Marseille," the mystical Sister Anne-Madeleine Rémuzat, who had been instrumental in introducing the cult of the Sacred Heart to Marseille.[78] These achievements led the Jesuits to transfer him to Toulon, seeing in him "a man capable of forming priests."[79]

With this reputation of making priests and saints, Father Girard arrived in a deeply religious community still reeling from hardships. The Jesuit's presence thus gave Catherine and Toulon the spiritual fulfillment both craved. His commitment to a life imbued with spiritual devotion soon appealed to Catherine, her family, and members of her *dévote* social circle. Given Catherine's religious inclinations and Father Girard's success with female penitents, the relationship between the young penitent and this experienced spiritual director seems natural and, indeed, almost inevitable.

Nevertheless, as a Jesuit, Father Girard was an automatic object of envy and suspicion. His ability to become a prominent spiritual leader almost upon arrival fit the perception of Jesuits as usurpers, outsiders who appropriated authority and power that belonged to others. For those who sympathized with Jansenist teachings or, at least, hated Jesuits, Father Girard's spiritual instruction was intrinsically suspect. Even as segments of the local population hailed him as a spiritual beacon, others closely scrutinized his actions and words. Any irregularities, anything out of the ordinary, could turn the story of a young woman's transformative spiritual journey into a firestorm of contestation and conflict.

THE MEETING OF TWO SOULS

This intense relationship between Catherine Cadière and Jean-Baptiste Girard originated in a community founded on faith, and it flourished under the benevolent gaze of public approval. But the same faith also had a more inward-looking side. Over the course of the seventeenth century, French elite women increasingly regarded rigorous introspection as indispensable to a meaningful devotional life.[1] Like many *dévotes* in Toulon and throughout France, Catherine accepted the notion that, as a woman, she needed a male spiritual director—a priest or friar—to guide her soul to God and toward perfection. In 1728, she found that experienced spiritual mentor in Father Girard. *His* commitment to spiritual direction exemplified the Jesuit mission to make confession and self-examination the center of religious life.

Toward the end of 1729, Catherine began experiencing mystical outpourings and physical torment. However unusual and dramatic, Catherine's visions and convulsions echoed other early modern forms of female Catholic expression. To the wonder of her community,

Catherine seemed to mirror the experiences of renowned holy women such as Teresa of Avila and Marguerite-Marie Alacoque. Moreover, her close relationship with Father Girard was condoned and even admired by family and friends because it appeared to replicate the exemplary spiritual friendships between famous female penitents and male confessors. For many, Catherine was becoming Toulon's very own "saint."

THE CONFESSOR AND HIS PENITENT

The act of confession conjures up shadowed figures and whispered words hinting of inner turmoil, of fervent exchanges between confessor and penitent. A young woman like Catherine enters the church. First, she approaches the altar and kneels before the image of Christ; eyes closed, hands folded, the believer prays feverishly in anticipation of a cathartic ritual of expiation. She then rises and heads to the dark edges of the church, disappearing into one side of a small, tight booth. Very soon, a cassocked figure enters the other side. To anyone else in the church, the only sign of these two individuals is a susurrus of murmured confidences.

The exchange remains elusive, known only to confessor, penitent, and God. If one could hear the penitent's outpouring, one might hear confessions of misdemeanors such as giggling during mass or harboring unkind thoughts about a neighbor or family member. The confessor might rebuke these transgressions with exhortations about temptation. But he might also push the penitent to speak more fully of "interior movements" within her soul. Did she have impulses tempting her to sin? Or perhaps, in the midst of prayer, the penitent felt the hand of God and experienced uncommon union with Him. The confessor might suggest: "Let us pray together and ask [God] for the clarity that we need."[2] In closing, the confessor would recommend formulas for penance and utter the words of absolution only an ordained priest could recite: "Ego te absolve a peccatis tuis, in nomine Patris, Filii et Spiritus Sancti"—"I absolve you of all your sins in the name of the Father, the Son, and the Holy Spirit."[3] Thus, the spiritually cleansed penitent was reconciled with God.

The centrality of the priest-confessor as mediator between God and penitent was based on unequal power. In Catholicism, confession was one of the seven sacraments, and the ability to absolve a sinner belonged exclusively to an ordained priest. Although it was rare, a priest could delay absolution until he was sure that the penitent was truly contrite and had undertaken acts of penance with sincerity.[4] On the other side, the priest also bore tremendous responsibility because the penitent had entrusted him with her soul. As a sign of that trust, the priest submitted to the inviolable seal of secrecy, which prohibited him from revealing the penitent's confession. Thus, power, trust, and secrecy—central elements of confession—shaped the Girard/Cadière relationship in ways that would play out less benignly in a few short years.

When Father Girard became Catherine's confessor in 1728, he also acted as her spiritual director. Spiritual directors did not necessarily confess the penitent, who could have a separate spiritual director and confessor. The director prepared the individual's state of mind for confession through sustained dialogue.[5] He offered the penitent personal instruction on how to live a Christian life and assisted her in examining her conscience. For penitents, the relationship with a spiritual director demanded rigorous self-scrutiny, and invariably, the male cleric became deeply embedded in one's personal life.

From the late sixteenth through the seventeenth century, more than six hundred confessional manuals were published, with titles such as *Pratique du confesseur* (Practice of confessors) or *Conduite des âmes dans la voie de salut* (Conduct of souls on the path to salvation).[6] Whereas in the Middle Ages such manuals, written in Latin, were designated solely for confessors, now authors—often confessors and directors themselves—wrote in the vernacular, addressing both confessors and penitents. These early modern manuals provided a script that standardized practices of self-examination and influenced the laity's expectations of spiritual directors and confessors.

One of the most popular French confessional manuals, the *Introduction à la vie dévote* (1609) by François de Sales (1567–1622), reflected the prominence of elite women in early modern European penitential culture. What drew women to an all-consuming devotional life? Perhaps the satirical depictions of absent wives busy attending mass or confession were correct—going to church meant escaping the confines of the home. However, this explanation fails to take the sincerity of female piety seriously. Nor does it take into account how women were viewed in contradictory ways. Women may have been attracted to a penitential culture because they believed that they *needed* to do more penance since, all their lives, they had been taught that as Eve's descendants, they were inherently more sinful than men. Paradoxically, women were also thought to be more devout, a notion that seemed substantiated by the famous examples of medieval and early modern holy women.[7]

In the *Introduction à la vie dévote*, de Sales's main character, Philothée, provided a model of female spiritual self-examination that captured these gendered paradoxes. While he chose a woman to be the exemplar worthy of imitation, like his contemporaries, François de Sales assumed that women were inferior and inherently weak. Thus, Philothée necessarily engaged a spiritual director. De Sales exhorted Philothée to "place not your confidence in his human learning, but in God whose minister he is, and who speaks to you by his means . . . so that you ought to pay as much attention to him as to an angel who would come down from heaven to conduct you thither."[8] De Sales may have believed that female spiritual introspection was a worthy goal, but he could not imagine this process without the guiding presence of a male spiritual director.

While de Sales's text remained important for the committed penitent, in the end, it was the Jesuits who dominated the field of spiritual direction. For the Jesuits, confession was more than just a sacrament: "The Jesuit discipline of general confession was understood as a devout method of self-examining and self-knowledge."[9] According to Ignatius of Loyola, "for just as strolling, walking and running are exercises for the body, so 'spiritual exercises' is the name given to every way of preparing and disposing one's soul to rid herself of all disordered attachments, so that once rid of them one might seek and find the divine will."[10] Moreover, Loyola adapted the rigorous program to meet the needs and constraints of a dedicated laity. He insisted that a director act as the believer's constant guide, and the Jesuit order worked tirelessly to put the spiritual director, who often acted as confessor, at the heart of an individual's spiritual life.

But the Jesuits' success as confessors and spiritual directors also made them objects of suspicion to their archenemies, the Jansenists. During the 1620s, the Jansenist theologian Jean du Vergier de Hauranne, the abbé de Saint-Cyran (1581–1643), established a rigorous penitential program for believers. Operating within a set of beliefs that emphasized humanity's corrupt nature, Saint-Cyran proposed that penitents withdraw from worldly society so they could contemplate their sins and God's greatness. Only then could they achieve genuine contrition and potentially benefit from God's grace. So severe was Saint-Cyran's method that some of his followers avoided communion for months, waiting until they had achieved a state of true contrition.[11]

This uncompromising approach to confession and penance contrasted sharply with the Jesuits' embrace of casuistry, a form of reasoning that allowed confessors to evaluate the depth of the sin on the basis of individual circumstances. What events or conditions led to the person's sinful act? Were actions intentional or accidental? This approach sought to lessen the burden on the sinner. However, for Jansenists, this flexible method signaled moral laxity or, indeed, depravity. In the satirical *Provincial Letters*, Blaise Pascal argued that the Jesuits sought to "govern all consciences. . . . Thus are they prepared for all

sorts of persons, and so ready are they to suit the supply to the demand that
. . . they suppress the offence of the cross and preach only a glorious and not a
suffering Jesus Christ. . . . [Y]ou will see so many crimes palliated and irregularities tolerated."[12] From this point of view, then, the Jesuits demonstrated a
shocking willingness to excuse sin, and as a result, they jeopardized their penitents' salvation.[13]

These suspicions regarding Jesuit penitential practices presented hidden
dangers for Girard and Cadière. No doubt local Jansenists kept a sharp eye
on this new Jesuit. What forms of devotional exercises did Father Girard ex-
pect from his penitents? How rigorous was the Jesuit in directing their prayers?
Did his penitents take communion too often, or not often enough? At the moment Jean-Baptiste Girard arrived in Toulon on April 8, 1728, these questions
remained buried. Father Girard appeared to radiate virtue—to the extent that
he "became alarmed at the slightest sin and could not suffer any imperfec-
tion."[14] This paragon of rectitude seemed destined to raise the moral standards
of Toulon's citizens.

With his fame preceding him, Father Girard quickly acquired a sizeable
following of *dévotes*, who met him at church and in their homes, confiding
all the movements of their innermost souls. The lengthy testimonies from the
trial reveal a group largely comprising Toulon's lower bourgeoisie and artisans,
the world of shopkeepers to which Catherine Cadière belonged. They included the fifty-year-old widow Thérèse Lionne, also known as l'Allemande; Anne
Batarelle, the twenty-two-year-old daughter of a sailor; a dressmaker's daughter, Marie-Anne Laugier, who was Catherine's contemporary; Claire Gravier;
and Anne-Rose Reboul, thirty-five, the unmarried daughter of a shopkeeper.
Father Girard's closest confidante was Anne-Marie Chauvet Guiol, the forty-
five-year-old wife of a joiner whose daughter was a nun in Toulon's Ursuline
convent. Clearly, none of these women was wealthy, but they all possessed two
things: a deep desire for spiritual improvement and sufficient leisure time to
spend many hours under Father Girard's personal supervision. And they regarded the confessor as a saint. Contact with the hem of Father Girard's habit,
perhaps even the brush of his fingers, would provide a blessing.[15] He could lead
them into lives of holiness.

The testimonies also paint a somewhat contradictory image of how Father
Girard directed his entourage of *dévotes*. According to Madame Guiol, the Jesuit
confessor administered "penances [that were] very difficult for her state"; these
penitential acts included reciting the offices to the Virgin Mary, which involved
a rigorous daily prayer schedule. He seemed to have required the women to

practice different forms of abstinence, such as fasting or simply living on bread and water.[16] There were, however, also stories of Father Girard and his penitents picnicking in the countryside, where they danced and sang.[17] There seems to be no explanation for this somewhat conflicting image of a Jesuit director who, on the one hand, advocated a rigorous spiritual lifestyle and, on the other, indulged his penitents in what some regarded as frivolous activities. Whatever his motivation, Father Girard maintained close (and apparently almost constant) relations with his followers.

In this core group of eight to ten women, one individual stood out: eighteen-year-old Catherine Cadière, who would rapidly become the shining star of Girard's coterie. How did she manage to attract the attention of a cleric who had so many other commitments? How did this obscure daughter of a shopkeeper's widow develop such a close attachment with a renowned and learned Jesuit? Such questions would ignite heated debates three years later as each side attempted to claim innocence while denouncing the other as guilty.

The first meeting between Catherine and Father Girard became a point of contention, as both sides argued about who sought out the other first (fig. 3). In the pro-Girard narrative, Catherine had pursued Girard, determined to distinguish herself from other penitents. They first met when Catherine had just exited the Carmelite church where she had attended a ceremony honoring the recently canonized Spanish mystic, Saint John of the Cross (1542–1591). At that moment, God announced to Catherine: "Behold the man I have destined to conduct thee to me, Ecce Homo."[18] The expression "Ecce Homo"—"behold the man"—was the declaration Pontius Pilate made when he presented a scourged Christ, wearing the crown of thorns, to the crowd.[19] For Father Girard's supporters, this episode proved that Catherine's penchant for visions predated her relationship with Father Girard, and it underscored her arrogance and ambition. Believing herself chosen by God, "Catherine Cadière, a young girl from an inferior order of the bourgeoisie of Toulon," deigned to appoint an eminent Jesuit as her director.[20]

The account favoring Catherine Cadière emphasized how Father Girard had singled her out from among his female followers. Both Catherine's lawyer, Jean-Baptiste Chaudon, and her brother François noted that she looked to Father Girard partly out of necessity, because her confessor M. Dolonne was very busy. Furthermore, she was enticed by the *dévotes*, who gathered around the Jesuit and "publicized his experience in the paths to God."[21] François, himself a priest, became Father Girard's "panegyrist" within the Cadière household.[22] According to Catherine, during their initial meetings, "he [Girard]

FIGURE 3
Jean-Baptiste Girard and Catherine Cadière. Father Girard wears his priestly habit, and it is likely that Catherine is holding a religious book. Both images suggest how faith shaped their relationship. The print originated in Dijon. Courtesy of the Musée Paul Arbaud, Aix-en-Provence.

spoke to me about God in a manner that did not rid me of the longing to have him as my Director."[23] From the moment he began supervising her spiritual journey, Father Girard was extremely attentive, making himself privy to details about Catherine and her family. According to Catherine, "no matter how busy he was, he never was so for me, and when I asked for him, whether it was at the door [of the rectory] or the confessional, I never met with any of the slowness that causes chagrin in people of our sex, who naturally love distinctions."[24]

For the first year, the relationship drew no unwelcome attention, and Father Girard became a familiar presence within the Cadière household. He appears to have visited the Cadière apartments on the rue de l'Hôpital frequently, apparently unperturbed by the contrast between the spacious Jesuit seminary, facing the sunny harbor, and the dark, narrow, and no doubt rank streets ten minutes away. Out of reverence and gratitude, the pious Cadières welcomed his presence. They had other reasons for inviting Father Girard into their home, independent of his marked kindnesses to Catherine. It appears that near the end of 1729, Étienne-Thomas Cadière, a Dominican friar, had lent a nun a Jansenist volume that critiqued Jesuit morality. Father Girard's colleague Father Sabatier, a longtime resident of Toulon, threatened to take Friar Cadière before church authorities. To the family's relief, Father Girard intervened on Étienne-Thomas's behalf; according to the Jesuit, his penitent later thanked him while at confession.[25]

To us and even to some of Catherine's contemporaries, the growing attachment between a young woman, not yet twenty, and her Jesuit director, nearing fifty, suggests a certain irregularity if not illicitness. However, the Cadière family's acceptance of the growing closeness between Catherine and Father Girard reflected the fluidity of gender hierarchies within the practice of early modern spiritual direction. Although most confessional manuals emphasized how men should maintain a strict vigilance over a woman's fickle nature, there were notable instances when the relationship between female penitent and spiritual director developed into a friendship of equals, defined by respect and reciprocity. The most prominent example was the emotional connection, based on "mutual love, trust, and frankness," between François de Sales and Jeanne de Chantal (1572–1641).[26] De Sales's letters capture the degree to which he depended on Chantal: "It will be impossible for anything to separate me from your soul. The bond is too strong."[27] The pair exchanged confidences, sought one another's advice, and together, they founded the female religious order of the Visitation in Annency. Similarly, the Visitation nun Marguerite-Marie Alacoque described her Jesuit confessor, Claude de la Colombière, as a "perfect friend."[28] By the early eighteenth century, print culture—in the form of letters, spiritual biographies, and memoirs—gave the educated faithful access to these celebrated spiritual liaisons.[29]

Some of the most popular devotional books were about or by female mystics who were exceptional because they were women who had achieved a spiritual union with God. This union, in fact, bypassed the traditional confessor/penitent relationship. The spontaneous outpouring of devotion replaced the official language of the Church: prescribed prayer, theological discourse, and catechism. Instead, mystical expression often assumed the form of loving "conversations" with God or Christ that went beyond speech; during these moments, the *dévote* often experienced intense spasms of pain and pleasure to the point of losing consciousness. Despite their lack of theological training and despite their sex, these women now became chosen vehicles for God's voice. On occasion, mystical women even acquired a certain authority *over* other believers, including male clerics.[30] Their spiritual directors did not so much guide them as preserve their visions and words, which then became available to the literate faithful.

Since its publication in France between 1601 and 1602, Saint Teresa of Avila's autobiography had become a canonical guide for perfecting one's inner and outer spiritual life.[31] Was Father Girard's lawyer Pazery right? Did works by or about such mystic women do more harm than good? He would argue that Catherine wanted not only to imitate these saints but also to surpass them.[32] However, clerics like Father Alexis, Catherine's *previous* confessor, held a different opinion. They urged their penitents to study Saint Teresa's autobiography because it highlighted how she maintained a vigilant state of self-scrutiny in the face of possible temptation and possession.

We do not know what books Father Girard assigned his charges, but he did provide Catherine with a mystical model when he lent her the letters he had exchanged with Anne-Madeleine Rémuzat between 1720 and 1730. The Visitation nun's letters contained all the elements associated with mysticism. Sister Rémuzat described herself as "filled with the knowledge of God by his own Understanding . . . I see nothing, feel nothing, taste nothing and I speak of these things as one speaks of the mysteries of faith that one believes in without seeing them." When referring to her physical agony, Rémuzat wrote, "I have discovered only in general an alliance with Jesus Christ that makes me participate in his state as victim and his joy at the same time."[33] The love of God brought on unbearable suffering, and the thirty-three-year-old nun died on February 10, 1730. Surely, family and friends viewed Catherine's growing closeness with the Jesuit as a privilege and a replication of his relationship with the "saint of Marseille."

CATHERINE AS MYSTIC

Nearly a year later, Catherine began to experience the tumultuous emotions and anguish that echoed those described by Sister Rémuzat and Saint Teresa. Catherine now entered into a rarefied world of extremes, moving violently from blissful ecstasy to acute physical agony. As her spiritual director, Father Girard knew that Catherine was joining a perilous realm in which her soul was vulnerable to evil spirits. But there was another kind of danger—the possibility that church officials would dismiss these episodes and denounce Catherine as an abomination, a threat to religion.

By mid-1729, Catherine's soul and body had become a contested field between good and evil. At different times, Catherine maintained that she could no longer pray, and her visions contained blasphemous images of nude men and women. One moment, Catherine would flail uncontrollably, as if possessed by demons, and then suddenly she would become absolutely rigid. When she again became aware of her surroundings, she was physically exhausted, as if she had engaged in backbreaking labor. In a vision that occurred just before Lent in 1730, the recently deceased Sister Rémuzat, accompanied by angels, delivered Catherine from demons, giving her some weeks of peace until the next set of visions and ecstasies began.

Yet soon after, Catherine's chosen status was spectacularly revealed, as the young penitent again vacillated between spiritual ecstasies and profound physical torment. The detailed accounts of this period come from her Lenten journal or *mémoire*, the subject of much controversy during the trial. According to Catherine's *mémoire*, God "wished [her] to be nourished not with the bread of man but the bread of Angels."[34] Like Christ in the desert, Catherine supposedly survived on water for forty days during Lent. At another point, God communicated to her by raising two of her ribs and elevating her whole body. During Holy Week, these episodes intensified while Catherine underwent the passion of Christ—indeed, becoming Christ's partner in suffering, similar to Sister Rémuzat, who had also felt a deep affinity with Christ's agony.

But Catherine was more than a witness to Christ's anguish—she was a participant in the crucifixion. On the eighth day of Lent, Christ showed the young woman His Sacred Heart, pierced by the sins of men. Immediately, Catherine suffered the same pain from an exterior wound that bled profusely. This blood loss and excruciating pain was all for the sake of "ungrateful and rebellious humans."[35] Toward the end of this period, Catherine observed the Last Supper and spent the night with Christ in the garden of Gethsemane, awaiting the Roman soldiers who would arrest Him. Her journal described how a crown of thorns was pushed down on her head, causing blood to run down her face; at the same time, her feet bled as if pierced by the same nails that crucified Christ. Now Catherine had become the personification of "Ecce Homo."[36]

Miracles soon followed the Lenten visions—Catherine mysteriously found two wooden crosses in her bed.[37] Father Girard and the Cadière brothers widely proclaimed that the crosses were surely signs of God's grace. She appeared to have acquired the gift of prophecy. Madame Guiol would later swear that Catherine had told her how the king was on the verge of war. God had revealed to Catherine that if she sacrificed herself, it would circumvent such devastation.[38]

But this tumultuous mystical state also raised the troubling question of how to distinguish between divine ecstasy and demonic possession. These two states operated within "a sliding scale of rapture" in which "at one end was the ecstatic spiritual who had surrendered her will to that of God and was rewarded . . . [with] a possible reputation for sanctity. At the other end was the witch, whose renunciation of her will, and her baptism, in exchange for extraordinary powers . . . aligned her totally with the devil."[39] Catherine's revelations and gyrations operated precisely within this spectrum. The young woman displayed all the traits of the ecstatic saint, but she sometimes appeared overwhelmed by temptation and the devil. During this intense and undoubtedly difficult period, the Cadières must have been alarmed as they watched Catherine undergoing acute distress, accompanied by bouts of illness. She had been a girl whose childhood was full of near-death experiences, and holy women did not seem to live long lives.

As a result, the family welcomed Father Girard's careful attentions. After all, Catherine had seen his namesake, John the Baptist, in a vision during which he had shown Catherine the Book of Life in which was inscribed "MARIE CATHERINE JEAN BAPTISTE."[40] While Catherine went to church for confession whenever she was physically able, the Jesuit visited the Cadières often and spent hours in Catherine's room with the door shut. Her visions and torments increased in intensity and duration. If Father Girard and Catherine followed the guidelines established in confessional manuals, their conversations would attempt to determine whether God in heaven was revealing Himself, or whether these visions were temptations from the devil, full of men and women performing unspeakable acts. A year later, during the trial, the nature of these lengthy exchanges would be a matter of bitter debate. At this point, however, there appears to have been no effort by the Cadières, Catherine, the Jesuits, or Father Girard to bring these meetings to an end.

Father Girard's close supervision of Catherine followed a codified process known as "discernment," in which trained clerics scrutinized a penitent's interior to assess whether the spirit inhabiting an individual was demonic or divine.[41] Significantly, discernment was often a gendered system. Dating back to the fourteenth century, proponents of discernment, such as Jean de Gerson (1363–1429), were motivated less by fear of the demonic and more by the conviction that female passion, vanity, and unpredictability made women the ideal vessels for demonic possession. In light of this widespread suspicion of woman's intrinsic nature, clerics increasingly used discernment not only to determine possession but also to authenticate mysticism.

The very nature of mysticism aroused anxiety. For some, it was an inherently dubious form of religious expression, unreliable and uncontrollable. Arguably, mysticism represented a feminized form of spirituality precisely because it defied the boundaries between the rational and the emotional. By the early eighteenth century, intellectuals, theologians, and medical practitioners increasingly questioned the validity of mysticism as a religious experience. Was female mysticism just a mutant product of the female intellect, itself incapable of reason and captive to "melancholy" and passion?[42]

The growing skepticism toward female mysticism was illustrated in the Jansenist attack on Marguerite-Marie Alacoque. Significantly, for some, she was an object of suspicion because the Jesuits had promoted her devotion to the Sacred Heart. A year before the Girard/Cadière affair, Alacoque and the Sacred Heart had become the center of a controversy thanks to a recent biography. The author was the ultramontane bishop of Soissons, Jean-Joseph Languet de Gergy (1674–1750), whom Jansenists despised because of his zealous support of *Unigenitus*.[43] Languet de Gergy's excessive language describing divine caresses transformed Alacoque into a figure of derision. Her expressions of devotion repulsed many Jansenists precisely because of their visceral physicality, their sensual articulations of love and self-surrender. The Jansenist periodical, *Nouvelles Ecclésiastiques*, described the bishop's style as more "romanesque than episcopal"; Christian women could hardly be permitted to peruse such a book, which read less like a devotional work and more like an erotic novel.[44]

The controversy around Languet de Gergy's biography was a reminder that when Catherine Cadière entered the mystical world, she may have taken a road well traveled, but it remained a perilous one. Popular songs mocked Alacoque, and Catherine, too, risked being denounced as a fraud. It would not have been unprecedented if she had been hauled before ecclesiastical courts, denounced as a deluded hysteric, and locked away in a convent for life. Similarly, Father Girard, as Catherine's spiritual director, was in a potentially precarious position simply for allowing Catherine to participate in mystical excesses. If Catherine were to be declared a charlatan, his reputation would be irreparably damaged. Like the bishop of Soissons, Father Girard could easily have become the target of satirical verses such as the following:

> Monseigneur de Soissons assuredly mocks himself,
> With his Marie à la Coque,
> Whom he sells to us.
> The discourse of his Angélique
> And the good God
> Are those of a public woman
> In an evil place.[45]

Given these anxieties about gender and religious authenticity, how was it possible that an unknown young Toulonnaise achieved such an elevated status in a few short months? Certainly, visions gave mystical women an authoritative position within their immediate social world by placing them so close to the divine. This had been the case with Sister Rémuzat, who had a deep influence over Henri Belsunce. Admittedly, her family belonged to the municipal elites of Marseille, whereas Catherine's father had married the daughter of a modest olive oil merchant; Sister Rémuzat was associated with the respected Visitandine order, while Catherine had no institutional support or powerful patron. Despite these disadvantages, word began circulating that Toulon might, in fact, have its own holy woman.

Toulon's acceptance and, indeed, celebration of Catherine's mysticism may be attributed to several factors. First, neither Father Girard nor his colleague Father Sabatier expressed any public skepticism. On the contrary, Father Girard appeared ready to validate the young woman's mysticism as a sign from God. Second, Catherine's dramatic displays of devotion did not deviate from the history of female religiosity that continued to find support within *dévote* circles. Third, Catherine appeared to be a direct spiritual descendant of Marguerite-Marie Alacoque and Sister Rémuzat. And finally, perhaps it was simply the case that this depressed town yearned for its own saint.

In the meantime, the Jesuits, Father Girard's other penitents, and the Cadière brothers enthusiastically spread the news of Catherine's miracles and visions, triggering curious crowds to visit the young woman.[46] By the late spring of 1730, Catherine Cadière's status as a "saint" was beginning to cement itself in the minds of her friends and neighbors. What could go wrong? Catherine and Father Girard appeared to have complete faith in one another, and their community celebrated their relationship as a divine gift.

Like the sunny Toulon days when the harsh mistral winds seemed unimaginable, the clouds of doubt gathering around mysticism seemed remote.

UNRAVELING AND BETRAYAL

The successful spiritual alliance between Catherine Cadière and Jean-Baptiste Girard reflected their ability to play well-established roles assigned to them in the script celebrating such religious partnerships. Their relationship depended on an unwavering, mutual trust and their capacity to project the sincerity of this religious collaboration. Its viability hinged on personal compatibility and consensus, as well as public acceptance and, indeed, complicity. In the spring of 1730, Catherine's family, the Jesuits, and her community fervently embraced her as a mystic on the path to sainthood. But the marquis d'Argens provided a more cynical interpretation of the couple's shared goals: "the reputation for making saints was as precious to him [Girard] just as the desire to be seen as one was violent for Cadière."[1]

D'Argens's sardonic comment was a reminder that although these partnerships were revered, they remained fragile (fig. 4). In the fall of 1730, Catherine revealed a shocking story of seduction and bewitchment. Director and penitent, once inseparable, became adversaries who

FIGURE 4
Jean-Baptiste de Boyer,
marquis d'Argens (1704–1771).
The marquis is considered by
many to have written *Thérèse
philosophe*. His father, Pierre
Jean-Boyer d'Éguilles, was
one of the magistrates in the
Grand'Chambre of the par-
lement of Provence. Courtesy
of the Musée Paul Arbaud,
Aix-en-Provence.

could not agree on a single aspect of their former relationship. Had Father
Girard abused his authority as spiritual director and used the secrecy of the
confession to seduce Catherine? Or had this vain and unstable young woman
used the authoritative voice of the mystic to deceive her confessor in order to
promote herself?

The two versions of what precipitated the rupture reflect the overlapping dangers of mysticism and the confessional. Mysticism and confession
were two different forms of devotion—the former unmediated by a cleric and
the latter impossible without one. However, both were intrinsically personal
and hidden from the view of others, much like the Divine Mysteries of God.
These two opaque practices invited suspicion and speculation, giving free
rein to malicious tongues and libidinous imaginations. Catherine's accusations against Father Girard were reminiscent of the archetypal cultural narrative of the lecherous priest and the virginal penitent in which "libertinism is
clothed with the appearance of piety."[2] At the same time, Catherine's trances

and prophetic utterances could easily be discredited as the product of a young woman's delusions.

GROWING APART

In early June 1730, Catherine Cadière would leave home and enter into a convent in Ollioules, just a few miles from Toulon. Although she was separated from her family, residing in the cloister did not mean that Catherine's relationship with her beloved director ended. Father Girard visited his penitent several times a week, and they corresponded frequently. Despite this contact, the distance began to make a difference. Later, the Jesuit would claim that his doubts about the authenticity of Catherine's blessed state had existed all along and only grew stronger when Catherine entered the convent. And as for Catherine, she described how "the good examples I had before my eyes in the convent of Ollioules, and the holy practices of this house, began to raise my suspicions of my state."[3]

Convents in the Catholic Church were revered enclaves for devout women who pledged their lives to Christ. Forsaking the world when they entered the cloister, these women "married" Christ, pronouncing vows of obedience, chastity, and poverty. This renunciation bestowed a hallowed status. Thus, Catherine's removal to a convent represented a natural step in her pursuit of spiritual perfection. However, it was not her decision but Father Girard's.

Events began to unfold after Catherine's return from a weeklong pilgrimage to the mountains of Sainte-Baume, twenty-five miles east of Aix-en-Provence, during which Catherine again had manifested various ecstasies and minor miracles. Immediately after, in the third week of May 1730, Father Girard wrote to the abbess of the convent of Sainte-Claire in Ollioules. He loftily described his penitent as not being a "common soul" and claimed that "our Lord has a singular predilection for her." He was "persuaded" that if the abbess were to admit Catherine into her convent, God would bless the community with the "greatest gifts."[4] The Jesuit urged the superior to keep these plans to herself because he feared that Catherine's family would protest her removal to Ollioules. Nevertheless, he expressed confidence that the Cadières would submit to the "will of God" once Catherine had left.[5]

Delighted at the prospect of having this exceptional "soul" in her community, the abbess, Madame Françoise d'Aubert, promptly agreed to the arrangement, and Catherine departed for Ollioules on June 6. She carried with her another letter from Father Girard to the mother superior in which he made two requests. First, he asked that the abbess not read his letters to Catherine since they dealt strictly with the "economy of her interior."[6] Father Girard also requested permission to visit Catherine periodically and to continue as her confessor, although this role traditionally fell to the Franciscan monks affiliated with the convent.

Catherine may have maintained her connections with Father Girard, but she was about to leave the only world she knew, perhaps forever. Given Father Girard's comment about the Cadières' reluctance in seeing the youngest family member leave for a cloistered life, we may easily imagine an emotional, tearstained farewell scene. Neighbors may have stood at doorways or looked out of windows, perhaps coming over to bid Catherine goodbye. Father Girard may have attempted to pacify Catherine's mother even as he was trying to get the daughter into the carriage.

Catherine had journeyed from home infrequently, and when she did it was with family or friends such as Madame Guiol, with whom she had visited Sainte-Baume. And now she was about to enter into a world of strangers who operated within a very different set of rules. Catherine prayed avidly and frequently, but now the convent community determined when she should pray. She would have to get out of bed at a set time and would have specific tasks assigned to her. She must have left Toulon unsure and perhaps a bit frightened of what she would find in Ollioules.

Catherine traveled inland on dusty roads to the small town of Ollioules, less than five miles west of Toulon. She was joining the order of Saint Clare, whose members were called Claristes (or Clarisses). A female offshoot of the Franciscans, the Claristes emphasized contemplation and poverty. Despite their principles regarding worldly wealth and enclosure, financial concerns often forced even the most austere of female convents to look for resources beyond their walls. Established in 1634, the Claristes of Ollioules numbered about fifteen, which made them dependent on the ruling elite of Toulon to provide daughters who came with convent dowries.

The nineteenth-century historian Jules Michelet provides an unflattering, although unsubstantiated, description of the community and its mother superior, Madame d'Aubert.[7] He paints a portrait of a thirty-eight-year-old woman who was ambitious and had a mercurial temper. She apparently governed badly: the community observed enclosure poorly, as nuns and novices frequently went in and out of the cloister. Now, Madame d'Aubert accepted Catherine because she wished to "exploit the young saint for the profit of the community"; her plan included expanding her influence over Catherine and diminishing that of the "old Jesuit director."[8] When the abbess failed, she developed a deep hatred for Catherine that would materialize in the deposition she gave against the young Toulonnaise. But in the meantime, Madame d'Aubert's rival, Madame Lescot, the mistress of novices, warmly welcomed Catherine. Michelet's depiction of convent life, full of intrigue and loose morals, remains unreliable and unsubstantiated. Nonetheless, his account reflects popular eighteenth-century perceptions of hidden convent life found in *Thérèse philosophe* and other novels, such as Diderot's *La Religieuse* (*The Nun*) of 1796. For skeptics of religious devotion and even for sincere believers, the convent could easily transform from a site of holiness into a disorderly arena seething with unruly passions.[9]

During the sixteenth and seventeenth centuries, female convents became notorious locations of mass possession. In Lille, Paris, Aix-en-Provence, and Toulouse, nuns "exhibited supernatural physical strength, developed aversion to sacred objects such as the Eucharist, cursed their confessors, priests, or mother superiors, screamed and shouted but also fainted, vomited, suffered fits, paralysis, contortions and convulsions, lost consciousness, and even sank into coma."[10] The most famous example remains the Ursuline convent of Loudun, where nuns, including the superior Jeanne des Anges (1602–1665), accused a parish priest, Urbain Grandier (1590–1634), of introducing Satan into the convent. Grandier burned at the stake in 1634, purportedly for witchcraft, but also because he had made enemies with the local clergy and Louis XIII's minister Cardinal Richelieu (1585–1642). As for Jeanne des Anges, she recovered from multiple possessions and died a famous mystic.[11]

The convent was the perfect stage for Catherine's spiritual agonies and ecstasies. Within a month after her arrival, Catherine began exhibiting the same astonishing behaviors that her family and neighbors had witnessed months earlier. On July 6, Catherine predicted that "extraordinary things" would take place.[12] Early the next morning, Madame Lescot and another nun found her in her cell, motionless, her face covered in blood, and her body prone in a manner that recalled the crucifixion. Witnesses also reported that Catherine said mass, a privilege reserved for ordained priests, and she appeared to have received a portion of the communion wafer through invisible means (fig. 5). Madame d'Aubert promptly sent a courier to summon Father Girard, who arrived soon after the porter's departure.

A crowd of nuns greeted the Jesuit, anxious to tell him about the miraculous events they had witnessed. When asked whether he had encountered the courier, Father Girard replied, "No." But he added that his "good Angel" had

FIGURE 5
Miracle at Ollioules. In *Historische print- en dicht-tafereelen van Jan Baptist Girard, en juffrou Maria Catharina Cadiere*. Courtesy of Bibliothèque Méjanes, Aix-en-Provence.

alerted him to these episodes while he had been saying mass in Toulon. Father Girard also claimed that *he* had been uttering a blessing on that same host, a portion of which had flown into Catherine's mouth in Ollioules.[13] Before going into Catherine's room, he suggested that the nuns keep the water used to clean her blood because it could have "miraculous effects." The Toulonnaise's physical union with Christ now gave her thaumaturgic or miraculous powers, and apparently the Clariste nuns were ready to believe in their effectiveness.[14]

But perhaps the nuns at the Ollioules convent were a little too willing to believe in Catherine's miracles. During the trial, Father Girard's lawyer, Claude-François Pazery de Thorame, would recount a less flattering "miracle."[15] The convent's garden boasted a peach tree, and toward the end of the summer, it appeared that the tree's fruit was rapidly disappearing, undoubtedly because of theft. The abbess took action by posting a spy to catch the thief during the middle of the night. To everyone's embarrassment, the culprit was none other than Catherine, who had been claiming that her ecstatic state made it impossible for her to eat. Now, she was caught stealing into the garden, where she proceeded to devour the peaches while squirreling away a reserve supply in her pockets. Desperate to salvage her reputation, Catherine declared that it was a miracle.

Christ had "inspired" her with gluttony to teach her humility. Moreover, her act of humiliation would cause the tree to bear more fruit. Pazery drily noted that the Ollioules nuns were not sufficiently conversant in the mystical inner ways to seize upon this spiritual "refinement." Luckily for Catherine, the contrite nuns believed her and thanked her for her sacrifice.

If there were signs that Catherine's heightened spiritual state was not genuine, they had no impact on her reputation that summer. News of her latest miracles spread to the neighboring area and to Toulon, and people soon bestowed Catherine with the title "the Saint of Ollioules."[16] Curious about this holy woman and perhaps eager to partake in these miraculous events, lay people and ecclesiastics journeyed to the humble convent to visit the saint. In these meetings, Catherine seemed to know "the secrets of their consciences," and some individuals even consulted her about their future.[17]

Catherine's most important visitor was none other than the bishop of Toulon, Louis-Pierre de La Tour du Pin-Montauban, who had just returned to the region after having been away for nearly two years on "indispensable family affairs."[18] Known for his absence as much as he was for his presence, La Tour du Pin-Montauban was somewhat less admired by his flock than Belsunce, his peer in Marseille, was. Appointed in 1712 during the final years of Louis XIV's reign, La Tour du Pin-Montauban, like the majority of bishops, originated from a noble family. He came from the town of Valence in the province of Dauphiné, northwest of Toulon in the Alps. Perhaps La Tour du Pin-Montauban's absence could be attributed to his roots outside the province.

But now the bishop resumed his role as Toulon's spiritual leader and decided to discover more about this "saint" residing in his diocese. The bishop first met with the Cadière family, who praised Catherine's virtues. She was "an Angel on earth" who could speak about the Holy Trinity more authoritatively than learned theologians; she had stigmata on her feet and fell into ecstatic states "five or six times a day."[19] La Tour du Pin-Montauban then descended upon the Clariste convent, where he met a pale-faced Catherine for the first time. Again, the accounts of what the prelate thought about Catherine and the legitimacy of her mystical experiences were shaped by the partisan nature of the trial. Catherine's supporters argued that the bishop had viewed Catherine as "a fruit of sanctity";[20] only later, under pressure from the Jesuits, did he maintain that Girard had expressed doubts regarding Catherine's visions.[21] Those who argued in the Jesuit's favor painted the prelate as somewhat hapless, duped by Catherine's brother Étienne-Thomas and then by Father Nicolas Girieux, who succeeded Father Girard as Catherine's confessor.[22]

Although public acclaim and the bishop's blessing contributed to Catherine's rising status, the young penitent still depended on Father Girard to authenticate her mystical state. On the surface, the partnership between spiritual director and penitent continued to thrive. Father Girard made the five-mile journey from Toulon to Ollioules two or three times a week, and the two exchanged letters. Writing letters was not simply about maintaining contact. The cornerstone of Jesuit confession and direction, writing also required the penitent to provide a detailed account of her interior movements.[23] Father Girard demanded that his penitent write to him "incessantly," reminding her that Heaven had designs for her.[24] Catherine promised to write twice a week and record her visions and illnesses, which she did in great detail.

Written between early June and early September of 1730, these letters provide one of the few direct clues about their relationship. The correspondence between Catherine and Father Girard provides a window onto how their relationship was shaped by mysticism and, at the same time, was inherently unequal. The letters do not answer exactly why the relationship fell apart, but they suggest tensions—impatience on his part, resistance and stubbornness on hers.

Their correspondence reveals a mutual commitment to mysticism and to one another. Catherine described how the "spirit of God fills me like an ocean with its immensity" and how the "interior flame" consumed her, all expressions that were standard mystical fare.[25] For his part, Father Girard continually urged Catherine to submit to her sufferings because God demanded she "abandon herself absolutely."[26] She would sometimes end her letters declaring herself to be in perfect union with Christ's Sacred Heart; similarly, Father Girard would conclude his letters, "I am all yours in the Sacred Heart of Christ."[27]

But in another letter, the Jesuit director somewhat petulantly chastised Catherine for not writing. He demanded that she answer him, but in a distinctly plaintive tone: "For the love of God, deliver me from this uncertainty."[28] Two days later, Catherine placated the unsettled confessor, reminding him that "in this life, only you, my dear Father . . . give me the first moments of joy, gentleness, and tranquility of which I have lost sight since the first moment that I entered this House."[29] Girard's letters also reveal his eagerness to see Catherine, sometimes expressed in visceral terms: "I have a great hunger to see you again and see everything."[30] This letter, dated July 22, 1730, became key evidence for the argument that Father Girard's attachment was more than spiritual.

Were these simply fervid letters between a priest and a penitent, or were they the impassioned communication between lovers? Not surprisingly, Chaudon and Catherine's supporters would later interpret Girard's letters as those written by a controlling lover and an immoral cleric. However, the letters exchanged between François de Sales and Jeanne Chantal resonated with a similar language of affection and, indeed, passion.[31] One anonymous pamphlet, the *Dénonciation des factums de M. Chaudon*, contained samples of François de Sales's letters, thus encouraging readers to evaluate Father Girard's letter in the context of accepted religious partnerships.[32] But perhaps unintentionally, this anonymous writer had also identified how much religious language borrowed from the vocabulary of love and longing and potentially could serve as a screen for an illicit relationship.

Whatever the nature of the relationship, the letters hint at growing tensions between Catherine and her beloved confessor over a variety of matters, especially her distaste for convent life. Although Catherine remained her confessor's "humble" and "obedient" daughter, she could not adapt to the prescribed routine of convent life. She claimed that her sufferings were made worse when God revealed the sins of the nuns and monks around her.[33] Catherine also complained of being denied the Holy Sacrament on a daily basis, a practice Father Girard had initiated and encouraged. Ironically, she found herself unable to take communion with the community and sometimes incapable of getting out of bed at all.[34] Father Girard responded to Catherine's unhappiness by insisting that it was God's will, and he appeared angry after she had spoken to his colleague Father Sabatier and the bishop's representative about the possibilities of leaving Sainte-Claire. He was determined to prevent this false step, which "the glory of God, the honor of virtue, the graces of Jesus Christ, absolutely forbid."[35] The Jesuit asserted his authority by reminding Catherine that "submission, obedience, abandon: this is what must be practiced today."[36]

The disagreement over whether Catherine should remain in the convent persisted, precipitating acrimonious exchanges. A letter dated September 15 indicates that during Father Girard's visit the day before, the two discussed the possibility of her finding another confessor. Father Girard now agreed, especially since his duties in Toulon made frequent travel to Ollioules difficult; moreover, he acknowledged that having two confessors could be awkward for Catherine.[37] The next day, Catherine left Ollioules and took up residence at a relative's nearby country estate. Catherine would later claim that the bishop of Toulon had been behind her sudden departure. According to this version, La Tour du Pin-Montauban became angered when he heard of Father Girard's plans to move Catherine to a Chartreuse convent outside the diocese of Toulon, either in Prémole or Salettes near Lyon.[38] He then sent a hired vehicle to transport her to her relative Monsieur Pauget's home; she was accompanied by the bishop's own chaplain and her brother Étienne-Thomas. The bishop also as-signed Catherine a new confessor, Father Nicolas Girieux, who had recently arrived from Avignon and taken up the position of prior at Toulon's Discalced Carmelite convent.

The great spiritual friendship between Catherine Cadière and Jean-Baptiste Girard, which had been the talk of Toulon for over nine months, was at an end. It appears that confessor and penitent disagreed over whether Catherine should remain in the convent. Nevertheless, the reasons why the two parted ways are still somewhat obscure because the two versions of what happened were not simple explanations but accusations made nearly a year later. As a result, the accounts on either side were embedded in a larger campaign to destroy the op-ponent's reputation and character. But what remains undisputable was that all the elements that had nurtured the Girard/Cadière partnership—trust, obedi-ence, and a mutual goal—had disintegrated.

THE RUPTURE COMPLETED

By the late fall of 1730, the rift between Catherine and Father Girard would degenerate into a series of accusations that reflected the dangers inherent in the penitent/director relationship and in the excess of mysticism. Catherine would recount a familiar narrative of how Father Girard had used the cover of confes-sion to seduce her. On the other side, Father Girard and his supporters would tell the story of a misguided young woman who fabricated tales of mystical ecstasies and possession to deceive her well-intentioned director.

Ironically, Catherine's claims about how Father Girard had seduced her using the secrecy of confession first surfaced within the confession itself. When Catherine departed from Ollioules, she was left without any spiritual coun-selor, probably for the first time in her adult life. But Father Girard's shoes were quickly filled, as it were, by Father Nicolas Girieux. Pazery suggested that it was the Cadière brothers who introduced their sister to the Carmelite prior; Father Nicolas had been their mother's confessor for the past month.[39] But according to Father Nicolas, the bishop of Toulon first approached him because he no longer trusted Girard. In this version, the prior was reluctant to take up the task of directing Catherine because he feared offending the powerful Jesuits.[40]

Who was Nicolas Girieux, whom many described as handsome, and how did his presence affect what would happen? He was a member of the male branch of the female Carmelites—the Discalced or Barefoot Carmelites (Carmes déchaussés), founded by Saint Teresa of Avila and Saint John of the

Cross. The Carmes déchaussés, like the Jesuits, sometimes acted as confessors and spiritual directors. Like Father Girard, Father Nicolas was an outsider who had just arrived in Toulon with a reputation that preceded him. According to Pazery, the thirty-eight-year-old Father Nicolas was enterprising, ambitious, and apparently brilliant, becoming a prior at a young age. The Jesuits had tried to recruit him, "but the most noble of Sentiments had raised him to the very summit of Mount Carmel, from where he boasted that he had confounded the Jesuits more than once, and that he had revealed some of their heresies in public disputes in Lyon."[41]

While the Discalced Carmelites of Provence were not virulently anti-Jesuit, it appears that Father Nicolas personally loathed the Jesuits, and most observers also tagged him as a Jansenist.[42] Thus, he met Catherine predisposed to think the worst of Father Girard. The relationship between Catherine and her new confessor, then, was framed by monastic rivalries and theological differences, which would shape events over the next several months. Father Nicolas was the linchpin of the Girard/Cadière scandal because it was through him that the private interactions of confession became the object of public scrutiny.

Soon after Catherine's arrival at Monsieur Pauget's *bastide*, Father Nicolas assumed his new responsibilities. Witnessing Catherine in various states during which she first appeared dead and then awoke with an account of visions and "celestial favors," the prior became increasingly doubtful that these episodes were gifts from God.[43] Determined to uncover the cause of such inner turmoil, the prior subsequently engaged his new penitent in a series of soul-searching conversations. How many hours had the Jesuit spent with Catherine? Were they alone? What kind of advice did her former director offer during her turbulent battles against demonic possession? Father Nicolas was shocked to learn that Catherine had not uttered a single prayer in the past year. Instead of resisting possession, she had followed Father Girard's orders to submit to it completely. She gushed that "he [Father Girard] was so intimately united with her that they carried each other in their hearts."[44]

Declarations such as these aroused the friar's suspicions. He learned that Father Girard had shown Catherine "marks of special predilection."[45] During their third conversation, Catherine told of the "maxims that Father Girard instilled in me, the principles on which he set his direction," and then she described "a part of the liberties which the Father had taken with me."[46] According to Father Nicolas, these disclosures confirmed what he had feared. It was the story that had made Abelard and Héloïse famous in the twelfth century—the story of a clergyman seducing a young woman. Similarly, the priest Urbain

Grandier had made enemies in Loudun after first seducing Philippa Trincant, who became pregnant, and then pursuing Madeleine de Brou: "The confessional, the site of forgiveness, had become the site of Grandier's approaches to the women of Loudun, a centre of lechery."[47]

Both the Church and the laity obsessively feared that the intimate practice of confession could hide a multitude of sins. One solution had been the invention of the confessional booth in the sixteenth century, although it would not be used consistently in France until the late seventeenth century. The architect of this innovation, Charles Borromeo (1538–1584), cardinal-archbishop of Milan, wanted to protect confessor and female penitent from one another. Thus, within the confessional box, a lattice grille, sometimes called the Borromean grille, separated the kneeling penitent and seated confessor from one another.[48] In his specifications, Borromeo required that the grille's holes be "about the size of a pea."[49]

Given these anxieties, the very nature of early modern confession depended on trust. The confessor counted on the penitent's sincere desire to enrich her inner spirituality, and the penitent placed her confidence in the priest's genuine commitment to guiding her through this journey. But that faith between Father Girard and Catherine Cadière had been betrayed. Catherine's version of events tapped into the larger concerns about confession when she described how her once-beloved confessor had taken advantage of her innocence and faith to seduce and bewitch her. On the other side, Father Girard portrayed Catherine as a false mystic; her visions and ecstasies were the designs of a silly young woman whose insatiable desire to be noticed led her to misuse confessional practices.

In spring 1731, the first public narrative of Catherine's version of events appeared in the *Justification de damoiselle Catherine Cadière*, "a faithful account of all that took place between this young woman and Father Jean-Baptiste Girard." It was the first salvo in the war of pamphlets and legal briefs that would come to define the Girard/Cadière affair. Despite the general disapproval of women writing for the public, Catherine spoke in her own "voice." Given her education and the restrictions placed on her movements, it is unlikely that Catherine actually composed this pamphlet. The probable author was the abbé François Gastaud (d. 1732), a cleric and lawyer from Aix-en-Provence known for his fierce opposition to *Unigenitus* and his hatred of the Jesuits.[50] Gastaud already had some experience transforming guilty women into women of virtue. In 1699, he had written a defense of Madame Tiquet, who had been executed for murdering her husband; the story he told was of a woman who moved witnesses because "her actions and her countenance showed a moral fortitude, a simplicity, and a tranquility that had been suppressed by her wicked past, but that now re-emerged."[51]

The *Justification* reinforced Catherine's status as an innocent and un-suspecting victim. No doubt, many eighteenth-century readers asked why Catherine had failed to recognize the truth behind Father Girard's words and actions. Was she, in fact, complicit? The *Justification* responded to such skepti-cism by showcasing her sheltered life and her unwavering obedience to her spiritual director. In contrast, Father Girard had used the practice of confession and the mysterious language of mysticism to disguise his true intentions.

To reinforce the image of Catherine as Father Girard's victim, the pam-phlet provided a linear narrative in which Catherine's life story was divided into two distinct parts: before and after the Jesuit director's arrival in Toulon. Prior to being Father Girard's penitent, the pious young woman had practiced a simple and unexceptional faith. As we saw earlier, piety defined Catherine's family life and childhood: "the example of my father and mother had taught me to love the poor, my Directors made it my duty; I followed their advice."[52] Catherine's words echoed Teresa of Avila's characterization of *her* father: "My father was a man of great charity towards the poor, and compassion for the sick, and also for servants . . . his life was most pure."[53] However, there was one significant departure from Saint Teresa's autobiography. Whereas the saint's narrative described temptations and illness as signs of her chosen status, such episodes were entirely absent in the *Justification*'s account of Catherine's child-hood. Instead, the pamphlet emphasized the intimate world of a modest family whose spiritual practices and inclinations did not deviate from the norm.

This familial serenity evaporated soon after Father Girard took charge of Catherine's spiritual inner life. Catherine marked the precise turning point. In late November 1730, the Jesuit supposedly blew a strong puff of air into his penitent's mouth. According to Catherine, "the change that I felt in that in-stant never appeared natural to me."[54] Soon, she found herself unable to say the words of the Paternoster, the Hail Mary, or any other prayers and offices. But Girard told her not to worry and "that the important thing was to give oneself to God, and once one had delivered oneself to Grace, one should not do any-thing other than leave the rest to God."[55] Catherine was not to fight temptation but to yield to indecent visions, obsession, and ecstasies, which were all a divine test of her worthiness (fig. 6).

It was through this guise of spiritual submission that Father Girard initi-ated a sexual liaison with Catherine. When Catherine voiced her doubts about certain lewd visions, Father Girard replied, "in this tone of the Master," that "it

FIGURE 6

Clearly in a trance, Catherine has no control over either her mind or her body. Father Girard assumes a pose that is both worshipful and amorous. In *Historische print- en dicht-tafereelen van Jan Baptist Girard, en juffrou Maria Catharina Cadiere*. Courtesy of Bibliothèque Méjanes, Aix-en-Provence.

was the will of God, that I must deliver myself to all that he [Girard] wished of me."⁵⁶ In the midst of her convulsions, the Jesuit seized opportunities to shut himself up with her alone in her bedroom. One day, he ordered Catherine to kneel while he held a discipline, a whip often used for self-mortification, in order to show her the "will of God."⁵⁷ After her "accidents," the term used to refer to ecstatic states, Catherine would regain consciousness and find herself in "indecent postures" and in a state of undress. At another point, the Jesuit supposedly embraced her from behind. According to Catherine, "I don't know what he did, but I felt a sort of pain I had never felt before." He then placed her on the bed, touching and kissing her "without reserve, always assuring me that this was a new way of achieving sublime perfection."⁵⁸ Father Girard often spoke to her while kneeling and used "the most tender language," perhaps reserved for mistresses and not penitents. No one knew better than Father Girard how to disguise "libertine sentiments under a specious jargon of affectionate devotion and sublime contemplation."⁵⁹

Father Girard's sins seemed to multiply in the *Justification*. Very soon after having had intercourse with Catherine, "the slowness of Nature undoubtedly troubled the tranquility of Father Girard."⁶⁰ In response, the Jesuit purportedly ordered Catherine to drink a concoction that terminated the pregnancy. Soon after, Catherine went to Ollioules, and during the first several weeks, Father Girard visited her frequently in the convent. His ardent desire apparently led him to sully the sanctity of the cloister; in one instance, the convent's turnkey saw the confessor kissing Catherine through the choir grill. He assured Catherine, more than once, that it was unnecessary to confess one's "impurities" because it confused the devil, who endeavored to tempt believers away from God by creating false scruples.⁶¹ These episodes worked together to illustrate how Father Girard had corrupted religious spaces and practices, betraying both his vocation and Catherine's confidence.

Not surprisingly, Father Girard, his lawyer, and the Jesuit's supporters all repudiated this version in the months to come. But denial was not enough of a defense. It was necessary to offer a counter-narrative that cast Catherine as the guilty party. In the months after the *Justification* appeared, Pazery and pro-Jesuit pamphleteers launched a campaign that borrowed directly from the attacks against female mystics who were targeted precisely because they were women, irrational and incapable of self-control.

Pazery and "an ex-Jesuit" pamphleteer, the abbé Pagi "from Lambesc," took great pains to establish that Catherine's predilection toward mysticism predated her encounters with Father Girard.⁶² What drew Catherine to mysticism?

Her family's humble background "condemned her to live in obscurity, without rank, birth, little wealth, little attraction." In Pagi's trenchant opinion, "her little person had the ambition and desire to shine in the world." Mysticism was the vehicle by which Catherine could win fame by becoming a saint.[63] Importantly, Catherine had visions and swoons even prior to Father Girard's arrival in Toulon. Her previous confessor, Father Alexis, had "called them the Caresses of the Divine Spouse, and her Companions called them Strokes of Divine Love." The same Father Alexis, so Pazery claimed, had declared that Catherine was another Catherine of Siena.[64] Under Father Alexis's direction, Catherine had consumed the lives of mystical saints such as Catherine of Siena, Teresa of Avila, and Angela de Foligny, all in an indiscriminate fashion.[65]

To underscore the extent to which Catherine's mystical bent illustrated her unstable character, Pazery and other Girard proponents claimed that Catherine's real model was not these genuine saints but Jeanne Guyon (1648–1717), the consummate false mystic, who seemingly defied all prescribed gender norms.[66] The widowed Madame Guyon had embraced mystical Quietism, a heretical practice involving the passive acceptance of all interior movements. Unlike Marguerite-Marie Alacoque or Anne-Madeleine de Rémuzat, Guyon did not live in a convent. Nor did she have a powerful patron, like the Jesuits or Henri Belsunce.[67] More alarmingly, she had acted as a spiritual director and mentor to priests—including well-known individuals such as François Fénelon (1651–1715), archbishop of Cambrai and tutor to Louis XIV's grandson. Moreover, Guyon had published a theological tract, the *Moyen court* (1685), which violated deep-seated Christian beliefs that women should never speak about theology. The bishop of Meaux, Jacques Bossuet (1627–1704), evoked well-worn constructions of female deception and duplicity when he wrote, "It's important to warn the faithful against a seduction that still exists; a woman who is capable of deceiving souls by such illusions, must be found out, especially when she has admirers and defenders and a lot of support for her."[68] Bossuet clearly regarded Guyon as a threat to social order. According to Pagi, Catherine imagined herself to be another Guyon, with Father Girard playing the role of her dedicated confessor.[69] Thus, Pagi characterized the Toulonnaise as a false mystic, a possible heretic, and a woman who violated fundamental gendered social norms.

In contrast, Father Girard appeared as the consummate confessor and spiritual director, painstakingly examining his penitent's soul while attempting to guide her away from perdition. But why did Father Girard, famous for his spiritual direction, allow Catherine to pursue her mystical ambitions? In

Pazery's assessment, "he was pious, an inward-looking man, full of God's good will for his creation, [who] believed these sorts of events possible."[70] Therefore, the Jesuit could not immediately dismiss Catherine's visions because he genuinely regarded his penitent as a "privileged soul." As a man of deep faith, he began by sincerely believing in what Catherine had told him.

But by the late spring of 1730, Father Girard began to suspect the extravagant manifestations of the divine and demonic that plagued Catherine. A conscientious director, he sought to exercise caution, keeping constant vigil over Catherine's interior state. He urged his penitent to maintain silence about her possessions and visions. Instead, Catherine almost immediately informed her family, friends, and neighbors. And there were other factors that raised Father Girard's doubts. It was after having read the Lenten memoir that he began to piece it all together: "Little by little, he conceived with such horror her hypocrisy and foolishness."[71] The handwriting in the journal was inconsistent—it was clear that there were other authors involved. To his displeasure, he discovered that the chronicle of the Lenten visions was being circulated throughout Ollioules and Toulon. But for the moment, Father Girard said nothing, because he wished to protect Catherine's reputation.

For Father Girard, his special friendship with Catherine was drawing to a close. In a letter to his penitent, he threatened that if, indeed, she had been responsible for publishing these episodes, "he had nothing more to say to her, that she might do as she pleased, that he was resolved to leave her."[72] Attempting to pacify the director, Catherine wrote him a number of times in early September, and although he did not respond, he did come to visit her on September 14. Father Girard possibly confronted Catherine with her lies. She may have begged his forgiveness while repeating how unhappy she was in the convent. According to Pazery, the Jesuit then admonished the errant penitent "that the only means she had left to save her Soul and her Reputation, was to have no communication with anybody out of the convent, but to bury herself forever in the obscurity of retreat."[73] Father Girard left, determined to cut off his relationship with Catherine. But because he was a charitable and pious man, he would not speak out against her. His intention was to remove himself from Catherine's life and hope that she would cease to act so recklessly.

So which version of these two stories was the truth? Had Father Girard seduced Catherine in the privacy of the confessional? Or had Catherine enacted a series of sensational episodes to retain her director's attention and win acclaim? There is the faintest hint that their interactions may have tested accepted boundaries.

A month after the trial ended, Father Girard wrote to a fellow Jesuit, "Although I have nothing to reproach myself with respect to the crimes imputed to me, I find myself with many other miseries with which to reproach myself and to expiate, that I must be careful not to say to the Lord 'why have you treated me thus.'"[74] It is possible that Father Girard was referring to sins in a general sense, sins that reflected the human condition. Or perhaps he felt that he had not been vigilant in guarding against Catherine's excesses. A third possibility is that while he did not commit the crimes of which he was accused, Father Girard had crossed certain lines in his relationship with Catherine.

In the end, we cannot know what happened, but in my opinion, these are some possible scenarios. Father Girard did seduce Catherine, but their feelings were ultimately mutual, a fusion of desire and religiosity. From all accounts, she was attractive, possessing a fervent personality. For Catherine, the Jesuit's attentions were flattering, and she was drawn to a man, however much older, who was charismatic, especially in matters of faith. If the two did embark on a passionate affair, they ran the risks of being caught. Perhaps they concocted the narrative of possession together, especially since it allowed them to meet unchaperoned. Or perhaps Catherine's ecstasies were genuine. But instead of being signs of God's will, they were manifestations of guilt. Or of sexual trauma. We cannot discount the possibility that while the feelings the two shared may have been mutual, Father Girard's initial attentions may have been forced on a young, inexperienced woman unable to resist a man whose vocation she had been taught to revere since childhood. Whatever the origins of the relationship, the intensity of emotion probably took its toll on both confessor and penitent.

Father Girard may have thought that the convent would help cool things down. Instead, the separation precipitated a rift, and now it became a question of how to retreat without damaging their reputations. It appears that Father Girard may have taken the route of silence, but since the two had ceased communication, how could Catherine be sure? If the truth came out, the Jesuits would protect Father Girard, a fact that certainly played out in the months to come. But she had no one—no man would marry her, no convent would accept her. And so, I believe, Catherine made a preemptive strike. All of this remains pure conjecture, since the relationship remained hidden. Father Girard and Catherine's divergent accounts of what had happened concurred on one important point. Their partnership, which once had led Catherine to new spiritual heights and had enthralled Toulon, was based on treachery and deceit.

For Catherine's and Father Girard's immediate associates, the two had represented the ideals of a Christian community. How would the community respond when they learned of the rupture? Perhaps no one guessed that when Catherine went public with her accusations against Father Girard, she would set off a chain of events that would begin as a local scandal and transform into a national obsession.

The TRIAL

BECOMING A *Cause Célèbre*

On January 23, 1731, the Paris lawyer Mathieu Marais wrote to Jean Bouhier, a magistrate in Dijon, that he too had heard rumors about "the provençal Jesuit" and that the affair was becoming "very serious."[1] As Marais's comment indicates, the story of Catherine Cadière and Jean-Baptiste Girard was no longer local gossip. How, in a matter of two months, did a scandal originating in a modest neighborhood in Toulon become a news item five hundred miles away?

The transformation of this local, provincial scandal into a national *cause célèbre* was essentially a three-stage process. It began with rumors and gossip about Catherine's possession by demons. In November 1730, Father Nicolas and the Cadière brothers performed a series of spectacular exorcisms on an ailing Catherine; alarmed, the bishop of Toulon sent his official representatives to investigate. Their harsh interrogation immediately prompted the Cadières to seek justice from secular authorities. The second stage began when the affair entered into the tortuous litigation system of the Old Regime. The Jesuits soon realized that the interrogation of more than one hundred witnesses was not going to stifle gossip anytime soon, and they turned to the king, who ordered the parlement of Provence to hear the case. In this final stage, the king's intervention effectively transformed the Girard/Cadière case into one of the most widely discussed trials in France and Europe, as the public showed an insatiable curiosity regarding the people and events related to the case. Soon, the public itself became a major feature of this *cause célèbre*.

EXORCISM AND SCANDAL

The gossip in Toulon began mounting in November 1730, when Catherine underwent a series of exorcisms, purportedly to rid her of demons. According to the ex-Jesuit abbé Pagi, Father Nicolas enthusiastically embarked on this course when he concluded that Catherine's series of "accidents" were, in fact, the "Devil's play."[2] Exorcism was a perilous process because it was initiated at the point of demonic possession.[3] By the early eighteenth century, theologians, church officials, and urban elites increasingly viewed exorcism with doubt and distaste. Thus, Father Nicolas opened Catherine and himself to mockery and scrutiny by engaging in what many elites dismissed as extravagant acts of superstition.

Early modern exorcism was a malleable ritual shaped by the exorcist's own inclinations, the possessed individual's symptoms, and local customs.[4] Practitioners invoked prayers, scripture, reading, and perhaps the names of saints commonly known for battling demons. They might also have used burnt herbs, fragrant oils, precious stones, and holy water. We might imagine a dark, smoky room, lit perhaps by a few candles, exuding a variety of strong smells.[5] The most powerful weapons were crosses and the Eucharist, whose presence and touch were thought to be unbearable for demons. By the late sixteenth century, priests also incorporated practices of discernment so they could ascertain the state of the possessed person's inner self. Disturbing sounds might have been heard, which included periodic shrieks, lewd diatribes, or gibberish issuing from the mouth of the possessed, perhaps in accents very unlike the person's normal voice. Through it all, the exorcist spoke with the demon, demanding to know its name, its purpose and chosen targets, and whether other demons were present.[6] It was only in 1614 that the Church published the Roman Rite, the official guide for performing exorcism rituals properly.

By the end of the seventeenth century, theologians and church officials began expressing skepticism regarding possession and exorcism in much the same way as they raised doubts about the authenticity of mystical experiences. In the wake of the mass possessions in the convents of Loudun and Louviers (1647), men of law and members of the clergy questioned whether these trials had been just.[7] Had inquisitors involved in these cases acted too indiscriminately and sent innocent men to the stake? Many church officials and elite observers came to regard exorcists as gullible and weak, falling prey to women and susceptible to superstition.[8] Such attitudes did not simply reflect growing doubts regarding demonic possession or even exorcism in principle. They also suggested an effort to define the boundaries of legitimate religious rituals and faith.

Father Nicolas adopted his new role of exorcist at the end of September, a few weeks after taking charge of Catherine's tormented soul. Here again, two conflicting stories would emerge. La Tour du Pin-Montauban and Father Girard's lawyer, Claude-François Pazery de Thorame, described how Father Nicolas, along with Étienne-Thomas Cadière, insisted that Catherine had been bewitched.[9] The Carmelite friar then carried out the ritual "without form, without any of the preliminaries that the Church requires in such a case."[10] However, during the trial, Father Nicolas's version focused on the bishop. La Tour du Pin-Montauban "saw with holy indignation that he had been fooled, and that she whom he had regarded as a Saint, was nothing but an abused creature."[11] The next step would be to censure Father Girard and prohibit him from continuing on with his duties. "No," replied Father Nicolas, "no, Monseigneur, it is necessary to avoid a scandal."[12] The bishop relented, but he ordered that the friar perform an exorcism not just on Catherine but also on Father Girard's other penitents.[13]

Catherine returned to Toulon on October 14, seemingly cured of her "accidents" and rid of all signs of stigmata and other wounds. Soon after, Father Nicolas performed more exorcisms on two of Father Girard's penitents. According to Pazery, Catherine urged her fellow penitents to undergo exorcism, while Father Nicolas went door to door and offered his services to these women. In the end, only two participated: the sixty-five-year-old Madame Lionne ("l'Allemande") and Mademoiselle Batarelle, "a young woman of about three and twenty, who has a weak head, and a strong imagination."[14] Moreover, in this version of the story, the bishop had no inkling of these rites.

News of these exorcisms as well as unflattering stories concerning Father Girard's duplicity began to circulate throughout Toulon. His colleague Father Sabatier insisted that La Tour du Pin-Montauban stop the exorcisms because of these rumors. In response, the prelate sent *grand vicaire* Jean Camerle to investigate the matter. Meanwhile, on November 10, Father Nicolas and Étienne-Thomas were suspended from performing their spiritual functions.

Despite this injunction, both clerics would be involved in another exorcism that became one of the most widely discussed episodes during the trial. In this instance, most of what we know comes from pro-Girard accounts, which used the incident to demonstrate how the Cadière family and Father Nicolas planned to destroy Father Girard's good name.[15] On the night of November 16, Catherine's brother François awoke the entire neighborhood by yelling out the window that his sister was being strangled by the devil. Neighbors poured into Catherine's bedroom. There, they found Catherine "stretched out upon the floor of her room, senseless and motionless, with her neck swelled, and the swelling still rising towards her mouth." Meanwhile, Étienne-Thomas, who had only been a priest for two months, was dressed in a nightgown, wearing a clerical stole around his neck. He carried holy water while Father Nicolas bore a large crucifix. The two men insisted that the witnesses kneel in prayer to assist in rescuing the tortured Catherine. Two curés and a surgeon arrived on the scene, and they declared that Catherine was not possessed; indeed, Catherine appeared to return to normal when they suggested cupping her. Father Nicolas would later defend himself by noting that these clerics were already there when he arrived. He had come to the house in the spirit of concern and charity, but only *after* he had been summoned.[16]

The ordeal continued through the night. Catherine supposedly spoke Latin, and when her brothers queried her on what devil was inflicting such pain, she replied "Jean-Baptiste Girard" and then, a bit later, "the Devil of Uncleanness." The next day, the "possessed" l'Allemande arrived at the Cadière house, and Catherine, who had been sleeping, joined her. Witnesses now saw the two women writhing and convulsing, a scene worthy of Loudun. According to Pazery, "the spectacle lasted until Night, the door of the house always open; so that the house was filled with a succession of persons of both Sexes, of all Ages and of all Ranks, Citizens, Artisans, and Officers of the Navy."[17]

For the Jesuits, the publicity surrounding the exorcisms and the accusations against Father Girard had disastrous possibilities. Father Sabatier was pivotal in the efforts to suppress rumors and to silence Catherine Cadière. We do not know much about this aged Jesuit who, so the Cadières and Father Nicolas would argue, played a key role behind the scenes. Perhaps using satirical verses as his sources, Jules Michelet depicted Father Sabatier as an old and bitter man who had committed a number of well-known indiscretions, including having a married mistress.[18] A few days earlier, Father Sabatier had insisted that the bishop suspend Father Nicolas and Étienne-Thomas. And now, seeking to prevent the scandal from escalating, the old Jesuit returned to the bishop's palace next to the Église Sainte-Marie and convinced him to make official inquiries about the events that had taken place on the rue de l'Hôpital.

Two days after the notorious exorcism, La Tour du Pin-Montauban sent three officials to question Catherine Cadière. They included the bishop's *grand vicaire* Jean Larmodieu (an administrative assistant directly under the bishop), the *promoteur* or investigator and prosecutor Esprit Reybaud, and finally, the episcopal *greffier* or record keeper Maître Pomet.[19] As the bishop's representatives, they were members of the diocesan *officialité*—the ecclesiastical courts—whose purview embraced all matters pertaining to religion and the Church. When the three men arrived at the small house, Elisabeth Pomet immediately rushed upstairs to summon her daughter, who was in bed, although it was daytime. Half awake, Catherine discovered that she had to submit to a lengthy interrogation about her various obsessions as well as the supposed miracles and prophecies.

The questions posed in this session quickly revealed that the representatives of the *officialité* regarded Catherine, and not Father Girard, with suspicion. For Catherine, Elisabeth Pomet, and the rest of the Cadière family, these proceedings were a shock. Catherine "saw herself dishonored, believed that she had nothing to lose, and that since her honor was lost, it was just to pursue vengeance against all the crimes that her Director had committed against her."[20] If she was to obtain justice, she needed to look elsewhere.

CATHERINE CADIÈRE AND LITIGATION IN THE OLD REGIME

At first glance, it might appear nearly impossible for the Cadières, a humble bourgeois family, to have any legal recourse against the powerful Jesuits. But in fact, early modern France was a litigious society in which people from all ranks had access to the complex court system. Marginal groups, such as peasants and widows, could avail themselves of the legal system and even succeed in obtaining justice against the powerful.[21] Litigants benefitted from the fact that in the Old Regime, there was no single judicial system, but tribunals with overlapping jurisdictions. The Cadière affair exposed this complicated and bewildering legal terrain, comprising civil and clerical institutions that sometimes competed with one another.[22] Importantly for Catherine, while the French Catholic Church had its own courts for cases involving clerics or religious issues, lay individuals could bring their grievances against clerics by going before the local *lieutenant-criminel*, a secular judge who functioned in the king's name.

FIGURE 7
Cardin Le Bret (1675–1734)
served as Provence's *intendant* and the *premier président* of the Grand'Chambre.
Courtesy of the Musée Paul
Arbaud, Aix-en-Provence.

Just hours after the bishop's officials had departed, Catherine went to Toulon's *lieutenant-criminel*, Joseph Marteli Chautard. This first deposition contained the key elements of the narrative that people throughout France would discuss over the next year.[23] Catherine stated that she developed an intense passion for her spiritual director immediately after Father Girard breathed into her mouth. Increasingly, temptations and evil spirits threatened to consume her whole being. The director exhorted her to yield to these sensations with the promise that it was a part of God's design for her. Catherine's deposition included a detailed account of their physical intimacy, her subsequent pregnancy, and its abrupt termination. As evidence of the Jesuit's inappropriate intentions, the Cadières attached five letters from Girard, two written to Catherine and the others to the abbess of Ollioules. These complaints to the *lieutenant-criminel* "began this great affair, which eventually attracted the attention of France and even all Europe."[24]

Once Toulon's ecclesiastical and secular officials initiated an inquiry, the Cadière family soon became aware that the justice system was not neutral. The

accused Father Girard remained at large, without any guard, and he continued to fulfill his clerical duties as confessor and preacher in the Jesuit church.
However, Catherine was essentially incarcerated in various convents. In a series
of formal protests that would later be printed, the Cadières also complained
that the Jesuits were suborning witnesses so that their testimonies reflected
badly on the "saint."[25] During the summer, Jean-Baptiste Chaudon, Catherine's
indefatigable lawyer, elaborated on the ways in which the Jesuits had tampered
with the testimony, devoting two legal briefs exclusively to this issue.[26]

It seemed that the odds were against Catherine, who found herself caught in
a systematic miscarriage of justice involving authorities at every level. Catherine
later argued in an *acte protestatif*, or petition of protest, that during her interrogation, she found herself "unjustly oppressed, suffering a great deal during the
examination."[27] This complaint seemed justified, as authorities did appear to be
closing ranks. In a letter to the comte de Saint-Florentin (1705–1777) in Paris,
Cardin Le Bret (1675–1734), Provence's royal commissioner, explained how he,
the bishop of Toulon, and Toulon's governor Dupont were working to contain
the scandal; however, Dupont certainly felt that by early December it was too
late.[28] As the royal *intendant*, Le Bret used a *lettre de cachet*, a sealed order, to
have Catherine imprisoned without any due process (fig. 7). Treating her as the
"guilty person," authorities placed her in Toulon's Ursuline convent, which was
known for its strong ties to the Jesuits; Father Girard had confessed a few of the
Ursuline nuns.[29] Officials also put l'Allemande and Batarelle in *maisons de force*,
convent prisons used to incarcerate unruly and unyielding women.[30]

When Catherine first lodged her complaint before the *lieutenant-criminel*,
she technically placed the case before the local civil court and therefore out of
the clergy's purview. But Toulon's *officialité* still remained in charge. Unusually,
secular and ecclesiastical officials questioned witnesses together, and an administrator for the *officialité* recorded testimonies. Who was working on Catherine's
behalf now that her "natural" judge, the *lieutenant-criminel*, seemed to be at
the beck and call of ecclesiastic officials?[31] The official procedure, designed to
protect individuals who had conflicts with the clergy, was being modified in a
manner that clearly benefitted Father Girard.

Ecclesiastic and secular authorities, which were supposed to "punish him
[Father Girard] for his crimes that so dishonored the Church and Religion,"
were subverting the entire process.[32] Sitting in a room right next to the one in
which witnesses were being questioned, Father Sabatier worked to dissuade
certain individuals from giving evidence that corroborated Catherine's accusations. Their options were either to withdraw or alter their statements. The Jesuit

and his assistants cajoled and supposedly threatened witnesses with impunity. And when he did not succeed, Father Sabatier confiscated the copies of the testimonies so that they would not be entered into the record.[33]

These testimonies contributed to a narrative designed to shatter the reputation of Ollioules's "saint." Once Catherine's friends, Madame Guiol and Mademoiselle Laugier now denied that they had experienced stigmata and obsession. Catherine's stigmata wounds were allegedly nothing but dried hemorrhoid blood, and her fits were, in reality, epileptic seizures. Supposedly living on water during Lent, Catherine had gorged on pâté, choice meats, and jam behind closed doors. She had confided to Madame Guiol how "it was not difficult to fool Father Girard."[34] Even the imprisoned Batarelle retracted her charges against the Jesuit, and as a reward, she was released. Catherine and Chaudon emphatically rejected their claims, stating that these women, as loyal penitents of Father Girard, were "accomplices of their director's crimes."[35]

Officials were also busy in Ollioules ensuring that the Clariste nuns now repudiated Catherine's dramatic miracles. Spearheading this effort was the Observatine monk Father Aubani, recently accused of having raped a thirteen-year-old girl. The officialité now dropped these charges with the understanding that Aubani would testify against Catherine and help with the proceedings. With apparent enthusiasm, Aubani assembled a group of assistants, including an uncle and a sister, who alternatively intimidated and coaxed nuns who might speak against Father Girard.[36] In addition, a nun from Toulon's Ursuline community, Sister Cogolin, wrote to Sister Beaussier on January 28, 1731, outlining the kind of evidence witnesses were supposed to provide when questioned. Apparently, the deposition of four Clariste nuns conformed to this "model."[37]

Aubani and his team concentrated much of their efforts on discrediting Marie Matherone, the convent's gatekeeper, who claimed to have seen Father Girard and Catherine kissing and embracing. Aubani threatened to have Matherone expelled from the convent if she did not withdraw her statement. Apparently, she responded that the bishop of Toulon would have to pay her a pension so that she would not starve. According to Jean-Baptiste Chaudon, this request proved that the Cadières, contrary to Pazery's claims, had not bribed her.[38] The story of Matherone's deposition, the treatment of the Ollioules nuns, and the testimony provided by Father Girard's loyal penitents seemed to point to one thing: a plot to preserve Father Girard's reputation at all costs.

The depositions also reveal how Toulon's dévotes, once united in their reverence for the Jesuit, were irrevocably estranged, which was made even more apparent in the "confrontations" between different witnesses. In his encounter with Madame Guiol, Étienne-Thomas suggested that she had had an unsavory past; in addition, she had gone deliberately to monasteries in Aix and Marseille "to defame his Sister." When he asked if Madame Guiol had commanded Father Girard's other penitents not to reveal the "liberties" the Jesuit had taken with them, she snapped back at his "atrocious calumny."[39] Other confrontations between Catherine and her fellow penitents, and between Father Nicolas and the penitents, must have been similarly dramatic, involving raised voices and sometimes devolving into shouting matches. For the community in which Catherine had spent her entire life, these emotional exchanges signaled a crisis that seemed to destroy the bonds created by shared goals of spiritual perfection.

Despite her friends' betrayal and the officials' hostility, the Cadière family continued to press Catherine's case. On December 20, 1731, Elisabeth Pomet wrote to Cardin Le Bret protesting procedural irregularity. First, the Jesuits and the bishop of Toulon had suborned witnesses. Second, the *officialité's greffier*, or scribe, Pomet, had recorded the testimonies in an irregular fashion. Third, Catherine had no counsel at all. And fourth, the Ursulines were treating her daughter in an insulting and unfair manner. They had placed her in a malodorous room, which once had housed an insane nun and now was furnished with only a straw mattress and thin blanket.[40] Catherine's "attendant" was the daughter of Madame Guiol, Father Girard's most loyal penitent. Whenever Catherine left the convent, guards escorted her to make sure that she would not escape. In addition to these indignities, the bishop of Toulon refused to provide her with a confessor until she had ceased targeting "a holy man."[41] Ominously, Le Bret did not respond.[42]

Elisabeth then looked to Paris for justice. On numerous occasions, she sent pleas to the keeper of the seals, Chancellor Henri d'Aguesseau (1668–1751), and once to Cardinal Fleury himself.[43] Elisabeth reiterated the complaints she had made to Le Bret about how the justice system seemed to favor Father Girard while condemning her daughter. She described herself as a mother "overwhelmed by grief" who was acting "to save the honor of a family exposed to public defamation."[44] While these affecting words may have been rhetorical flourishes designed to elicit sympathy, they probably reflected real fears. Was Elisabeth going to lose her only daughter and youngest child?

Elisabeth's correspondence to authorities in Paris indicates that the matter had now gone out of local hands. On January 16, 1731, Louis XV (1710–1774) issued an *arrêt du conseil*; this edict placed the case before the parlement of Provence in Aix-en-Provence, some thirty-six miles away.[45] This shift in procedure indicates that local officials—ecclesiastic and secular—had failed to bring closure in a manner that was satisfying to either party. How did the king, seated in Versailles, become involved in a scandal taking place so far south, in Toulon? According to the marquis d'Argens, whose father was one of the presiding judges, Louis XV's confessor, the Jesuit Father de Linière, wrote to his fellow Jesuits, urging them to consult with "their friends." As the parlement's highest-ranking magistrate, its *premier président* (as well as Provence's *intendant*), Le Bret met with judges, sympathetic to Father Girard, who agreed that the hearings should take place before the parlement.[46] This secret deliberation produced the king's intervention. His decree was meant to bring the scandal to a conclusive and speedy end in Father Girard's favor.

The effects of Louis XV's edict were felt in February, when representatives of the parlement of Provence were put in charge. An *arrêt* of February 16 charged two commissioners—Louis Bouchet, sieur de Faucon (1680–1766) and councilor of the parlement, and the abbé Augustin de Charleval (1677–1732)— with the task of collecting testimonies in preparation for the hearing before the Grand'Chambre, the parlement's highest chamber. To the Cadières' consternation, the commissioners' arrival did not signal a departure from the harsh treatment Catherine had received from Toulon's officials.

Like the Toulonnais officials, the two commissioners seemed equally determined to affirm Father Girard's innocence. The confessor continued to enjoy his freedom while Catherine remained virtually imprisoned in the Ursuline convent, although now she was allowed to seek counsel for her defense. On February 23, Faucon and Charleval, along with the parlement's attorney general, served Father Girard a *décret d'assigné*, a summons that required only his lawyer's presence. Although desirable, the Jesuit's presence was not obligatory, and he would only have to pay fines if he failed to comply with the summons. However, Catherine, Étienne-Thomas Cadière, and Father Nicolas all faced more serious writs, *decréts d'ajournement*, which mandated that the three appear for questioning. Failure to obey the writ allowed officials to take them into custody.[47] Not surprisingly, Girard replied to his summons with alacrity because he knew that "he would be among friends."[48]

But it was the commissioners' interrogation of Catherine on February 23 and 26 that added even more drama to the affair. During the first two interviews with Faucon and Charleval, the young woman steadfastly maintained her allegations against Father Girard. Before the third interview, her "keeper," Sister Guiol, insisted that the exhausted Catherine drink some wine to revive herself; Catherine later stated that she did so reluctantly. Immediately after consuming the wine, she felt that she was on fire and "outside of herself." As if in a fog,

Catherine heard the convent's superior, Madame Gerin, threaten her, telling her that if she persisted in her accusations, the Cadière family would be lost. But Catherine would not perish at the stake if she "revealed" that Father Nicolas was behind the accusations. The abbé de Charleval reinforced this intimidating message, and Catherine described his aggressive behavior as "torture to my spirit." "From eight in the morning until seven at night," the commissioners relentlessly interrogated the disoriented young woman, who increasingly gave contradictory responses.[49] At the end of the session, Catherine retracted her accusations. She had been wrong. She had lied. Father Girard was innocent of seduction and bewitchment.

Catherine stood by this new version of her story while the commissioners moved rapidly to terminate the case, reexamining witnesses, including Father Girard. On March 6, confessor and penitent had a meeting during which Catherine confirmed the Jesuit's version of the story.[50] She also blamed Father Nicolas, who, Catherine now claimed, invented much of the story she had previously told. At this stage, Father Girard was clearly exonerated, the victim of a slanderous ruse to tarnish his saintly image. It seemed to be over. According to the Jansenist newspaper *Nouvelles Ecclésiastiques*, the Jesuits made sure that news of this recent development was made known throughout the realm almost right away.[51]

However, on March 10, Catherine issued a retraction of her retraction and returned to her original story. According to the young Toulonnaise, the wine Sister Guiol had given her had tasted "salty." Soon after swallowing the beverage, Catherine entered into a state in which she could not even recognize "her own mother."[52] Thus, her responses to the commissioners' interrogation on February 26 and 27 were neither "free nor voluntary" but really the result of a plot to silence her. Who were the perpetrators? Although Sister Guiol had served her this questionable wine, it was Father Girard who "well knew by what means one can agitate the spirits of people, and is not a novice in the composition of beverages."[53] All the statements Catherine had issued for the last few weeks had been made under duress.

After this astounding reversal, Catherine was removed from the Ursuline convent, "like a prisoner of state," and taken to Ollioules, where the commissioners were preparing to question the Clariste nuns.[54] At Ollioules, Catherine was placed in quarters so squalid that her mother was forced to go to Toulon to procure a mattress. Elisabeth Pomet did more than that. She lodged another official complaint regarding her daughter's treatment and repeated how the tainted wine had resulted in the "derangement of her [Catherine's] senses."[55] Before leaving for Ollioules, Catherine herself signed an *acte protestatif* on March 15 that charged the *officialité* of Toulon and the Ursulines, respectively, with judicial mismanagement and mistreatment. The next day, she made a statement about the episode of the infamous beverage used to coerce her into withdrawing the charges against Father Girard.[56]

Despite these complaints, Catherine's situation did not materially improve. The commissioners denied Elisabeth's request that Catherine be restored to her, stating that they had instructions to remove her daughter to Aix-en-Provence, where the parlement would soon hear the case. Catherine described a humiliating journey from Ollioules to Aix in which she and her mother had to endure uninvited attentions from the archers escorting them. When they arrived in Aix on March 18, the superior refused them entry, despite the orders she had received to house Catherine. Once in the convent, the situation worsened. Male guards patrolled outside Catherine's door, and the nuns continually taunted the young Toulonnaise; hostile passersby serenaded her with "defamatory songs" right underneath her window.[57] At one point, Catherine discovered a mysterious letter on her bed. Addressing her as "ma chère" (my darling), the anonymous author threatened Catherine with further public opprobrium if "thou continuest to inform the rest of the world about your folly."[58]

However much Catherine and her family must have despaired, they still had one legal defense available, the *appel comme d'abus*, a special appeals process that had grown in political importance over the last few years. Designed to prevent clerical abuses, the *appel comme d'abus* enabled an injured party to bring an *ecclesiastical* superior or a *clerical* judgment before a *secular* court like the Grand'Chambre of the parlements.[59] Catherine's use of the *appel* had added significance in the spring of 1731, because the appeal had become an important political weapon in the controversies surrounding the anti-Jansenist bull *Unigenitus*.

Starting in 1727, Cardinal Fleury (1653–1743) stepped up his campaign against Jansenism, which he regarded as a political threat because its proponents consistently defied the authority of both Church and State (fig. 8).[60] He replaced Jansenist prelates with ultramontane bishops, who then targeted suspected Jansenist parish priests. These policies resulted in a reinvigorated use of the *appel comme d'abus* protesting such episcopal zeal. Furthermore, in January 1731, forty lawyers from the parlement of Paris wrote a fierce defense of the *appel* after the General Assembly of the Clergy had denounced the process. In a remonstrance issued on September 3, the parlement followed up by sharply reminding the king that the *appel* was "an invincible rampart to stop the

FIGURE 8
The king's prime minister,
Cardinal André-Hercule de
Fleury (1653–1743). Courtesy
of the Bibliothèque de la
Société de Port-Royal, Paris.

enterprises of ecclesiastic powers on the legitimate and immutable rights of royal authority." And it was the parlement's sacred duty to protect this right from the encroaching reach of the clergy.[61]

Unlike the public, when Catherine Cadière used the appeal on April 11, 1731, she was probably unaware of the explosive politics surrounding the *appel comme d'abus*.[62] In her *appel* against Toulon's *officialité* and the commissioners from the parlement of Provence, Catherine protested the inequities that were impeding justice. The *promoteur* Reybaud had violated Catherine's rights as a royal subject, especially when he entered her house without a warrant or any official charges. The clerical judge had acted in bad faith, desiring nothing less than to "favor crime and oppress innocence."[63] An innocent girl had been transformed from the accuser into the accused. In addition to the *appel comme d'abus* against clerical officials, Catherine lodged an appeal protesting how Father Girard had been served the *décret d'assigné* while she and her brothers had to endure the indignities of the harsher *décret d'ajournement personnel*.

Despite these protests, the process continued to work in Father Girard's favor. On April 8, the parlement of Provence's Grand'Chambre received the papers relevant to the case.[64] Obeying the king's wishes to silence public opinion, Le Bret ordered that the proceedings take place behind closed doors. Going against custom, he commanded guards to prevent anyone from entering the Grand'Chambre, "even the sons of the presidents and counselors."[65] On May 21, Le Bret, in his capacity as the leading judge in the parlement, rejected the appeals regarding the *décrets*.

In the meantime, Catherine and her mother, Elisabeth, pressed their case further by writing again to Chancellor d'Aguesseau on May 2.[66] They pleaded with the chancellor: "Deign, Monsieur to use your authority, so that one can at least save the appearance of rules, and that neither the time nor the means of self-defense are taken away."[67] Perhaps the Cadières had been advised that Henri d'Aguesseau had once been a fierce proponent of parlementary prerogatives, such as the *appel*; he had been rumored to be pro-Jansenist, characteristics that might make him less sympathetic to the Jesuits.[68] But the chancellor whom Cardinal Fleury had only recently recalled from exile was now a different man.[69] In a June 10 letter to commissioner Faucon, d'Aguesseau gave assurances that the king desired nothing more than to silence the scandal and to protect Faucon's reputation. Unfortunately for d'Aguesseau, the *Nouvelles Ecclésiastiques* printed the letter in August, which added to the public's growing perception that authorities were actively working on Girard's behalf and against Catherine. At the same time, the king had issued a June 11 *arrêt* upholding Le Bret's rejection of the appeals against the *décrets*; the edict reaffirmed the royal order that the Grand'Chambre hear the case.[70]

Like Catherine, Father Nicolas and Étienne-Thomas Cadière encountered setbacks in their efforts to defend themselves. Both contested the *officialité*'s actions and the parlement's *décret d'ajournement*; they also refused to accept the evidence the commissioners had amassed.[71] In his appeal, Father Nicolas noted that when he received his *décret*, he "believed that the proceedings had confused one confessor with another, or that one imagined that one could replace an accused Jesuit with another monk who had no other support but his innocence."[72] Clearly, justice could not be found in Provence.

At the end of May, the Carmelite friar and Étienne-Thomas took a more aggressive approach and left for Paris "to take their complaints against the injustices of the parlement, notably the commissioners, before the Throne."[73] They made the arduous journey from Toulon to Paris, hoping to persuade the powers in Paris to present the case before the Grand Conseil, the King's Council.[74] Perhaps they hoped to find more sympathy from those removed from the politics of Provence. It must have been an overwhelming journey, given the strain of the last six months. The two clerics were welcomed by the Paris Dominicans, especially the anti-Jesuit head prior. But they got lost in the busy Palais de Justice, the seat of the parlement of Paris, where they hoped to meet with some of the most powerful lawyers of the day. Father Nicolas and Étienne-Thomas were unsuccessful in their efforts to meet Chancellor d'Aguesseau and the archbishop of Paris, Charles-Gaspard de Vintimille-Luc (1655–1746).[75] They may not have been surprised that Vintimille did not see them—before becoming archbishop of Paris in 1729, Vintimille, the former archbishop of Aix, supported *Unigenitus* and was a friend to the Jesuits.

The king's repeated intervention in the Girard/Cadière trial, the letters to Chancellor d'Aguesseau, and this trip to Paris suggest the different ways in which the affair was no longer taking place at the periphery of the kingdom. On a fundamental level, the king's decree took a provincial trial and made it a national affair. With the use of the *appel comme d'abus*, Catherine's trial became linked to anxieties about a clergy that consistently appeared to be overstepping its defined jurisdiction and thereby infringing on the rights of French subjects. But if the Jesuits succeeded in getting the judicial courts to favor Father Girard, they found themselves at a decided disadvantage before another court—the "tribunal of public opinion."[76]

PUBLIC OPINION

In the second paragraph of his first *mémoire judiciaire* for Catherine Cadière, a brief close to two hundred pages, Jean-Baptiste Chaudon praised the public as a "Judge, so upright and so fair."[77] Chaudon's comments reveal that by the early summer of 1731, the public became an important element of the Cadière trial. Letters and police records indicate that the public was eager to obtain the numerous legal briefs pertaining to the trial; elites and non-elites closely followed the deliberations taking place before the parlement of Provence. While there was a public comprising a hodgepodge of people representing different social groups, there was also "the public"—a unified, abstract entity. This public functioned as a rhetorical counterweight to the institutions and authorities of the Old Regime. During the early 1730s, the controversies over *Unigenitus* and the Cadière affair gave this public new life, especially in the pages of the Jansenist periodical *Nouvelles Ecclésiastiques* and the trial's many *mémoires judiciaires*.

Who were the individuals and groups following the Girard/Cadière scandal, and how did they obtain news? Letters circulating throughout France illustrate how members of the aristocracy, the legal world, and the literary world followed the Cadière affair. Joseph de Seytres, marquis de Caumont (1688–1745), a respected man of letters in Avignon, got his information from a variety of correspondents who reveal a network from Paris to Provence. They included Henri-Joseph de Thomassin de Mazaugues (1684–1743), a magistrate in the parlement of Provence, who first informed Caumont of the affair in late December 1730.[78] Caumont himself exchanged news with his friend d'Anfossy, affectionately called "Kiki," who was Cardinal Fleury's secretary in Paris. Caumont's other correspondent was Pauline de Grignan (1674–1737), marquise de Simiane and the granddaughter of the seventeenth-century aristocrat Madame de Sévigné (1626–1696), the celebrated letter writer. Speculating about Father Girard and Catherine's relationship, Madame Simiane noted, "but it is all rumor, and this affair has varied so often for and against, that it would be rash to form and establish a judgment based on gossip."[79] Mathieu Marais remarked to his friend Jean Bouhier that he was somewhat surprised that the *Nouvelles Ecclésiastiques* had not yet written about the scandal.[80] Thus, elites took advantage of oral, written, and printed venues to obtain news.

Moreover, the letters and diaries of elites help us imagine milieus in which individuals from different walks of life gathered to exchange information. Barbier observed that the *mémoires* were being openly distributed at the doors of public walkways and theaters.[81] Police spies gathered information from "different places"—smoky cafés, public gardens such as the Palais Royal in Paris, theaters like the Comédie Française, or even markets by the Place des Prêcheurs in Aix. These were spaces inhabited by simple bourgeois, artisans, students, and priests, women as well as men. The police referred to anonymous "nouvellistes" who gathered information about events in Provence.[82] Their records also reveal how people shared material in more intimate ways, as neighbors. In November 1732, one Montenaut, a notary in Aix, moved into the rue Saint-Sauveur in Paris, where he offered to make his neighbor a copy of the anti-Girard *Motifs des juges du parlement d'Aix*; this task needed to be completed quickly, since a friend had lent Montenaut his copy.[83] Such records suggest a public composed of elites (including men and women), laity and the clergy, professionals belonging to the bourgeoisie, and non-elites ranging from artisans to workers.[84]

While letters and police files reveal a public that was anything but homogenous or cohesive, the "public" evoked in print gave the impression of a "unitary tribunal capable of distilling reason and consensus from the mass of conflicting individual opinions."[85] Chaudon implicitly argued that the Cadière case galvanized this public because its issues were so universal: "This cause, which is the subject of discussion and attention throughout the entire Christian world, is very important because it interests Religion and the entire public so deeply."[86] Chaudon was, of course, conveniently ignoring how *Unigenitus* and the Jesuits produced divisions within the public. Importantly, in calling the public a judge, Chaudon endowed the "public"—or more precisely, "public opinion"—with authority. His appeal to the "public" reflected the growing importance of public opinion in two arenas: the reignited conflicts around Jansenism in the late 1720s and the growing importance of the public within the pages of the *mémoires judiciaires*.[87]

As we saw, Cardinal Fleury's anti-Jansenist operation reinvigorated the Jansenist quarrels. The most recent controversy was a 1727 ecclesiastical council in Embrun, some 115 miles away from Aix.[88] The council's hidden purpose was to punish bishops who had led the charge against *Unigenitus*, and its target was the eighty-year-old Jean Soanen (1647–1740), bishop of Senez, a seat 55 miles northeast of Aix. Soanen was a hardened Jansenist, renowned for his unrelenting fight against the bull. Moreover, he came from an obscure, non-noble background and therefore had no powerful family or patron to protect him. As a result, the Council of Embrun used the bishop as a scapegoat to warn outspoken opponents of *Unigenitus*; it effectively stripped Soanen of his clerical status and exiled him to Auvergne.

The Council of Embrun gave new life to a sporadic newsletter, the *Nouvelles Ecclésiastiques*, which now became a regular periodical reporting on the persecution of those who opposed *Unigenitus*, especially its recent martyr, Soanen.[89] Started by the brothers Jean-Baptiste and Marc-Antoine Desessart, the polemical *Nouvelles* had two clear goals: to publicize the persecution of Jansenists and to undermine the Jesuits. It meticulously recorded how unknown individuals—artisans, nuns, and shopkeepers—willingly suffered for their faith in their resistance to the bull.[90] The growing importance of the laity within the Jansenist movement was also reflected in the events in the Parisian parish of Saint-Médard. Starting in the late 1720s, hundreds of visitors flocked to the tomb of the deacon François de Pâris, a Jansenist known for his charity, austerity, and fierce opposition to *Unigenitus*; on August 4, 1731, a woman named Lorme went into a paralytic state, which ushered in the convulsionary movement.[91] The *Nouvelles* kept faith with the Saint-Médard *convulsionnaires* by naming individuals in their detailed accounts of miracles. Whether reporting on appellants or the faithful of Saint-Médard, the periodical repeatedly appealed to the public as "a judge" with an unprecedented urgency.[92]

For the *Nouvelles Ecclésiastiques*, the Girard/Cadière affair appeared at a critical moment when authorities had Jansenists against the rails. There is no indication that Catherine Cadière herself was a Jansenist, although her brother Étienne-Thomas belonged to the Dominican order, whose Toulon house had Jansenist leanings. If anything, the Jansenists abhorred the mystical excesses that had made Catherine such a celebrity in Toulon. For many Jansenists, the convulsionary movement was a deep embarrassment made worse when Louis XV closed the cemetery in January 1732.[93] Regardless, what mattered to the *Nouvelles* was that Catherine was the victim of Jesuit perfidy, and her case was not an isolated affair. It was a reflection of Jesuit immorality and the Society's dominance over the king and his subjects. The Jesuits systematically maligned their enemies "without proof, without foundation, without truth" while going so far as to justify their fellow Jesuits' crimes.[94] Not surprisingly, the periodical provided painstaking details of the legal proceedings and included long excerpts of the various legal briefs.[95]

These briefs, also known as *factums* or *mémoires judiciaires*, occupied a unique place in a world of censorship and clandestine publishing.[96] Composed by lawyers in defense of their clients, the briefs were included in a parcel of papers, the *sac du procès* or "trial bag." They were intended exclusively for the presiding judges who were supposed to read the documents within the confines of the courtroom. The Bibliothèque Méjanes in Aix-en-Provence possesses a bound copy of a judge's annotations of the *factums* from the Girard/Cadière trial. Unfortunately, we do not know the identity of this judge—a man of "great merit" and with "a great reputation in the Republic of Letters." However, the meticulous annotations illustrate the seriousness of the trial and provide an example of how most judges earnestly approached their tasks.[97] These *factums* were not public documents; by definition, they were sealed official documents and were therefore uncensored.

Yet this institutional policy had nothing to do with practice. For well over a century, lawyers made their briefs accessible to the reading public through their prose and publication in print. We think of legal briefs today as dry, full of legal jargon that makes the contents tedious and often incomprehensible. In contrast, early modern French legal briefs provided entertaining stories of bigamy and murder, as in the case of the country nobleman Louis de la Pivardière, who was thought to have been killed by his unfaithful wife but then reappeared with a second wife and children.[98] Moreover, by the time the Cadière affair exploded onto the scene, there was an *expectation* of public disclosure. Writing to Bouhier in late September 1731, Marais questioned the Provençal court's criticism of Chaudon: "one reproaches him for having had the interrogations printed: isn't it a document thought to be public?"[99]

These legal briefs became events in and of themselves. Marais wrote to Bouhier that "la Cadière's great *factum*" had at last arrived, and copies were being snatched up at the Palais Royal.[100] On three occasions, Thomassin de Mazaugues informed the marquis de Caumont that the first *mémoire* for Father Girard, which was being written in "great secret," still had not appeared.[101] Soon eager readers were struggling to keep up with the avalanche of *factums*. Madame de Simiane asked Caumont: "Do you have them? Do you want them, and at what address?"[102]

When the trial finally ended in October 1731, Caumont and Thomassin de Mazaugues planned on binding together a collection of the *factums*.[103] But printers were well ahead of them. Over the next few years, collectors could acquire multivolume sets of different sizes containing all the *mémoires*. These sets were given the title "recueil général" (general collection) and were printed in Aix, Paris, and abroad in Holland. By 1732, the briefs had been translated into English and German.[104] As Marais remarked, "at present, all the universe knows about the trial and in all the languages."[105] Over the course of six months, there were sixty-six different legal documents printed, some of which were over two hundred pages in length.

Although the *factums* produced during the trial fit into the category of those exposing the private lives of subjects, those pertaining to the Cadière affair intersected with a different use of *mémoires* that had gained political traction over the previous two decades. By the late 1720s, some of the most prominent Parisian lawyers used the *mémoires judiciaires'* immunity from censorship to defend appellants protesting *Unigenitus*. During the Council of Embrun, twenty Parisian lawyers wrote a variation on the *mémoire*, a *consultation*, for Jean Soanen. Jacques-Charles Aubry (1688–1739) authored a theoretical *consultation* that conveyed a vision of the Church based on the "rights" of the believers. Similarly, Chaudon and the lawyers defending the Cadière brothers and Father Nicolas argued how certain clergy—namely, the Jesuits—posed a threat to those rights.[106] When, in the early 1770s, François Richer began editing François Gayot de Pitaval's *Causes célèbres et intéressantes* (1734–43), he devoted an entire volume to the Girard/Cadière trial.[107] Richer's thorough treatment of the Cadière affair had political roots. After all, his mentor was Louis-Adrien Le Paige (1712–1802), a Jansenist lawyer who was at the center of the fight against *Unigenitus* and the Jesuits during the second half of the eighteenth century.[108]

Gossip and rumor, a complicated legal structure, and different forms of print made a local scandal into a national preoccupation. Significantly, they brought in an important player: the public. Within the pages of the *mémoires judiciaires* and the *Nouvelles Ecclésiastiques*, the public appeared as an independent entity, an impartial judge who possessed the ability to discern the truth. However, this public was not the public associated with the Enlightenment, an oppositional voice from the outside. Rather, this public emerged out of Jansenist dissent and from loopholes within the legal system of the Old Regime.

ARGUING THE CASE

The twists and turns of the Cadière affair riveted the public's attention. The sheer volume and intensity of *factums* stoked its curiosity, and the bitter war of words between lawyers further captivated the public. In addition to Jean-Baptiste Chaudon and Claude-François Pazery de Thorame, three other barristers participated: Bourgarel (for François Cadière), Jean-Louis Fouque (for Étienne-Thomas Cadière), and Jean-Jacques Pascal (for Nicolas Girieux). Through the summer and fall of 1731, no *factum* went unrebutted. Chaudon even answered Pazery's second 201-page *mémoire* with *two mémoires*. Toward the end, both lawyers consolidated their arguments into shorter *précis*, perhaps realizing that they might exhaust the judges' patience and public sympathy.[1]

Not satisfied with picking apart and restitching Catherine's accusations, the lawyers heavily embellished the evidence with character studies and claims of conspiracy. Father Girard was the libertine confessor who abused his position to control his penitent's body and soul. Catherine was the charlatan whose unsubstantiated charges wove a web of delusional lies. Moreover, Pazery contended that, to protect Catherine, her brothers and Father Nicolas had hatched a conspiracy to ruin Father Girard and embarrass the Jesuit order. But Chaudon, Fouque, Bourgarel, and Pascal countered that the Jesuits were the real conspirators, subverting justice and threatening innocent families. These charges acquired further toxicity through vitriolic pamphlets by partisans on both sides.

A *cause célèbre* like this begins with a particular crime or scandal, but its staying power hinges on its connections to larger issues and anxieties. All five lawyers successfully demonstrated how the crimes imputed to Catherine and her brothers, to Father Girard and Father Nicolas, were linked to broader concerns about ecclesiastical authority and the sanctity of religion. These arguments gained additional urgency because they were intertwined with those articulated during ongoing political conflicts about *Unigenitus*.

THE WANTON JESUIT

At the time of the trial, Jean-Baptiste Chaudon was forty-eight years old, a native of Moustiers in the Aquitaine, directly west of Provence. Like a number of barristers attached to the parlement of Provence, he had been reluctant to take this case against a Jesuit. However, once committed, Chaudon threw himself into Catherine Cadière's defense, "at the expense of his life, if necessary."[2] But the lawyer was no Jansenist; indeed, he had always gone to Jesuits for confession.[3] The *Nouvelles Ecclésiastiques* emphasized that Chaudon's motives were pure and nonpartisan: he was "so convinced of this Father's crime that since he was already defending the girl's innocence, he did not believe that her defense should be abandoned to another."[4] However, rumors did circulate that Chaudon received assistance from the abbé François Gastaud, a vocal opponent of *Unigenitus*.[5]

Chaudon was an indomitable presence in court. According to Thomassin de Mazaugues, in early July Chaudon spoke "with a fire and a vehemence" for three and a half hours.[6] During a fierce altercation between Chaudon and Pazery, Cardin Le Bret, "who is as phlegmatic as he is taciturn, was stunned by Chaudon's yelling and even more, his boldness."[7] This passion asserted itself in thirteen *factums*, to which he devoted "all the force and liberty of his ministry."[8]

Chaudon's *mémoires judiciaires* expounded on the four central charges against Father Girard: witchcraft, Quietism, spiritual incest and abortion, and as we saw earlier, subornment of witnesses. His long discussion of the first three accusations demonstrated that Father Girard's relationship with Catherine was a story not simply of sex but of power. The lawyer liberally used stock characters—the innocent, unsuspecting virgin seduced by the libertine Jesuit—to convey Catherine's helplessness against a man who exploited his status as priest and confessor to dominate her completely. Significantly, Jean-Baptiste Girard's crimes fit into a larger history in which "many priests have been executed after the discovery that their crimes passed for models of virtue."[9]

Chaudon inherited the accusation of witchcraft from Étienne-Thomas Cadière and Father Nicolas, who had presented these charges to the bishop of Toulon earlier in the fall of 1730. *His* strategy involved comparing Father Girard to Louis Gaufridy, a Marseille parish priest convicted of sorcery in 1611: "The example of Louis Gaufridy can well serve to justify the same approach taken by the accused [Girard], who so well imitated it in every way."[10] Gaufridy's supposed crime took place in a cave near Aix-en-Provence where he caused over thirty demons to enter the bodies of two young women, Madeleine Demandols and Louise Capeau, nineteen-year-old novices in Marseille's Ursuline convent.[11] Like Father Girard, Gaufridy infamously exhaled a breath into the mouth of another penitent, Madeleine de la Palud. He then took the pregnant Madeleine, "his penitent and mistress," away from her father's house and placed her in a convent in Aix. The parlement of Provence condemned Gaufridy, who perished at the stake, accused of rape, blasphemy, magic, and witchcraft. These comparisons, of course, directed readers to conclude that Father Girard deserved the same fate.

Using the testimony of multiple witnesses, Chaudon presented Catherine's "accidents" as clear evidence of demonic possession. Asked to reveal the demon's name during the exorcism of November 18, Catherine repeatedly yelled, "Jean-Baptiste Girard." "Does all of this not prove that the link of this fateful union of a director with his penitent was sorcery, the object, indecency, and the author, Father Girard?"[12] The lawyer attempted to inject logic into the claim: "Indeed, without witchcraft, could a young girl of eighteen years, like demoiselle Cadière, have become enamored to the point of madness of a fifty-year-old director who himself had nothing glamorous or seductive for a young girl?"[13]

While Catherine's neighbors may have eagerly witnessed the November exorcisms, Chaudon's opponents and educated readers were skeptical. In his second *mémoire judiciaire* for Father Girard, Pazery gleefully emphasized the inconsistencies in Chaudon's accusations of sorcery.[14] He dismissed the idea that Father Girard had made a pact with the devil forty years before: "In truth our fathers' nurses put them to sleep with similar tales: but their children, little affected by such frivolous amusements, wish for something more solid to content their spirits, which were instructed and formed early."[15] Similarly, the marquis d'Argens ignored the witchcraft charges in his memoir: "I leave the idea of witchcraft aside; it must be the height of ridiculousness for whoever has the least notion of a little philosophy."[16]

These skeptical attitudes reflected a growing trend in the second half of the seventeenth century in educated circles—in the Church, aristocratic drawing rooms, and the government.[17] In 1682, Louis XIV had issued an edict that "declared all magical practices to be false and identified its practitioners to be nothing but 'so-called magicians.'"[18] Without affirming or denying the existence of witches, the edict made witchcraft prosecution suspect. Even before, the parlements had been reluctant to prosecute supposed witches who confessed under duress. Increasingly, church officials suggested that priests treat accusations of witchcraft with reason and incredulity. Lines seemed clearly drawn: superstitious beliefs in witches, magic, and supernatural forces belonged to the world of the uneducated.[19]

Derision of witchcraft probably caused Chaudon to retreat and focus on the "pernicious maxims of Quietism" as the source of Catherine's supposed miracles and visions.[20] In the late 1680s, the Church had condemned mystical Quietism as a heresy because it defined an individual's relationship with God as something internal, unmediated by priests and independent of the community. This emphasis on interiority was reflected in a mystical style of prayer known as orison, which contrasted sharply with two other accepted forms of prayer. The first was vocal prayer located in the mass or religious processions— in other words, all the forms of communal worship associated with "baroque piety." Often practiced by adherents of Jansenism, the second form, meditative prayer, was more inward looking and rigorous in its efforts to overcome temptation and individual weakness. While these two methods of prayer were active, orison emphasized complete abandonment, passive acceptance of all that God offers a person.[21] Jansenists despised orison because its passivity did not discipline the mind to contemplate God and His mysteries.

In the late seventeenth century, Quietism gained notoriety because of Jeanne Guyon, whom we encountered earlier, but also thanks to a libertine Spanish priest, Miguel de Molinos (1628–1697). Molinos urged followers not to resist temptation because "the greatest of all temptations was to have none at all." This was the road to "pure love" of God.[22] However, his focus on the individual's spiritual union with God, without priestly assistance, implicitly challenged the Church's hierarchical emphasis on male clerics. Not surprisingly, the Jesuits, who stressed the confessor's importance, thought that Molinos threatened moral and social order, and they led the campaign against him. Molinos was charged with heresy in 1687.

Yet the pages of *Nouvelles Ecclésiastiques* indicate that the tables had turned on the Jesuits. The order became linked, at least by Jansenists, with Quietism, thanks to the charge against Father Girard. In June 1731, the *Nouvelles* reported that Quietism was "making progress" in Provence, and that "the devotion to Sacred Heart of Jesus is always the preliminary step [toward Quietism]." Fourteen months later, the curés of Rhodez, nearly 160 miles northwest of Marseille, accused another Jesuit, Father Lamejou, of Quietism.[23] The timing of these charges, during and just after the Cadière affair, strongly suggests that for Jansenists, at least, the Jesuits' questionable moral and theological inclinations manifested themselves as a form of heresy.

Chaudon devoted an entire *factum*, the *Parallèle des sentimens du p. Girard avec ceux de Molinos*, to crafting a lineage between Father Girard and Miguel Molinos (who also had questionable relationships with female penitents).[24] Giraud, one of Catherine's earlier spiritual directors, testified that Catherine and a number of Father Girard's other penitents could no longer say their prayers. Anne Batarelle admitted to experimenting with a "cessation of prayers"; Catherine herself had reassured her that once union with God was achieved, all other forms of worship were unnecessary.[25] Father Girard's penitents also took communion often, without preparation through appropriate prayer and fasting. In contrast, Jansenists distrusted frequent communion, believing that the sacrament could only follow true repentance, achieved through rigorous meditative prayer. Only then was one worthy of the Holy Sacrament.

But instead of insisting that his penitents battle sin, Girard encouraged them to abandon self-control. At the core of Father Girard's teachings was a phrase that would become infamous as the months wore on: "oubliez-vous, laissez-vous"—"forget yourself and let yourself go." Through this language of faith, Girard led Catherine to sin by exhorting her to surrender to whatever visions she saw or voices she heard. Chaudon specifically identified this doctrine as "carnal Quietism": "One can say that carnal Quietism is the great highway to impurity. Thus, Quietists, under the pretext of pure love, of Divine love, give in to all types of dissolution."[26] Thus, "he [Father Girard] told her: 'My daughter how can you doubt that the good God does not wish us to live together in a state of conjugal union' . . . He successfully persuaded her that she should regard it like the caresses of Divine love."[27] Girard used his theological training to transform desire into a form of worship. Through this dialogue, Chaudon illustrated the chilling mechanics of "carnal Quietism," which enabled Father Girard to access, violate, and control Catherine's body *and* soul.

Quietism was the vehicle through which Father Girard committed his principal crime—"spiritual incest." Unlike the phrase "carnal Quietism," which Chaudon had manufactured, the term "spiritual incest" was derived from canon law. The very phrase conveys how sexual liaison between a spiritual director and his penitent encompassed a multitude of sins.[28] The director not only had physical relations with his penitent but also betrayed the implicit trust that was purportedly the foundation of that relationship. As evidence, Chaudon focused on a letter of July 22, 1730, which contained another phrase Chaudon repeated often: "I have a great hunger to see you again and to see everything."[29] Hunger signaled visceral, insatiable physical desire. The letter also included another ambiguous statement: "I will tire you; oh, well, don't you tire me as well? It is right that everything is divided in half."[30] Chaudon commented that it would be difficult to explain this statement without hurting "chaste ears" and that perhaps these words were more appropriate to describe a "conjugal union" between husband and wife.

Father Girard's yearning letters were not the only evidence of his passion. Chaudon repeatedly highlighted how Father Girard had been sequestered behind closed doors in Catherine's bedroom in Toulon and in her cell at Ollioules. His own excuse was that he had been alone with Catherine for just a few minutes and only four or five times, with the sole purpose of authenticating her supposed stigmata. The wound that attracted the greatest speculation was the one on Catherine's side, located "four fingers" below her left breast (fig. 9). Chaudon noted that for the confessor to judge the wound properly, he must have undressed her. Why was Catherine's mother absent during this investigation to ensure all proprieties?[31] After examining her bare side closely, the Jesuit then had kissed the gash, following the "example of Saints." "Could we not ask him how he kissed this stigmata without touching a tit?"[32] Did Father Girard see himself as another Saint Aldhelm, "who in order to triumph over the Demon of Impurity, and to gain a certain victory over him, lay with pretty girls, and took leave without emotion or peril?"[33] These questions mocked Father Girard's denials, and Chaudon sealed his arguments by reminding readers that both canon law and Jesuit rule forbade priests to be alone with women and certainly to touch them.[34] These cautionary laws reflected the dangers of the confession, where intimacy might move to fornication, then pregnancy.

According to Catherine, this natural course of events precipitated another of Girard's crimes—abortion. For a priest to father a child was certainly not

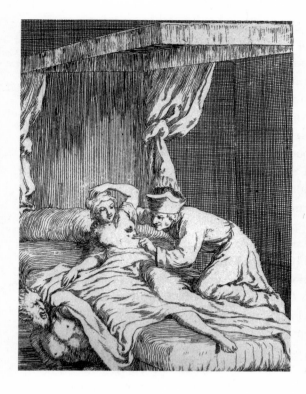

FIGURE 9

As if preparing to climb into bed, Father Girard intently inspects possible signs of stigmata "four fingers" below her breast. The satyr-demon below the bed reveals the Jesuit's true intention. Catherine's expression in this image suggests possible complicity and even pleasure. In *Historische print- en dicht-tafereelen van Jan Baptist Girard, en juffrou Maria Catharina Cadiere.* Courtesy of the Bibliothèque Méjanes, Aix-en-Provence.

unheard of, and throughout Catholic Europe, stories circulated of rural priests whose housekeepers functioned as wives and mothers.[35] However, by the 1730s, after more than a century of Catholic reform of priestly conduct, Father Girard knew that Catherine's pregnancy spelled his ruin. In Catherine's version of the story, the Jesuit then hatched a plan to circumvent scandal by terminating the pregnancy.

Early modern abortion involved consuming an abortifacient or chemical substance that induced miscarriage. Catherine claimed that over the course of several days, Father Girard administered a beverage, assuring her that it was "water." According to testimony by the Cadières' servant, he insisted that only he could prepare this concoction. But as Girard's lawyer Pazery would rightly point out, no one saw him prepare it. If he had, did the Jesuit go to the local apothecary and ask for a collection of dried herbs, such as thyme, lavender, or substances like the "Jesuit" or Peruvian bark that, ironically enough, Jesuit missionaries had brought back from the Americas?[36] Perhaps Father Girard went out alone and collected the evergreen plant rue, a known abortifacient common throughout the Mediterranean.

Whatever was in the beverage, it worked. After severe bleeding, Catherine passed large quantities of tissue and blood, which Batarelle and l'Allemande verified in their testimonies.[37] Girard then took the "mass of flesh" over to the window and inspected it with some satisfaction before its disposal—another sign of Father Girard's guilt.[38] Subsequently, when Catherine went to the Clariste convent, Father Girard asked the abbess and the mistress of novices to alert him if Catherine lost large amounts of blood. In a letter of July 30, Father Girard also inquired about Catherine's period.[39] Thus, Chaudon presented detailed, yet circumstantial, evidence that effectively painted a compelling image of a ruthless man attempting to cover up one crime with another.

How was Father Girard able to satisfy his lust and maintain power over his penitent? Jean-Louis Fouque, Étienne-Thomas Cadière's lawyer, suggested that the Jesuit used the confessional shadows: "while a white sepulcher outside, and ravaging wolf inside, he [Girard] practiced in secret only actions of shadow, works of death, only operations of flesh and blood."[40] The bestial connotations of this remark only made Girard more sinister. Further, Fouque's remarks suggest a different interpretation of the well-worn tale of the lascivious priest seducing the nubile penitent. Yes, Girard was unable to control his passions. But perhaps the confession itself was at fault because it remained hidden and unsupervised, enabling a predator to catch his unsuspecting prey.

But proving Father Girard's various crimes in the name of confession and mysticism was not enough. Chaudon was challenged to salvage Catherine's image as an innocent, virtuous woman even after her seduction. He depicted his client as a "simple" girl; it was "simplicity" that caused her to believe everything Father Girard taught.[41] "Simplicity" came with a multitude of meanings, as suggested by the different definitions found in the *Dictionnaire de l'Académie française*. The term meant naiveté and even gullibility, but it also suggested unaffectedness and purity.[42] "Simplicity" made Catherine an inherently passive figure controlled by her spiritual director. Thus, she bore no responsibility for her convulsions, visions, and blasphemous utterings. Catherine was, above all, a victim.

With some help from the codefendants' lawyers, Chaudon evoked a stark narrative of clerical seduction. In the end, Father Girard was the agent of all the fantastic goings-on in the Cadière household and at the Clariste convent of Ollioules. Sorcery and Quietism represented a systematic campaign, all the more sinister for being planned and executed in the confession. Father Girard had used his position and its authority to deceive Catherine, her family, and his other penitents.

THE WAYWARD SAINT

Girard's lawyer, Claude-François Pazery de Thorame (1678–?), had the burden of establishing that his client, not Catherine, was the true victim. As *sieur* or lord of Thorame, he was an established barrister and assistant to the parlement of Provence's judges. Étienne-Thomas Cadière's lawyer, Jean-Louis Fouque, tagged Pazery as the "Defender of the Society," an insinuation of corruption.[43] The *Nouvelles Ecclésiastiques* reported that he became involved in the case as early as Christmas 1730; supposedly, Pazery spent two days sequestered in the opulent Jesuit seminary in Toulon, strategizing how to crush the scandal.[44] Unlike Chaudon, who had to surmount numerous legal obstacles and uncooperative officials, Pazery had Jesuit power and influence behind him and the knowledge that at least half of the parlement was loyal to the Society. Rumors circulated about possible collaborators who may have helped the lawyer. There was the highly placed Pierre-François Lafitau, the ultramontane bishop of Sisteron (1685–1764), the abbé Jean de Vayrac, and the unknown "abbé Pagi, ex-Jesuit," author of *Histoire du procez entre demoiselle Cadière . . . et le père Girard.*[45]

In countering Chaudon's *mémoires judiciaires*, Pazery had to refute the charges against Father Girard and essentially to invert the contrasts Chaudon drew between his client and Catherine Cadière. Father Girard now became a devout religious, while Catherine was a woman of volatile, dubious character. Pazery also declared that the real criminals were Catherine, her brothers, and Father Nicolas. The three men had launched a *complot* or conspiracy to ruin Father Girard, or, more accurately, to humiliate the Society of Jesus.

Pazery's initial defense revealed inconsistencies in claims that Girard had bewitched Catherine. According to a number of witnesses, Catherine had experienced visions *before* her confessor's arrival in Toulon. And her wounds were not the product of possession: she had been susceptible to sores since childhood. Pazery also rejected the assertion that Father Girard had blown into her mouth. "Where is the proof of the specific virtue of this breath? In which nocturnal assemblies was he [Girard] discovered? Which magicians had he been seen to visit? Finally, what pact had he made with Devil?"[46]

Pazery questioned whether it was possible for Father Girard to be both a sorcerer *and* a Quietist. How could someone who had renounced God and religion then embrace a heresy, which, although full of doctrinal errors, did not deny God? Furthermore, Father Girard had "preached, he directed, he confessed for twenty-five years. Was there anyone who had ever risen up against his doctrine?"[47] Referring to the notorious phrase "oubliez-vous, laissez-faire,"

Pazery asked whether it was possible that the same priest who urged complete self-abandonment would then exhort his penitent to pray for God's guidance—especially since Quietists eschewed prayer.[48]

Father Girard's remarks about self-annihilation were not Quietist errors but, in fact, derived from accepted doctrine. The lawyer argued that Father Girard was "speaking only in the language of the *Imitation of Jesus Christ*," referring to Thomas à Kempis's devotional manual (1418–27), which emphasized how renunciation was necessary in order to open oneself to God.[49] In response to the supposedly amorous language in Girard's letters, Pazery pointed out that François de Sales had used words of affection and intimacy when writing to Jeanne de Chantal.[50] Even more outrageously, "the sisters à la Coque and Rémuzat are declared Quietists just like *la Cadière*, and the confessors of the two nuns, libertines and heretics like Father Girard because all three were Jesuits."[51] In other words, Chaudon had expressed shocking impiety by conflating authentic mysticism, exemplified by François de Sales and the cult of the Sacred Heart, with the false mysticism of Quietism.

Pazery's distinction between true and counterfeit mysticism indicates that rifts between the educated and illiterate over spiritual matters were not as absolute as we imagine. Indeed, the presence of the supernatural was indisputable for the vast majority of French society, regardless of rank, wealth, or region. Mathieu Marais, who consumed Enlightenment literature and shook his head over witchcraft, also celebrated the miracles around the tomb of the "blessed Pâris," the Jansenist deacon of Saint-Médard.[52] And despite his earlier remark about nursery tales, Pazery did not argue that witchcraft and magic were purely the fanciful imaginings of the uneducated. In a later *mémoire*, the lawyer stated categorically, "We agree with our adversaries about the power of demons. The difficulty thus is no longer about the principles but only in the application of those principles."[53] The statement suggests that Pazery found himself in an awkward, even dangerous position. A complete denial of supernatural forces implicitly questioned religious miracles, such as the priest transforming the communion wafer into the body of Christ. For the educated and uneducated alike, who all belonged to a Christian community, questioning the supernatural was, at the very least, unsettling, especially in the wake of the Quietist controversies and battles over *Unigenitus*. What was true Christian doctrine? And what role did priests play in one's spiritual life?

Pazery affirmed the centrality of the clergy as he dismantled accusations of spiritual incest and abortion. Chaudon had suggested that Father Girard's frequent visits to the Cadières' home revealed his predatory obsession with Catherine. Pazery countered, "In effect, if visits of this nature could be condemned, what disorder would it create for families? The sick, the indisposed and those who could not leave their homes, would perish without any assistance to their souls."[54] When inspecting Catherine's sides to verify her stigmata, Father Girard had touched her with "all modesty and all precautions imaginable"; a handkerchief was "folded twice" so he could lightly touch her neck and shoulders.[55] These were not a lover's caresses but the scrupulous ministrations of a conscientious priest authenticating a miracle. Since there had been no sexual intimacy, Pazery logically concluded that the abortion had not occurred.

Proving Father Girard's innocence depended on demonstrating Catherine's guilt as well as that of her brothers and Father Nicolas. In the *factums* and pamphlets written for Father Girard, Catherine was a somewhat protean figure. At some points, she appeared weak and misguided; at others, manipulative and malicious. The multiple crimes laid at Father Girard's door were "the system of *la Cadière*." But Catherine did not design this "system" alone.[56] In Pazery's version of events, her brothers and Father Nicolas had hatched a *complot*, a conspiracy against Father Girard. Their intrigue served two purposes: to salvage Catherine's reputation before she was exposed and to undermine the Jesuits regionally and perhaps across the realm.

Catherine Cadière was a bad character whose ambition to be a saint combined with what Pazery saw as an innate talent for fabrication. Her vanity led to a spiral of "duplicity" and "hypocrisy," words that Pazery sprinkled generously in his *factums*. Catherine used a variety of tricks to convince her confessor and those around her that God, in fact, had chosen her as a vehicle for his message. For example, she had applied rouge and opened up preexisting tumors to cover herself with blood.[57] He also noted that these episodes generally took place once a month; perhaps Catherine had used menstrual blood as stigmata.[58] The *Second mémoire pour le p. Girard jésuite* contained five pages, divided in columns, comparing Catherine's visions to similar episodes in the lives of Catherine of Siena, Agnes of Montepulciano, and Agatha of the Cross.[59] These saints merited "the veneration so just and so legitimate that all Christians should have for Saints recognized by the Church." However, Catherine was engaged in "sacrilegious imitation."[60]

Imitation implied theatricality. Pazery referred to the exorcisms of November 18 as a "comedy."[61] Certainly, the scenes in which Catherine underwent ecstasies and possession were made all the more dramatic by the audiences she attracted. References to theatricality were especially potent because the theater occupied an ambivalent place in early modern society. Louis XIV manifested his power through a staged life at Versailles and displayed his benevolence by generously supporting the theater. On the other hand, many considered the theater to be a source of distraction that used human frailty as a source of merriment. Plays lured people into make-believe worlds and encouraged audiences to suspend belief and judgment.[62]

Thus, accusations of theatricality automatically implied immorality and deceit. Pazery repeatedly denounced Cadière's vicious ruses, her "fourberies." She engaged in a form of playacting and therefore was an "actress." For church officials and many moralists, actresses were in some ways "public" women, or prostitutes, because they put themselves forward brazenly.[63] The abbé Pagi, author of the *Histoire du procez*, was hardly circumspect in calling Catherine Father Nicolas's "whore." Another pamphlet referred to Cadière as the "pretend virgin."[64] Catherine's different roles—innocent virgin, mystic visionary, possessed being—were not just a random assortment of lies. They were a "system" contrived to hold the attention of a priest whose blessing she needed to gain public recognition as a "saint."

Catherine's system, or comedy, needed a supporting cast. Pazery and Girard's other supporters insisted that the story Catherine brought before the bishop of Toulon in September was a larger *complot* or "cabal," involving Étienne-Thomas, François, and Father Nicolas. According to the lawyer, there were two plots. The first involved the Cadière brothers, who worked behind the scenes to cement their sister's reputation as a saint. Architects of the second conspiracy were Étienne-Thomas and Father Nicholas, who fabricated the accusations against Father Girard that Catherine presented first to La Tour du Pin-Montauban and then to Toulon's *lieutenant-criminel*.

In Pazery's narrative, by early 1730, the Cadière brothers were invested in their sister's fame as a "saint" because it gave them status in the community. They also recognized that Catherine's success depended on retaining Father Girard's approval. Catherine herself had devised her gyrations, convulsions, and other physical manifestations of the divine and demonic. But, during those same months, the brothers had manufactured written evidence showcasing Catherine's exalted state.[65] Catherine clumsily exposed her brothers' entanglement when she made the pilgrimage to Sainte-Beaume, near Aix, in May 1730. Her traveling companion, Madame Guiol, had walked in on Catherine, who was holding a just-finished letter to Father Girard. But there was no ink on her writing desk! In other words, the letter, which included details about the various ecstasies and visions Catherine experienced *during* her trip, had been written before the journey.

The most egregious example of forgery and deception was the famous Lenten memoir.[66] Father Girard had asked Catherine to submit a journal so he could discern the nature of the spirits tormenting her and determine the authenticity of her visions. To his irritation, Catherine had delayed writing the journal and only did so months later at Ollioules. When Girard finally received her journal, he might have had the unsettling experience of feeling he had read Catherine's account elsewhere. As noted earlier, certain descriptions of her miracles and visions matched almost exactly those found in the lives of well-known saints like Catherine of Siena. The journal also demonstrated a certain sophistication incomprehensible in "a girl raised in the bottom of a shop, who nevertheless used scholarly terms, and gives herself the airs of someone raised in philosophy and theology."[67] More to the point, Catherine's brother Étienne-Thomas, a Dominican monk and the family intellectual, was Sorbonne-educated.[68] The Jesuit's suspicions, once aroused, could not be allayed. After "the mask fell off, [he discovered] the Saint was only a hypocrite, [and] Father Girard left her right away."[69]

At this point, Catherine and her brothers panicked. What if Father Girard acted "to unveil their impostures"?[70] Catherine would be ruined, her honor irrevocably tarnished, and the family a laughingstock. The second *complot* was thus born in the fall of 1730. The Cadière brothers now drew in the Carmelite friar Father Nicolas, who invented the accusations against Girard that filled Chaudon's *factums* and the *Nouvelles Ecclésiastiques*.[71] The Cadières willingly followed their new accomplice's lead when he informed the bishop that Catherine was possessed by demons. By unleashing these demons, Father Nicolas set about destroying Father Girard's reputation.

What was the motivation for the friar in this tangled web of deceit? It was rivalry and jealousy. Two pamphleteers, Chiron de Boismorand and the abbé Pagi, argued that soon after Father Nicolas and Catherine met, they embarked on an affair: "Father Nicolas did not displease Mademoiselle Cadière, and Mademoiselle Cadière did not displease Father Nicolas."[72] It was rumored he had spent a night alone in Catherine's room, supposedly to monitor her spiritual state. However, Pazery opted for another version in which Father Nicolas immersed himself in the Cadières' affairs not because he took "a great interest in Cadière's honor, but to satisfy his ancient passion against the Jesuits."[73] Catherine's plight was a golden opportunity for the Carmelite priest to form his own coterie of *dévotes* and be the new spiritual icon of Toulon.[74] Father Nicolas and the Cadière brothers hoped to damage the Jesuit's standing in the eyes of the bishop, Louis-Pierre de La Tour du Pin-Montauban, and "a certain Public in Toulon," no doubt a reference to Jansenists.[75]

Thus, it was reasonable to believe that the Cadières and Father Nicolas expanded their campaign against Father Girard to encompass the entire Jesuit order. Indeed, Pazery noted that the "cabal" would not have even formed had not Girard been a Jesuit.[76] He observed that Chaudon's *factums* and published appeals, as well as verses, pamphlets, and newspapers, "not only were against Father Girard in particular, but against the Jesuits in general."[77] Another sympathetic pamphlet, the *Lettre d'un magistrat désinteressé*, bitterly remarked that "an infinite people," though ignorant of the facts and the evidence, hated the Jesuits so passionately that they condemned Father Girard before the magistrates had heard the case. Who were these people? For some, the answer was obvious. An anonymous pamphleteer declared that for the Jansenists, "it is a great blessing to find a Jesuit guilty and perhaps . . . all the Jesuits of the universe."[78]

Personal ambition and passion combined with broader political issues had transformed the innocent Father Girard into an object of hatred, the victim of a series of plots. Interestingly, Catherine sometimes appeared as a victim in Pazery's *factums*: "This girl, unhappy as well as guilty, victim of vanity, of shame, of the resentments of her brothers [toward Girard] and the Passions of the Carmelite father, thus became the odious instrument of their vengeance."[79] Why did Pazery excuse Catherine? Did he assume that since she was a woman, Catherine was incapable of devising such an intricate plot? Or perhaps the lawyer knew that by attacking this woman, whom the public quickly had come to regard as Jesuit prey, he would undermine his client's case. It might have appeared better strategy to go after men who could be shown to have larger, more dangerous motives.

BROTHERS AND FRIARS

These elaborate accusations against the Cadière brothers and Father Nicolas remind us that Father Girard and Catherine were not the only ones forced to defend themselves: François and Étienne-Thomas Cadière and Father Nicolas were also implicated. Thus, three more lawyers became involved. Bourgarel, the least known, wrote two *mémoires judiciaires* on behalf of the priest François Cadière. Jean-Louis Fouque composed two for Étienne-Thomas, the Dominican friar accused of masterminding the first plot. And the Provençal lawyer Jean-Jacques Pascal (no relation to Blaise Pascal, "a fatal name for the Jesuits") denied the charges against his client in the 168-page *Mémoire instructif pour le père Nicolas de Saint-Joseph*.[80] Their *factums* naturally included lengthy rebuttals of the accusations of *complot*. What distinguished them from Chaudon's diatribes was a more direct, expansive critique of the Jesuits.

Both Bourgarel and Fouque were at pains to disprove the accusations of forgery and fabrication against Catherine's brothers. Did François and Étienne-Thomas compose letters for their sister in order to pass her off as a saint? Of course not—she dictated them to her brothers whenever they visited Ollioules.[81] Jean-Louis Fouque countered the allegation that his client Étienne-Thomas had composed the infamous Lenten journal; Pazery claimed that the text reflected a specific Dominican mystical text found in the Dominican library in Toulon.[82] Fouque rebutted this attack with Anne Batarelle's testimony, which said Father Girard had lent her a copy of the Jesuit Jean-Joseph Surin's devotional works. In 1695, during the Quietist controversy involving Madame Guyon, Surin's *Spiritual Catechisms* (1654) was banned for its mystical contents.[83] Jesuit influences, not a Dominican treatise, appeared to have shaped Catherine's mystical experiences.

Similarly, Jean-Jacques Pascal sought to absolve Father Nicolas from any responsibility for Catherine's state of demonic possession. Pascal's Father Nicolas was a modest, obedient cleric with no interest in exorcism. Like Father Girard, the Jesuits, and, indeed, most of Toulon, the Carmelite friar had believed in Catherine's "heroic" mystical state. He had exorcised the possessed young woman because he had been told to do so by the bishop of Toulon, head of his diocese.[84] Thus, Father Nicolas had gone through the appropriate channels and exorcised these demons discreetly and according to protocol.[85] The accusation that Father Nicolas and the Cadière brothers had launched an elaborate conspiracy against the powerful Jesuits seemed built on unproven conclusions and circumstantial evidence.

The theory of this conspiracy may have arisen from the widely held conviction that Father Nicolas was a Jansenist. So did Jansenist beliefs, in fact, shape his defense? Persistent rumors, linked to Nicolas's trip to Paris, alleged that his *mémoire* was written by "four of the most famous lawyers in Paris."[86] These rumors identified two well-known lawyers, Jacques-Charles Aubry and Henri Cochin (1687–1747), who were engaged in the fight against *Unigenitus*; Aubry had played an important role in composing the *consultation* for Soanen after the Council of Embrun.[87] The two lawyers did not put their names to the *factums*, but that was hardly unusual. If Cochin and Aubry were involved, it is likely that Pascal consulted them, and they may even have contributed sections to Father Nicolas's *factum*.

More than any other *factum,* this *Mémoire instructif pour le père Nicolas* reflected a Jansenist outlook on life. The brief's opening reiterated the Jansenist conviction of humanity's inherent sinfulness: "Man's corruption is such, that it is not enough for him to abandon himself to the most obscene passions, [that] he wishes to do so peacefully and with impunity; he sometimes even goes so far as to sanctify them in the eyes of other men."[88] Pascal also adapted the arguments of his seventeenth-century namesake Blaise Pascal. The allusion to the sinner who pursued his activities under the guise of virtue suggested Jesuit casuistry. As Blaise Pascal had argued nearly eighty years earlier, casuistry profoundly failed to make clear distinctions between good and evil. Girard thus personified this casuistical method because his piety masked sin.

Jean-Jacques Pascal implicitly equated casuistry with Quietism. He fused anxieties about Quietism with well-worn stereotypes of the Jesuits—their moral laxity and their uncanny ability to insinuate themselves into the hearts and homes of trusting Christians: "The Director only spoke to her of God; he assures her that she is united with God; she participates every day in the most revered Sacrament [communion], she sees that one makes a kind of cult out of her stigmata, and that the will of God manifests itself in miracles; she is, however, *dishonored*, and it is the act of Quietist virtue that *dishonors* her."[89] The reference to frequent communion also linked Girard to another Jansenist complaint against the Jesuits.

While these insinuations critiqued Jesuit doctrine, the Jesuits' dealings with the bishop of Toulon were reminiscent of the persecution Jansenists experienced starting in the late 1720s. In his examination of the events of November 1730, Pascal focused on how Father Girard's colleague Father Sabatier had pressured La Tour du Pin-Montauban and manipulated the overall proceedings in Toulon: "Was Father Sabatier not always the master, and even if he were to cease being one, would there not be more Jesuits in the world to replace him?"[90] The old Jesuit had "remonstrated" with La Tour du Pin-Montauban for failing to act decisively and put an end to the scandal. When the bishop seemed unwilling to revoke Father Nicolas's status "to save the Society's honor," the Jesuit spent three weeks threatening him.[91]

For many contemporaries, the image of this indecisive bishop cowed by Father Sabatier struck a sinister note because of relations between the Jesuits and a number of ultramontane bishops. After all, Henri Belsunce, bishop of Marseille, and Pierre-François Lafitau, bishop of Sisteron, had both been Jesuits. Over the past few years, the parlement of Paris had tried to act against zealous bishops who sometimes went beyond Cardinal Fleury's policy of eradicating Jansenism within the clergy.[92] The magistrates of the Paris parlement had argued that ultramontane bishops and the Jesuits put themselves above French law. This pattern now surfaced in the Cadière trial. According to Pascal's colleague Jean-Louis Fouque, "the Jesuits believe themselves to be above rules." "Accustomed to respecting no one, it [the Society of Jesus] brutally insults the magistrates, the lawyers, God himself."[93]

Bourgarel, François Cadière's lawyer, added another group oppressed by the Jesuits: the family. He cast the Cadières as an honest family who unwittingly became victims of Father Girard's crimes and Jesuit domination. The Cadières' simplicity had led them to trust the "depraved Director."[94] The Jesuit had infiltrated the Cadière household to the point where Elisabeth Pomet regarded his commands as sacrosanct. When Father Girard's perfidy had been revealed, reverence gave way to fear of Jesuit retaliation. Indeed, when the bishop of Toulon first threatened to act against Father Girard, the Cadières pleaded with him not to do so.[95] Bourgarel drew a sharp contrast between the Cadières and the Jesuits to underscore the former's vulnerability: "An unfortunate family, the particulars, the simple people, without credit, without support, without experience, exposed to everything that a body as powerful as the Jesuits has[:] authority, intrigue and even force."[96] Now, legal proceedings justified their anxieties. Catherine had been incarcerated, drugged, and generally humiliated; her brothers had also endured assaults to their dignity. The Cadières would be "eternally an object of compassion in the eyes of the entire Universe."[97]

By invoking familial images, Bourgarel effectively made Catherine's story more universal, more personally relevant to the public. Both he and Chaudon suggested that the Cadières' fears extended to all families. If the marquis d'Argens is to be believed, the Girard/Cadière trial already had begun to take a toll on families: "the division augmented day by day: everything was combustible in families; each torn apart by the most atrocious gossip."[98] However, for Bourgarel, Jesuit infiltration into families was not simply about quarrels but represented a threat to the realm itself. After all, French society understood itself in terms of familial metaphors. Early modern French political theory embraced a patriarchal model where the king was father of his people. Bishops and priests were also supposed to act as benevolent father figures, not masters.[99] Both Father Girard and the Jesuits had failed to live up to this paternal model and, at the same time, had violated the laws that protected families.

The voluminous *mémoires judiciaires* during the Girard/Cadière affair represented a war of escalation that intensified as the two sides pulled further and further apart. But were these opponents as far apart as we might think? Despite the contentious debate about who was guilty, who was a victim, and who had instigated a plot, one theme was agreed upon: the Cadière affair represented a serious threat to faith and religion. Demanding that the magistrates punish Father Girard, Chaudon thundered, "If the crimes of the accused remain unpunished, what will happen to Religion? to the Sacraments? to the Public?"[100] In a similar vein, Pazery repeatedly urged his readers to direct their outrage at the Cadière cabal, whose "sacrilegious impostures" compromised "religion" itself.[101] Thus, the contested figure was the priest, who was at the center of early modern Catholicism.

On both sides of the case, priests had defiled the sacrament of confession. Father Girard stood accused of initiating a forbidden relationship within the secret confines of the confessional. But many, such as the polemicist Boismorand, also accused Father Nicolas of violating the seal of confession: "Do you know that a priest, that a minister of this sacrament owes him [the penitent] the same secrecy that God keeps for himself regarding our faults."[102] Pascal heatedly countered that the bishop of Toulon himself had done the same. Was the bishop then also involved in the supposed *complot*? What about Catherine's rights as a victim?[103] As one observer reasoned, the penitent Catherine was entitled "to make her confession public. . . . Without [this right], a girl or woman who had the misfortune of being seduced or violated by a lay person or a man of the church, even by a confessor, could not bring her complaint to justice and demand a just reparation."[104]

The Cadière affair thus aggravated doubts about the preeminent status of the priest. According to Girard's supporters, the elevation of Catherine to victim and martyr was at the expense of "a Priest, a Monk, a Preacher, a Confessor, all respectable characteristics that should put all conjecture on his side until there is convincing evidence."[105] Similarly, Bourgarel, François Cadière's lawyer, indignantly protested, "What's this! Priests, male religious, whose life and morals have always been irreproachable, would they have been capable of forging a calumny so atrocious?"[106] Each side contended that it was sacrilege to question male religious, but their *mémoires judiciaires* invited the public to judge these men and to pass sentence on them.

However much lawyers and pamphleteers appealed to the "tribunal of public opinion," justice ultimately depended on the parlement of Provence. The magistrates were in an unenviable position. They were to preside over one of the highest-profile cases in decades, and with all eyes of France fixed on Aix. The parlement was also judging the case of a Jesuit and was preparing to adjudicate weighty theological issues such as Quietism. Did preserving the sanctity of religion mean shielding the Jesuit or protecting the penitent?

BEFORE THE COURTS

Jean-Jacques Pascal concluded his *factum* for Father Nicolas with effusive praise for the parlement of Provence: "an august Senate that always distinguishes itself by the nobility of its sentiments, and by its inviolable attachment to the rules of Justice and the interests of Religion."[1] As this fulsome statement suggests, the magistrates were expected to resist social and political pressures, to preserve Catholicism, and to protect the innocent from the guilty. Pascal's comments were also a reminder that, however much a lawyer tapped into public opinion, the judges had the final word on who would walk free and who would face incarceration or even execution.

From late spring into early autumn 1731, the judges or *parlementaires* of the court's highest-ranking chambers, the Grand'Chambre, heard lawyers' arguments and sifted through testimony. The chamber's functions included hearing civil cases involving individuals of rank, appeals pertaining to municipal police courts, and the *appel comme d'abus* against ecclesiastical individuals or agencies such as the *officialités*. Despite Louis XV's wishes and Cardin Le Bret's efforts, the Cadière case dragged on. Even before the Grand'Chambre could debate whether Father Girard had committed the crimes Catherine laid at his door, the magistrates were confronted with Catherine's *appel comme d'abus* regarding alleged procedural irregularities on the part of Toulon's *officialité*.

But the proceedings before the parlement in Aix-en-Provence's Palais de Justice indicate that justice was neither blind nor impartial. Tempers ran high in August when the magistrates finally began to consider the accusations against Father Girard. The Girard/Cadière trial exposed fissures rooted in deep-seated, conflicting opinions about the Jesuits. This animosity was compounded by tensions regarding the contentious *Unigenitus*. Certain magistrates thought that the "constitution" *Unigenitus* undermined the independence of a French or Gallican church. However, those who stood by Cardinal Fleury's policies and the ultramontanism of a Belsunce or a La Tour du Pin-Montauban believed that the secular judges were infringing on the clergy's authority. These disagreements produced a verdict that, in itself, would be a torrid topic for years to come.

BEFORE THE GRAND'CHAMBRE

Aix-en-Provence, the "capital of Provence," epitomized the power and wealth of its ruling elite, the magistrates of the parlement (map 2). As the diplomat William Mildmay noted in 1730, "It cannot have any great pretence to trade, being inland without the conveniency of any River, but at the same time it does not want a good circulation of money, since Parlement is there establish'd, which . . . also draws to it for a time all Strangers who are parties in any of the Affairs which are brought into their Courts."[2] Travellers marveled at the newer section of town, specifically the Cours royale, today called the Cours Mirabeau, which the parlement had commissioned in the mid-seventeenth century. Unlike the dark narrow alleys of Toulon, the Cours royale and the streets of Aix's fashionable quarters of Saint-Jacques and Mazarin were built along a uniform grid, "well paved, even clean, and of a great breadth and length."[3] Philip Playstowe readily praised the four rows of trees that lined the Cours, forming three walkways and containing "four magnificent fountains." He admired the great buildings, "in which the nobility and gentry reside," along spacious streets.[4]

The nobility in question was Aix's *noblesse de robe*, the "robe" nobility, comprising high-ranking judges and councilors of the parlement. Of the thirteen parlements, the parlement of Provence ranked seventh, reflecting Provence's

MAP 2

Provence, ca. 1688. From *Atlas* (Amsterdam: Bij Frederick de Wit, [1688]). Courtesy of Special Collections, Vassar College Library.

incorporation into France in 1486.[5] "As magistrates of a high royal court, the *parlementaires* [of Aix] were local symbols of political authority derived from an almost mythical king at Paris."[6] Accordingly, the magistrates flaunted their rank and connection to the king. Every October, after summer recess, they returned from their country estates to preside over the new session. In a procession known as the *rentrée*, the parlement's lay councilors donned red gowns, while clerical members of the body wore vermilion. The parlement's leading members, the *présidents*, "wore round hats or *mortiers* of gold-trimmed black velvet with a pendulous tip, lace at the throat, and an ermine-trimmed mantle over a red robe held high by an attendant to avoid the filth underfoot."[7] After the procession, the magistrates went into the imposing Palais de Justice on the diamond-shaped square, the Place des Prêcheurs. Charles de Brosses, count of Tournay, commented that the Palais's exterior and public audience rooms were "of bad taste" and "ugly," but the chambers were "beautiful and well decorated"

109

with blue velvet hangings and gilded crown molding.[8] Catherine Cadière was unlikely to have seen much of this opulence when guards escorted her through the older streets of Aix, whose dim lighting and odors were probably more reminiscent of her Toulon neighborhood. She was no doubt anxious about her first hurdle: the Grand'Chambre's deliberation over whether Toulon's church officials had acted inappropriately to skew the procedure in Father Girard's favor.

When Catherine's lawyer, Jean-Baptiste Chaudon, came before the Grand'Chambre to argue for Catherine, he soon must have realized that a substantial number of the assembled members were unsympathetic to his client. As the son of one magistrate privately commented, although he believed the Jesuit was guilty, he would "bet that Father Girard would be exonerated and that la Cadière would be whipped in Aix and in Toulon."[9] There was some truth in this cynical assessment. Despite the Cadières' protest over how the two commissioners had acted on Father Girard's behalf while in Toulon, Faucon and the abbé Charleval still assumed their seats in the Grand'Chambre and were allowed to deliberate on the legitimacy of their own decrees. To counter what they considered a judicial breach, Catherine and her mother suggested to Chancellor d'Aguesseau that perhaps all four chambers of the parlement should assemble to hear the case; at least, the Grand'Chambre could meet with the Chambre de la Tournelle, which presided over criminal cases as well as "important provincial cases of treason, sedition, libel, heresy, sacrilege, and blasphemy."[10] Perhaps someone had tipped off Catherine or Elisabeth Pomet that members of the Tournelle saw the Cadières' plight more favorably.[11]

Despite these obstacles, the Cadières had important allies. On April 13, Catherine wrote to d'Aguesseau that the attorney general or avocat-général Jacques-Joseph de Gaufridy (1674–1741), known for "his integrity and his intelligence," would take up her cause before the Grand'Chambre.[12] A member of an established parlementaire family, Gaufridy, the baron of Trets, had both the status and experience to help the distressed Catherine.[13] After visiting her at the Visitation convent, Gaufridy described the scared Catherine as "rather pretty, and combined with much simplicity and spirit."[14] She told him how hostile individuals had said that "she should prepare herself" since the "stake had already been lit."[15] Despite his sympathies, Gaufridy queried her closely, probably to the point of tears, on the retraction she had made in February; he also doubted the Cadières' accusations of sorcery. At the same time, it had been proven to him that the confessor had "kissed and sucked her wounds" while his penitent was in her nightgown. The attorney general also concurred that the official investigation in Toulon had deviated from accepted procedure.[16]

But Gaufridy did more than lend a sympathetic ear. A year later, Le Bret would bitterly complain to Cardinal Fleury that although the *avocat-général* was scheduled to speak on June 25, he kept delaying. On July 28, Gaufridy sent a note to the Grand'Chambre that he was ill. Yet he had been seen strolling on the Cour royale the evening before and managed to attend mass at the Carmelite convent on July 29.[17] Why was Gaufridy stalling? It appears he felt the need to make the procedure more equitable. Earlier in May, Father Girard's lawyer, Claude-François Pazery de Thorame, had been informed about the proceedings three days before Chaudon had been advised of the timetable. Additionally, Jean-Louis Fouque and Jean-Jacques Pascal, lawyers for Étienne-Thomas Cadière and Father Nicolas Girieux, would barely have enough time to present their arguments, especially since their clients were in Paris. In light of these events, Gaufridy declared that he would not speak until July 20.

The *avocat-général* finally took the floor at the end of July. Lasting two and a half hours, the attorney general's speech was a highlight of the trial. The *Nouvelles Ecclésiastiques* certainly saw Gaufridy as a crusader for *their cause*, reporting that he delivered his speech "in a manner worthy of his position and his great reputation."[18] Similarly, a member of the Chambres des Enquêtes, Henri-Joseph Thomassin de Mazaugues, wrote to the marquis de Caumont that Gaufridy's presentation was "magnificent."[19] The drama of the speech was enhanced by the presence of a large crucifix hanging right next to him.[20] Gaufridy repeated Chaudon's charges against Father Girard and attacked Toulon's *officialité*, which, he argued, had exceeded its authority during the interrogations in late 1730.

Gaufridy's critique of Toulon's clerical officials centered on questions of jurisdiction and intent. He declared that these ecclesiastic authorities had overstepped themselves when they interrogated Catherine in her *house*; their powers were only legitimate in churches and ecclesiastical courts. This practice forced "subjects of the king" to submit to ecclesiastical jurisdiction, which technically did not extend to lay individuals outside those venues.[21] Esprit Reybaud, the *officialité*'s legal representative, was painted as overzealous in his efforts to protect Father Girard. Gaufridy restated the Cadières' claims that Reybaud had made Catherine into the criminal and systematically tampered with testimonies. Such procedural irregularities were nothing less than "oppression."[22]

Gaufridy was an important player because he was one of the five *gens du roi*, also known as the *parquet*, who were the king's prosecutors and, therefore, responsible for sifting through the evidence. But Gaufridy's personal convictions seemed to evaporate on July 30 when he rejected Catherine's *appel comme d'abus* against the *officialité* on the grounds that there had been no abuse. The *gens du roi* also issued the following rulings. The *décret d'assigné*, which only required the presence of Father Girard's lawyer, stood. At the same time, Girard was required, along with Étienne-Thomas and Nicolas, to remain in prison until the case was over. However, the writs against Catherine and her brother François were overturned, and they were both free. The *gens du roi* also ordered that witnesses who had been held back now give testimony. Another surprise was the order to imprison until further notice Father Girard's loyal *dévotes*, "la Batarelle, la Laugier and la Guiol, la Gravier, la Réboul and les Allemandes, mother and daughter."[23] These bewildering conclusions appeared to protect Father Girard even while they acknowledged irregularity in the judicial process.

How do we explain these variations and the discrepancy between this official pronouncement and Gaufridy's passionate speech days earlier? As the *Nouvelles* explained to its undoubtedly mystified readers, the parlement of Provence required that the attorney general's conclusions reflect the majority opinion of the *gens du roi*.[24] Gaufridy and the other attorney general, Jean-François de Séguiran, concurred that there had been abuse. But the other three members of the *parquet*, Gaspard de Gueydan and two chief prosecutors, Pierre-François de Ripert de Montclar and Pierre-Jean Boyer d'Argens (1682–1757), all favored Father Girard's case and declared that there was no abuse.

The Grand'Chambre's subsequent debate mirrored this division among the *gens du roi*. The same day, a vote confirming these conclusions narrowly passed—thirteen to ten—after three and a half hours of debate.[25] Cardin Le Bret led the vote in favor of the *arrêt,* or ruling, and most of those who had favored the decree concisely noted that they were "of the opinion of Monsieur the first President."[26] One of them, Honoré-Henri Piolenc (1675–1760), argued against Gaufridy's claims that clerical authorities could not enter a house. After all, if a priest had murdered one of his servants, it was expected that an ecclesiastical official visit that house. Nevertheless, there was an awkward moment when three judges, known to be Father Girard's supporters, were ready to alter the charges against the Jesuit from a simple *assigné* to the more serious *ajournement*. They withdrew their suggestion because it effectively incriminated Faucon and Charleval, who represented two votes on the Girard side.[27]

Although the pro-Cadière magistrates were in the minority, they vehemently favored Catherine's *appel*. Jean-Baptiste de Maliverny (1694–1766) declared that the ecclesiastical judge was essentially a liar. Charles Grimaldi de Régusse (1675–1741), who had more than thirty-five years of experience, spoke for half an hour. Referring to the *officialité*, "he could not, in honor and conscience, affirm a procedure teeming with abuse, nor contribute to punishing the innocent."[28] The magistrate also argued that the court must judge Father Girard first *before* debating the charges against the Cadière brothers and Father Nicolas. He was eloquent but also surprising—Grimaldi de Régusse had always been known as friendly to the Jesuits, and the order had counted on his vote.

On one level, this rancor among men who ordinarily worked side by side appears inexplicable. As members of the Grand'Chambre, the judges were keenly aware that they belonged to the most prestigious chamber of the three main courts in the parlement of Provence. They also represented a relatively homogeneous social unit.[29] They enjoyed wealth, owning impressive mansions or *hôtels* in Aix with estates in the nearby countryside. And these individuals were connected through marriage. When Geneviève de Suffren de Saint-Tropez married the son of Joseph Arnaud de Nibles in 1733, Madame de Simiane wrote that "it's as if Father Girard had married Mademoiselle Cadière," a reference to how Joseph-Jean-Baptiste Suffren (1651–1737) and Nibles had benn on opposing sides of the scandal.[30]

Despite these social connections, the Girard/Cadière trial intensified differences stemming from the hostilities between Jesuits and Jansenists. A number of judicial families had been educated in the Jesuit-run Collège Royal de Bourbon, now the University of Aix-Marseille.[31] The Meyronnet family was so close to the Jesuits that members of the family were buried in the college's chapel in Aix. Cardin Le Bret had personal and professional ties with the Society of Jesus. Conversely, according to Le Bret, Jean-Louis-Hyacinthe Esmivi de Moissac (1684–1740) had connections to the *Nouvelles Ecclésiastiques.*[32] And Gaufridy's opposition to the "constitution" *Unigenitus* dated back to the regency of Louis XV's reign in the late 1710s. When Gaufridy died in 1741, the parish priest would not administer last rites because the attorney general had refused to accept the bull as a rule of faith.[33]

The contrasting attitudes toward *Unigenitus* and the Jesuits were embedded in two different understandings of the relationship between Church and State and the location of authority in the Church.[34] France was, of course, a Catholic country, but for many, it was Catholicism grounded in the principles of Gallicanism—the long-standing belief that although the pope headed the Church, he had no temporal or material power over the French monarchy. In 1682, Louis XIV issued the Four Gallican Articles, which effectively denied the pope's authority over the Church *in* France.[35] For Louis XIV, the principles of Gallicanism were inextricably linked to his God-given absolutist authority.

In 1713, these same Gallican beliefs led Louis XIV to reconcile with the papacy in his campaign to suppress Jansenism. This new alliance bred *Unigenitus.*

Unfortunately, the bull had been put together hastily, containing propositions guaranteed to offend theologians and legal theorists alike. Proposition ninety-one stood out, stating that "the fear of an unjust excommunication ought never to deter us from doing our duty." This statement raised a troubling question: "Might popes again excommunicate French kings, the Parlement's *gens du roi* were to ask, and prevent their fearful subject from obeying them?"[36] The parlements saw themselves as gatekeepers of Gallican principles by virtue of being agents acting in the Crown's interest. They did not consider themselves as representative institutes but as intercessors or mediators between the king and his subjects. As "agents of the monarchy with the people," they reminded the king of his duties to his subjects' well-being.[37] For many lawyers and magistrates, *Unigenitus* undermined Gallican ideals and therefore peace in the realm.

Although the most intense conflicts over *Unigenitus* occurred in Paris, Provençal magistrates were as partisan as their counterparts in Paris. Like the parlement of Paris, on March 20, 1714, the parlement of Provence registered *Unigenitus* only after attaching modifications that signaled the courts' repudiation of the clause on excommunication.[38] This position brought them into conflict with the Provençal clergy. In 1716, the bishop of Toulon declared that his diocese would not allow individuals to enter the clergy if they had been educated in an institution that failed to accept *Unigenitus*. Later, Jacques-Joseph Gaufridy issued a pamphlet against La Tour du Pin-Montauban. The abbé François Gastaud, who later assisted Chaudon, then wrote in Gaufridy's defense; a decade later, he defended Jean Soanen in the aftermath of the Council of Embrun.[39] On February 16, 1728, the parlement also denounced the council on a technicality: it had not obtained certain patent letters that were necessary since the council was held within the parlement's jurisdiction.[40]

What did these positions mean in terms of the relationship between Church and State? Gastaud's 1716 defense of Gaufridy encapsulated the adamant Gallicanism of many *parlementaires*. Addressing the Jesuits directly, Gastaud marked them as anti-Gallican because of their papal affiliations and their dismissal of the Sorbonne, a distinctively French institution. Gastaud emphasized the importance of bishops working with "provincial" or "national" councils as opposed to alone or with the pope.[41] This conclusion reflected conciliarism, which centered on the whole Church—all members of the clergy, not just highly placed bishops and cardinals. Gastaud also made a case for the right of the parlements to intervene in religious issues. Parlements were the "depositories of his [the king's] authority, the parlements want bishops to be bishops, and you [the Jesuits] want them only to be the pope's vicars.[42] He concluded that the bishops had no right to excommunicate magistrates for their opposition to *Unigenitus*.[43] This spirited defense of Gaufridy, combined with his attack on the Jesuits, brought swift retribution: Cardin Le Bret exiled Gastaud in 1728.[44]

A friend of Cardinal Fleury, Le Bret represented voices favoring *Unigenitus*. But where the *intendant* himself was measured in his support of both the bull and the Jesuits, others were more inflexible. Unlike many of their colleagues, Piolenc and Paul de Meyronnet-Châteauneuf (1693–1767) backed the controversial 1716 *Pastoralis officii*, which refused communion to clerics who opposed *Unigenitus*.[45] Fittingly, Piolenc, Meyronnet, and others who shared their strictly hierarchical version of Catholicism defined themselves as "the party of bishops."[46] Their position was essentially political, since Le Bret and likeminded colleagues regarded clerical and royal authority as intrinsically connected. According to Bishop Bossuet, who had condemned the Quietist Jeanne Guyon, the king's authority was sacred because "it is the spirit of Christianity to make kings respected in a kind of religious way."[47] Within this framework, church and state existed in a symbiotic relationship. As a result, stubborn opposition to *Unigenitus* threatened schism and could potentially ignite a civil war as destructive as the sixteenth-century Wars of Religion (1562–1598).

These ideological tensions around *Unigenitus* ensured that the Girard/ Cadière case was a political scandal as much as a religious one. For Gaufridy and other Gallican magistrates, a Jesuit who had misused his powers in the confessional was the microcosm of a larger problem: abuse of clerical authority. Naturally, secular institutions had the right and responsibility to bring this errant Jesuit to justice. However, for the Le Brets, Piolencs, and Meyronnets, impugning Father Girard's reputation and questioning the bishop of Toulon's competency was blasphemy and, implicitly, political treason.

TOWARD A FINAL JUDGMENT

Immediately after the July 30 judgment, Father Girard went to prison. "Pale like death and carrying the proof of his crimes on his forehead," the Jesuit passed two thousand people waiting outside the Palais de Justice.[48] The *Nouvelles Ecclésiastiques* gleefully noted that individuals such as the dowager baroness of Châteaurenard and the wife of the marquis de Bandol yelled out names such as "Villain, Devil, Sorcerer."[49] Added to Father Girard's humiliation was the crowd's "demonstrations of joy" when they saw Étienne-Thomas Cadière.[50] Voices urged Étienne-Thomas to have courage because he was only going to prison to act as Father Girard's *concierge* or caretaker.[51] The excited crowds even turned on people only tangentially connected to the case. When Pazery's valet refused to participate in these events, the crowd dragged him across the hall and threatened him with a knife.[52] As they continued their deliberations in the waning summer weeks, the magistrates were keenly aware that the public was closely monitoring the case and judging *their* actions. Daily, on arrival at the courthouse on the Place des Prêcheurs, the men supporting Father Girard were greeted by whistles, taunts, or angry silence; their colleagues on the other side heard warm salutes.

As Catherine, Father Girard, Étienne-Thomas, and Father Nicolas each negotiated the pressures of confinement and litigation, the trial dragged on into the fall. Even before the magistrates could deliberate on Catherine's accusations against her spiritual director, they had to examine Chaudon's contention that witnesses had been suborned. This deliberation, known as the *jugemens des objets*, was delayed for a few weeks because Cardin Le Bret fell ill. Mathieu Marais reported to Jean Bouhier, "one says that the trial will kill him."[53] Another correspondent heard that the first president had complained to his doctor, Guirichet, how he wished he had never been embroiled in this affair, worsened by the intransigence of his colleagues, such as Moissac and Jacques Joseph de L'Estang (1673–1751), sieur de Parade, who were now opponents.[54] Finally, Le Bret returned on August 13, and on August 14, the courts ruled in Catherine's favor. Numerous witnesses were recognized as legitimate, and their testimonies were admitted into the record.[55]

With the question about procedure and witnesses cleared up, the case was returned to the *gens du roi*, who issued their "conclusions definitive" on September 11. Boyer d'Argens, Ripert de Montclar, and Gueydan voted for Father Girard's release and found that Catherine had "abused Religion and profaned the Mysteries." She was to be hanged just outside on the Place des Prêcheurs; her brothers and Father Nicolas were to be fined as her accomplices, and Jean-Baptiste Chaudon was also sentenced to prison.[56] Gaufridy and Séguiran voted for Father Girard to be hanged and burned and concluded that the other parties were innocent; however, they also stipulated that Catherine be placed in a convent of her "choice" for three years. Séguiran spoke for an hour and Gaufridy for ninety minutes, during which bitter words passed between the attorney general and Boyer d'Argens.[57]

The magistrates supporting Father Girard, now known as the "Girardins," became targets of public anger. The day the conclusions of September 11 appeared, an anonymous set of "bloody" verses aimed at Boyer d'Argens, Ripert, and Gueydan surfaced. And "when one saw M. *le premier président* [Le Bret], who was suspected of favoring the Jesuits, everyone turned their back to him; on the contrary, one accompanied another *président* (that is *président* Maliverny) to his house" because he was a Cadière "partisan."[58] When the gout-ridden "Cadièriste" baron de Trimond left the Palais on September 17, assisted by porters, he was greeted by well-wishing hordes that asked God to deliver him from illness and "give him the force to assist him in the final judgment."[59] In this tense atmosphere, it was rumored that Catherine was to be taken to prison. Crowds gathered around the Visitation convent where the "unfortunate girl" stayed. They spoke words of encouragement, and many stayed until five in the morning to prevent her from being taken. They cheered when Catherine waved a handkerchief to reassure them.[60] The people of Aix were making their opinions known loud and clear, no doubt adding to rising tensions inside the Palais de Justice.

Starting on Wednesday, September 12, the twenty-five magistrates began convening every morning at 8:15 A.M. to go over all the evidence. Details of the deliberations over the next month are available to us, thanks to a handwritten *relation*, an account of the proceedings within the Grand'Chambre. Although unsigned, the contents suggest an author sympathetic to Catherine. The copy housed in the municipal archives in Toulon was donated by "H. de Pierrefeu" and belonged to his great-uncle Martini St. Jean, whose grandfather had been a member of the parlement of Provence.[61] This magistrate Jean-Honoré-Estienne de St. Jean (1690–1755) decidedly favored Catherine, and *his* possession of the account suggests its partisan nature.

The first item the magistrates faced on September 12 was the reading of testimony, which, predictably, became a heated issue. In charge of organizing the evidence, François de Maurel (1679–1766), seigneur de Mons, tried to push through the testimony of over one hundred witnesses as rapidly as possible. When he suggested that it was "useless" to read Father Nicolas's testimony, St. Jean countered with "vivacity" that de Mons was to read it all and not skip anything. Later, André de Barrigue de Montvalon declared that Marie-Anne Laugier's testimony, which undermined Girard's case, should not be read because the penitent had been under the direction of Father Nicolas. Jean-Baptiste Le Blanc de Leveaune countered that Batarelle's testimony was equally inadmissible because Father Girard had been her confessor.[62]

Toward the end of September, the magistrates were ready for the final interrogations of key witnesses: Father Girard, Catherine, the Cadière brothers, and Father Nicolas. But on September 27, Catherine requested a *confrontation mutuelle*, a procedure allowing her to meet Father Girard one last time in a legal setting. Technically, the *confrontation* between Catherine and Father Girard had occurred on March 6.[63] But Catherine now claimed that it had taken place under duress just six days after her forced retraction. In that meeting, she had confessed that her visions resulted from an easily excitable imagination and certain influential books.[64] Why set such an awkward meeting now? Perhaps Catherine and the determined Chaudon calculated that a confrontation between the attractive, young Toulonnaise and the aging Jesuit might change at least one judge's mind, although both sides seemed as "inflexible" as ever.[65]

The question of the *confrontation mutuelle* gives us a glimpse of how the Cadière trial tested the lines between procedure and justice. Faucon commented that the request was "unusual" because only judges could make such recommendations; his fellow commissioner, the abbé Charleval, argued that this form of *confrontation* took place only in cases of *rapt de séduction,* when victims were seduced with promises of marriage. Maliverny countered that Charleval had failed to ensure that the appropriate *confrontation mutuelle* had taken place earlier in the spring. Not surprisingly, this accusation precipitated another heated exchange that ended only after Le Bret ordered silence. In the end, the Grand'Chambre granted Catherine's request to meet Father Girard, perhaps for the last time.

Before the *confrontation*, the court had to interrogate the Jesuit and Catherine individually. As *premier président*, Le Bret conducted the interrogation; all questions were channeled through him. On Friday morning, September 28, Girard answered questions for three hours and fifteen minutes. Even Le Bret, a known supporter, did not spare him, asking the confessor why, when he suspected Catherine of deception, he had failed to communicate his misgivings. Many of the magistrates hostile to the Jesuit, including St. Jean, Moissac, and Le Blanc, followed with their own queries. Had Father Girard been alone with Catherine in her room in Toulon? In her cell at Ollioules? Le Blanc asked why, if the Jesuit doubted the miracles and visions, he continued to administer communion to Catherine "every day." At another point, Moissac became so frustrated with Father Girard's denial of wrongdoing that he addressed the Jesuit directly. Piolenc immediately interrupted, hotly reminding his colleague that this direct query violated procedure.

As the judges' tempers showed signs of fraying, how did Father Girard hold up under such intense scrutiny? A contemporary eyewitness indicates that the Jesuit entered the courtroom fairly calm but, under questioning, turned "pale and trembling." But at other times, his face expressed "firmness, arrogance, and severity."[66] There were also moments of embarrassment when he was asked about his contact with Catherine's body. At another point, Father Girard wiped away tears when asked about his "desolation" and "despair," claiming that Catherine's deceit had precipitated this agony.[67] Despite some discomfort, Father Girard left in triumph.

A few days later, on October 2 and 3, it was Catherine's turn. Overall, her performance was much more successful than Girard's, although she arrived late, which provoked Piolenc to remark that for "a *dévote*, she takes a long time to get ready."[68] When asked by Le Bret why she acquiesced to Girard's Quietist teachings, she answered that she believed he was a "holy man." Catherine seemed nervous, wiping her face when Le Bret closely queried her about her Lenten visions and supposed elevation atop her bed. Still, she responded with a steadiness that surprised many. At another point, de Mons asked her to read Father Girard's letter of July 26, 1730—one of the supposedly secret letters in which he demanded Catherine's silence. Realizing that this evidence incriminated Father Girard, the magistrate maintained that Catherine was not reading the actual contents. The court clerk then watched over Catherine's shoulder as she reread the contents, and he authenticated her words, an episode that left de Mons in a state of "great confusion."[69] Nibles complained that such interruptions were tactics to intimidate Catherine. Nevertheless, the "judges"—no doubt those on her side—were "satisfied," and many concluded that the twenty-one-year-old had defended herself better than her lawyer had done.[70] Did Catherine successfully lay the groundwork for her *confrontation* with Father Girard the next day?

Catherine entered court on the morning of October 4 "with a serene air and with much modesty," while Father Girard's face was pale, almost resembling that of a "dead man."[71] It was a theatrical moment between two antagonists and an equally divided audience (fig. 10). For the next two hours, Catherine held the upper hand as she ticked off accusations: Quietism, obsessions, abortion, and spiritual incest. (The charge of sorcery was notably missing.) Catherine recounted different ways in which Father Girard had seduced her, even introducing new facts. Wasn't it true that Father Girard often prostrated himself before her, telling her that he adored her as "his idol"?[72] On another day, "he threw himself on his knees crying, and declaring that he had impregnated Mademoiselle Gravier."[73] She spared neither her former confessor nor her audience the details of how he had kissed her wounds and touched her.

In its account of the *confrontation*, published two months afterward, the *Nouvelles Ecclésiastiques* gushed about how Catherine shone on the stand: "The union of such modesty, spirit, and firmness, in a girl whose age, birth, and education does not allow for such performances, seemed a wonder."[74] Another

FIGURE 10
"L'aréopage d'Aix," or "The
Tribunal of Aix." This
Provençal engraving of the
confrontation between Father
Girard and Catherine is presented from the perspective
of the public. Magnified and
distinct, the public represents
the true judges of this case. In
the right-hand corner, two
men converse animatedly,
a reflection of the public's
engagement. Courtesy of
the Musée Paul Arbaud,
Aix-en-Provence.

observer confirmed the *Nouvelles'* version as he noted how Catherine was able
to speak of "obscene" matters without compromising her modest appearance.
He also described how the room recognized the "hand of God weighing down
on the guilty and seeking to support the innocent."[75]

Through all this, Father Girard appeared on the defensive, unable to make
persuasive rebuttals of Catherine's allegations. He attempted to interrupt her,
sometimes calling her words "false." These interruptions were frequent enough
that Le Bret had to silence him, and at one point, the magistrate St. Jean stepped
out of line and told the Jesuit to "shut up and let her speak."[76] Girard was also
observed shrugging his shoulders and shaking his head in denial of her accusations. When she described how the spiritual director had used her physically,
his pale face became "red like fire." In the heat of the moment, he cried out that
she was a "friponne," a minx or hussy.[77]

The *relation* suggests that betrayal and anger dominated emotions between
the two. As she catalogued "all the dreadful abominations" Father Girard had

committed against her, Catherine underscored all the ways in which her former spiritual director had misused his authority and deliberately misled her. Conversely, for Girard, Catherine's accusations, especially in this public venue, betrayed his authority as confessor and spiritual director. Their conflicting perspectives resonated in the Grand'Chambre's final deliberations.

These deliberations did not begin until six days later. On the night of October 4, Esmivi de Moissac's octogenarian father died of apoplexy. For the Cadières, this event was potentially catastrophic; Moissac was one of the twelve judges in their camp. Elisabeth Pomet went with supporters to plead with the bereaved magistrate not to withdraw from the case, because his vote could make all the difference. "People of consideration" and even members of his own family urged Moissac to return to the Palais de Justice. After much debate and a vote of fifteen to eleven, the Grand'Chambre closed the proceedings for a day after Moissac requested a two-day delay. When the magistrate returned to the courthouse, the crowd on the Place des Prêcheurs mobbed him and greeted him with "acclamations and demonstrations of joy."[78]

Despite the drama inside and outside the Palais de Justice, the judges of the Grand'Chambre convened for their final deliberation on October 10. The meeting began at six in the morning, just before sunrise, and almost two hours before the usual time. Archers were posted around the courthouse while crowds kept vigil on the Place des Prêcheurs, overflowing into nearby streets. Inside the courthouse, judges loyal to the Jesuits, such as de Mons and Piolenc, reiterated the ultramontane position emphasizing clerical authority: Father Girard was a preacher and confessor with an established reputation. Conversely, Catherine's judicial supporters spoke of her "oppression" and "vexation." Both sides remained intractable, and not one judge conceded a point.

The discussion first revolved around Father Girard. The Jesuit's allies emphasized his "extreme simplicity" as well as his unimpeachable piety.[79] If there was any crime, Piolenc opined, it was the confessor's "indiscreet zeal and excessive charity," which had allowed Catherine to dupe him.[80] Suffren was the only "Girardin" who interpreted Father Girard's gullibility as a crime; he concluded that the Jesuit should be banished perpetually. Twelve judges, including Le Bret, concluded that there was not enough evidence to condemn Father Girard and therefore voted to dismiss the case. The thirteenth pro-Girard magistrate, Suffren, went in a different direction and voted to suspend the Jesuit from fulfilling his priestly obligations.

On the other side, twelve judges were ready to condemn Father Girard. Indeed, one of them, Joseph-Paul Ricard (1665-1741), had come to the courthouse despite severe gout and the pleas of his wife and sister-in-laws.[81] For Montvert and his like-minded peers, Father Girard was an out-and-out "scélérat," a villain who should be punished for the "horrible abuse of his ministry that this Confessor had committed."[82] When the recently bereaved Moissac launched into an exhaustive litany of Father Girard's crimes, Montvalon, a "declared protector of the Jesuits," muttered in low voice: "Why lose so much time? The *arrêt* is done, and no one is going to come around." Enraged, Moissac thundered, "there are only too many wolves among the chickens, if I leave it at that, I would believe myself dishonored before God and before men."[83]

Four hours after the contentious debate on Father Girard's fate, the judges embarked on an even tenser deliberation over Catherine. The "Girardins" dismissed the penitent's accusations as nothing but "deceit," "full of madness and extravagance."[84] According to Faucon, she had demonstrated "a thoughtless impudence against a director of known integrity."[85] However, Le Blanc defended Catherine as "a young girl, who, before his [Father Girard's] direction, was an example of innocence and virtue."[86] What else could it be but seduction, since Father Girard was fifty and Catherine was nineteen?

While the two sides diverged in their assessments of Catherine's character, the decisions about how to punish a woman, however guilty, were less than clearcut. Thirteen opined for dismissing Catherine's case and returning her to her mother. Twelve of these votes were predictable, since these judges had consistently argued on the penitent's behalf. The thirteenth, the Girardin Suffren, stated, "Sirs, we just absolved the greatest criminal there ever was, and we will impose the smallest pain on this girl."[87] Suffren's words suggest a cynical vote that was less about justice and more about salvaging the Jesuits' reputation. Interestingly, many of the magistrates who had reviled Catherine now seemed reluctant to punish her harshly. A number of them believed that Catherine first should make an "amende honorable," a public apology, most likely with a rope around her neck, in front of Toulon's cathedral. What then? Six favored placing her in a *maison de refuge*, essentially a prison for prostitutes. But the other six suggested that Catherine be placed in a convent. Even here, there was disagreement. Le Bret and Valabres called for two years and ten years, respectively, while another suggested three years, and three other magistrates voted for five years. These different positions were so confusing that, in its coverage of the verdict, the *Nouvelles Ecclésiastiques* included a folio sheet with a list of the magistrates' names and their various decisions.[88] In sum, the verdict was as follows: twelve judges voted to send Father Girard to the stake, while thirteen judges voted in his favor; of the latter, one voted to suspend his clerical functions for ten years (see table 1).

TABLE I

Verdict and recommended punishment for Catherine Cadière and Jean-Baptiste Girard by the Grand'Chambre of the parlement of Provence

JUDGES	VERDICT ON GIRARD	VERDICT ON CADIÈRE
Faucon	Case dismissed	Life in *maison de refuge*
Villeneuve	Case dismissed	Life in *maison de refuge*
de Mons	Case dismissed	To *maison de refuge*
Valabres	Case dismissed	Ten years in the convent
Espinouse	Case dismissed	Five years in the convent
Estienne	Case dismissed	Five years in the convent
Meyronnet	Case dismissed	Five years in the convent
Le Bret	Case dismissed	Two years in the convent
Estang of Parade	Case dismissed	Life in *maison de refuge*
Montvalon	Case dismissed	To *maison de refuge*
Meyronnes-Courville	Case dismissed	To *maison de refuge*
Piolenc	Case dismissed and sent to the ecclesiastical judges	Three years in the convent
Suffren	Prohibited from all work for ten years	Returned to her mother
Boulie	Death by fire	Returned to her mother
Galice	Death by fire	Returned to her mother
Grimaldi de Régusse	Death by fire	Returned to her mother
Le Blanc	Death by fire	Returned to her mother
Maliverny	Death by fire	Returned to her mother
Moissac	Death by fire	Returned to her mother
Montvert	Death by fire	Returned to her mother
Nibles	Death by fire	Returned to her mother
Peyrolles	Death by fire	Returned to her mother
Ricard	Death by fire	Returned to her mother
St. Jean	Death by fire	Returned to her mother
Trimond	Death by fire	Returned to her mother

How might we interpret this indecision and the relatively mild sentences, especially given how strongly many of the judges had censored Catherine? Perhaps the judges thought that, given her age and gender, Catherine did not deserve a death sentence. Or perhaps some judges privately believed that Father Girard did, in fact, bear some responsibility for the events that precipitated the scandal. Or, as I believe, the "Girardins" were profoundly aware of the large crowds outside that overwhelmingly supported Catherine and who had, so far, not hesitated to express their discontent.

The divided ruling also reflected the failure of royal justice. As the king's *intendant* and the *premier président*, Cardin Le Bret was supposed to have prevented the Cadière scandal from becoming a crisis. How was an effective administrator, respected by both the Crown and his fellow magistrates, unable to circumvent a verdict that would make the Provençal parlement an object of mockery for several months? In part, Le Bret seemed unable to bridge the chasm created by personal loyalties and ideological differences. For a number of magistrates, Catherine Cadière's accusations against Jean-Baptiste Girard hardened their allegiance to the Jesuits. Their peers, who profoundly distrusted the Society, regarded it as the Grand'Chambre's duty, its jurisdictional right, to protect the king's subjects from clerical abuse—a position their opponents fiercely rejected. This conflict was magnified by the larger constitutional crisis in which the Crown and the parlement of Paris were engaged—a "politics of contestation" over precisely the same issues about ecclesiastical authority.[89]

Although it had been waiting for more than nine hours, the crowd outside the Palais de Justice showed no signs of dissipating. Periodically, couriers appeared, but nothing definitive was pronounced until seven that evening. Three couriers finally appeared, probably carrying torches in the dark, and cried out: "All cases have been dismissed." In disbelief, people asked the couriers whether this were true. Bursts of laughter were heard through the crowd. It appeared ludicrous and even impossible that both Catherine and Father Girard were found guilty and innocent.[90] Later, the crowd let out shouts of joy when the court's clerk sent out the orders to release Catherine, the Cadière brothers, and Father Nicolas; the judge Joseph-François Galice (1677–1765) had demanded their release when he discovered that Father Girard was already out of prison *before* the final judgment had been signed.[91] The expressions of enthusiasm were so loud that they reverberated inside the Palais. Le Bret was rooted "in his seat astonished."[92] The judges had spoken. But as the tumult outside the Palais de Justice indicated, so had the public.

BEYOND *the* GRAND'CHAMBRE

Seven

PUBLIC OPINION AND THE
STORY OF THE WANTON JESUIT

Some time before October 10, a short poem captured how the Girard/Cadière scandal had become a national obsession: "Everywhere one sings, and one publishes / The discourse and the counter discourse."[1] Scores of poems and songs that surfaced in 1731 and 1732 confirm the epigram's observation that everyone in France had an opinion about the affair. This running commentary circulated in print, through scraps of paper, and by word of mouth throughout France and beyond. As we have seen, pamphlets, such as the *Résultat des mémoires de la demoiselle Cadière*, appeared alongside the pamphlet-like *mémoires judiciaires*. And if readers tired of reading pamphlets, they might have attended an *opéra-comique*, *Le Nouveau Tarquin*, performed in August 1731. In addition to the songs performed in *Le Nouveau Tarquin*, verses floated around Provence, Paris, and other towns, such as Dijon. Collectors could purchase illustrations and portraits, and if they were willing to take the risk, they could buy erotic plates exposing the secrets of the confessional and Catherine's bedroom.

The dizzying world of songs, pamphlets, and other polemical literature reveals the complex "communication network" of eighteenth-century French society.[2] It took multiple forms, continually testing the boundaries between oral and print culture. But it was effective precisely because these forms often overlapped, generating commentary that was, at once, derivative and dynamic. Such dynamism was all the more astonishing because these pieces circulated undercover, hidden from the searching eyes of officials and censors.

Despite their shadowy existence, the different forms of commentary provide important clues as to how elites and non-elites connected the Girard/Cadière scandal to private and public life, to religion and politics. We cannot ignore the entertainment value of satirical verses and pithy epigrams. At the same time, they all reveal anxieties about the close relationship between a penitent and a spiritual director, especially a Jesuit. Verse after verse excoriated the pro-Girard judges for dishonoring the judicial system. Some had a decidedly Jansenist perspective, linking the Girard/Cadière affair to the persecution of appellants and *convulsionnaires*. The profusion of verses and their circulation throughout the realm reflect an eager market of readers. At the same time, in acknowledging this public, this polemical material gave it an authoritative voice.

PUBLIC OPINION AND MEDIA

The flow of news in the early modern era may appear sluggish and remote to us. However, eighteenth-century media—like today's social media—effectively spread the news, sustained public interest, and offered commentary on events. Eighteenth-century vehicles of communication shared another characteristic with twenty-first-century information exchange: hybridity.[3] Genres of writing were not always distinct. Songs, fables, and images were textual and oral, printed and transcribed by hand, circulating in a gray area between the learned culture of print and a more "popular" culture of gossip and rumor.[4] Regardless, they all reflected passionate points of view.

The desire to make one's perspective transparent certainly suggests another parallel between the media of the eighteenth and the twenty-first centuries, but such comparisons do not hold up when tackling questions of authorship. With today's "information superhighway," an author's celebrity or notoriety may appear inseparable from his/her opinions. But we are limited in our ability to identify eighteenth-century authors; not surprisingly, many writers preferred anonymity to a stint in the Bastille or any another prison. In any event, polemical pieces worked together to spread the story of Catherine Cadière and Jean-Baptiste Girard to a public beyond Provence, in streets, cafés, and elite salons. The circulation and consumption of this scandal in these spaces emphasize how real people, from various walks of life, formed a vibrant, engaged public.

Opinions of the trial were accessible to this diverse public because they were expressed in multiple forms, "oral, manuscript, and print."[5] While we might regard these as distinct categories, in the eighteenth century, they defied classification. As we have seen, the printed word played a powerful role in spreading details of the affair. Pamphlets and periodicals bridged the gap between the legal world and the larger freewheeling spaces inhabited by the public. Some pamphlets, such as the *Histoire du procez entre demoiselle Cadière*, were included in the multivolume collections of *factums*, while the *Nouvelles Ecclésiastiques* provided lengthy summaries of the briefs. But others resembled treatises or *factums* of more than two hundred pages.[6] Still other pamphlets appeared as letters, a format that fused private exchange and public discourse.

Whatever their form, most pamphlets were commentaries—opinionated and unrestrained. Indeed, the French terms for pamphlets were *libelles injurieux* or *libelles diffamatoires*, indicating that their authors intended to insult or disparage.[7] At the time of the Girard/Cadière trial, Jansenist authors often criticized ultramontane bishops and the Jesuits in pamphlets that commented on theological issues or events such as the Council of Embrun.[8] Pamphlets supporting or condemning the convulsionaries of Saint-Médard also began to appear. Nevertheless, the Girard/Cadière case stands out. In general, a court case involving private individuals rarely generated polemical material, a phenomenon not seen often until the 1770s.[9]

The world of print also included images. Almost overnight, intense speculation surrounding the Cadière trial made the two obscure figures at its center objects of fascination. The curious could readily purchase engravings of Catherine and Father Girard. Cardinal Fleury's secretary d'Anfossy noted that images, "under the name of Girardines," were being sold in the large fair of Beaucaire in the province of Languedoc.[10] The majority ridiculed or demonized the Jesuit confessor and in fact belonged to a larger set of anti-Jesuit images circulating since 1713.[11] Perhaps the most stunning images were a set of thirty-two erotic engravings without any text, suggesting that the engraver believed that pictures clearly were worth a thousand words. In 1735, a Dutch version, the *Historische print- en dicht-tafereelen van Jan Baptiste Girard, en juffrou Maria Catharine Cadiere*, began with a detailed explanatory preface and verses.[12] And in England, Jeremy Jingle's *Spiritual Fornications*, "a burlesque poem," contained risqué images, as did an English translation of the *mémoires judiciaires*.[13]

Verses dominated polemical outpourings on the Cadière affair, underscoring the importance of oral communication in eighteenth-century French society.[14] Indeed, when Édmond Barbier first referred to the Cadière affair, he immediately noted the appearance of numerous "bonnes plaisanteries," alluding to verses circulating in Paris.[15] Poems and songs were not isolated but coexisted in a world of constant exchange. Thus, one verse took the abbé Boismorand to task for his pamphlet *Résultat des mémoires de la demoiselle Cadière*, defending Father Girard.[16] A random assortment of short epigrams and *chansons*, or lyrics, were put to known popular songs, all of which were rarely printed.[17] Instead, writers would scribble them on bits of paper, perhaps in the privacy of their rooms or dimly lit cafés; authors gleefully borrowed from one another, "cutting and pasting." The verses probably passed from one person to the next, crumpled or folded, to avoid attracting attention from police spies under orders to monitor seditious views of the king, Cardinal Fleury, and the Jesuits. Memorization also played an important role, especially when familiar tunes were coupled with verses.[18] We can imagine, then, that as the verses were copied and recited, their contents subtly shifted—a word added, a name slightly altered, a line omitted.

However, certain verses survived and continued to be distributed decades after the affair because they went into print. Two groups stand out: the *calottes* and the *sarcelades*. The first set belonged to a definable group known as the *Régiment de la calotte*; satirical and strident, *calottes* and *brevets* parodied patent letters or warrants.[19] During the Cadière affair, a number of calottes targeted individuals, such as "Thérèse Bertot" and the "abbé Valbanette," most of whom were pro-Girard inhabitants of Aix.[20] Referring to a poem, the "Réflexions des habitans de Sarcelles, sur l'arrêt du parlement d'Aix rendu en faveur du père Girard," Mathieu Marais described it as a "*Sarcelade*, which is in peasant language, like the pieces against the archbishop [of Paris] by the inhabitants of Sarcelles, and from it comes this new word that has enriched our language and which might well stay like '*Ballade*.'"[21] During the early 1730s, some of these anti-Girard poems were published in small volumes containing other anti-Jesuit verses, such as "Method for becoming a good Jesuit in a short time."[22] Well into the 1750s, various editions of the *sarcelades* included a title page with this publishing information: "A Aix, Chez Jean-Baptiste Girard, rue de Bret." Both the *calottes* and *sarcelades* illustrate how the Girard/Cadière affair became a cultural flash point, especially with respect to the Jesuits.

Given the dramatic episodes of the scandal, narration of the affair made its way onto the actual stage. In late August, people in Provence and Paris were discussing a play, the *Nouveau Tarquin*, which drew its inspiration from ancient Roman history and retold the Girard/Cadière affair using the rape of Lucretia by Tarquinus. Indeed, the play achieved such notoriety that publishers included it in anthologies containing the trial's *factums*. Even plays unrelated to the scandal, such as Jacques Autreau's *Le Chevalier de Bayard*, were rumored to have "allusions to the affair of Father Girard."[23] In addition, there were other half-finished skits such as the "Parodie d'une scène de la tragédie d'Iphigénie de Racine" or "Minos et Rhadamante."[24] These two pieces seem local to Provence and were likely distributed in private, elite venues where, we might imagine, aristocratic men and women took turns reading parts.[25] Thus, the visual, in the form of performance, intersected with both print and orality.

The story of Father Girard clearly attracted English playwrights whose audiences were hostile to the Jesuits.[26] As early as 1731, a ballad opera, *The Wanton Jesuit*, a "faithful translation of the French Original," appeared; the original French piece remains unidentified, although it was "acted with Success before an Audience of Friends in private by Persons of great Rank and Figure."[27] Henry Fielding, the author of *The History of Tom Jones* (1749), produced a variation in the three-act *The Old Debauchees*, staged in Drury Lane on June 1, 1732. The audience made such loud disapproving sounds that Fielding was forced to cut speeches before he was awarded "universal applause"; however, one Grub Street writer commented that the play was "so far improper for an *English State*, or to be exhibited to a *polite*, an *honest*, and a *Christian* people."[28] In addition to these productions, there is evidence of an unpublished pantomime, *Father Girard the Sorcerer; or, The Amours of Harlequin and Miss Cadière*, that sometimes included songs and dance.[29]

Who was behind these audacious poems, songs, and plays that made audiences in drawing rooms and cabarets laugh uproariously while police officials nervously sought to suppress this *mauvais discours*? Generally, the individuals who scribbled verses remained elusive. On occasion, vague references appeared, as in the case of the "Vers sur l'affaire de Mademoiselle Cadière," which was attributed to "Sieur Artaud, a young man from Marseille."[30] Authors sometimes hid behind another identity, as was probably the case with "Mademoiselle Agnès," a boarder at the convent of Ollioules, who wrote a "response" to a letter disparaging Chaudon's trial briefs.[31] Anonymity invited speculation. For example, in Rouen, a false rumor circulated that Voltaire (1694–1778) had written the anonymous preface to a locally printed collection of Girard/Cadière *factums*.

Voltaire erroneously assumed that the printer Jorre had started this rumor in an effort to increase his sales.[32]

Sometimes the identities of certain authors were revealed well after publication. For example, the individuals behind the *calottes* and *brevets* belonged to a regiment of the king's musketeers; their leaders were Philippe Emanuel de Torsac, Théophile Aimon, and Amédée Paul Achille de St. Martin, who established "this illustrious corps" in 1702.[33] Nicolas Jouin (1684–1757), a failed banker, had published the *sarcelades*, escaping detection for two decades. Police finally arrested Jouin in 1754 when his own son turned him in, disgruntled because his parents had had his mistress incarcerated![34] Police arrest records illustrate how educated authors like Jouin had frequent contact with the clandestine underworld of *colporteurs* and printers responsible for distributing many songs and poems.

While the identity of someone like Jouin might be betrayed, other authors took advantage of their position to publicize their opinions; not surprisingly, they generally belonged to the Girard camp, which enabled them to publish with impunity. In 1732, Henri Belsunce, bishop of Marseille, wrote a "letter" to a Visitation nun that publicly condemned Catherine and Jean-Baptiste Chaudon.[35] What drove this exalted man to sully himself in the polemical quagmire of the Cadière affair? Belsunce certainly did not view the "public" in generous terms. In a letter to Cardinal Fleury, Belsunce seemed to equate the public to the "wild populace" of Toulon, who rioted in the days after the trial.[36] But the public could not be ignored. Thus, Belsunce wrote to Sister Greard that "it is up to me to disabuse the Public" about the lies that had tarnished Sister Rémuzat's reputation during the trial.[37]

Belsunce's frustration appears justified, given the avid consumption of polemical material that cropped up almost spontaneously. For example, Barbier painstakingly transcribed a number of songs, including the lengthy "fable" "La Girardière."[38] And he no doubt had to make choices, since the trial generated approximately 165 songs and poems.[39] The most famous collector was Jean-Frédéric Phélypeaux (1701–1781), comte de Maurepas, whose vast collection of eighteenth-century songs and poems was released in a ten-volume collection in the nineteenth century.[40] However, it is unlikely that any one individual could have obtained all of the poems. Archives and libraries in Aix-en-Provence and Toulon, for example, suggest that some pieces were exclusive to the region.

How did individuals evaluate all of this material that floated through the public spaces and private homes of eighteenth-century French urban centers? Not surprisingly, we see a range of views. Mathieu Marais wrote to Jean Bouhier in Dijon about certain "beautiful writings," including the fable "La Colombe et du corbeau," or "The Dove and the Crow."[41] However, the marquis de Caumont described "the verses, the songs, the *brevets*," appearing "everyday," as "mediocre."[42] Although the *Nouvelles Ecclésiastiques* eagerly included Chaudon's *factums*, it remained silent about these pieces of ephemera. With respect to *Le Nouveau Tarquin*, Bouhier flatly stated that while some aspects of the play were "bearable," the rest made him want to "vomit."[43] He was not alone in this view: the *opera-comique* inspired a verse, the "Ambigue Girardique," mocking it.[44]

Men and women also took their symbolic performances of sympathy and condemnation to streets and homes. Some actions were tongue in cheek. Fashion "à la Cadière" appeared—for example, muffs "à la Girard" could be purchased.[45] However, not all forms of opinion were so frivolous. Police records contain a copy of the poem "Au Parlement d'Aix" with the following heading: "Broadsheet displayed on the doors of those who belonged to the Jesuit party in the affair of Father Girard, Ignatien."[46] Clearly, the poem's critique of the Jesuits—"this horrible corps"—and the "unworthy" pro-Girard magistrates had a certain resonance. Posting this verse involved the risk of imprisonment. Whoever was responsible had appropriated the poem and transformed it into an act of defiance against the Jesuits and the authorities. At such moments, the public was more than an audience: it was an active voice of dissent.

In a climate where *Unigenitus* and the convulsionary movement of Saint-Médard provoked oppositional commentary, the Cadière trial opened another opportunity to express anger and discontent at the Jesuits and ultramontane bishops. Not surprisingly, then, officials sought to suppress related printed and transcribed writings through censorship, an intrinsic part of early modern print culture.[47] The *arrêt* of October 10 pointedly stated that a number of Chaudon's *factums* would be ceremonially brought to the court and torn up by the bailiff, a symbolic gesture of condemnation and suppression.[48] In Paris, authorities sought out those responsible for printing the *mémoires* and other subversive polemical literature. On March 11, 1733, a year and a half after the Cadière verdict, the Parisian police took Le Changeur, a "Jansenist," into custody for circulating various *libelles* on current affairs, including those about the Girard/Cadière trial.[49]

The risks *libellistes*, colporteurs, and consumers took to produce and obtain this ephemera illustrate that the Cadière affair struck a deep chord in eighteenth-century society. Historian Arlette Farge has argued that this was a public with mobile and fragmentary opinions.[50] She describes a populace "whose reactions were instinctive, emotional and invariable, and who were incapable of seeing the finer points and minute shifts which politicians were able to manipu-late."[51] Should this messiness be a reason to dismiss these varied opinions? I would follow Farge's lead and say no. As Farge notes, from the late 1720s, police spies and informers changed their own retelling of overheard conversations to reflect what they believed to be a shift in tone. By expressing their opinions, members of the public of the 1730s demanded accountability from both secular and religious authorities. Moreover, although their words, in verse and song, might appear to be an anarchic mosaic composed of tiles of different sizes, tex-tures, and colors, there were patterns, a series of themes, made clearer through repetition and interconnectedness.

"LE MONDE RENVERSÉ"

The title of one verse, "Le Monde renversé," or "The World Turned Upside Down," encapsulates how contemporaries interpreted the Cadière trial as a moment of crisis.[52] While the magistrates in Aix's Palais de Justice were evenly split, in the larger world, most writers appeared to believe that Jean-Baptiste Girard was a villain and Catherine Cadière his victim. For Catherine's support-ers, Father Girard's crimes against his penitent and the Jesuits' ruthless efforts to protect him represented a reversal of morals and of justice. These themes surfaced mainly around two topics: the relationship between Catherine and Father Girard and the parlement's verdicts of July 30 and October 10.

Poems and other writings often cast Father Girard in the role of a hypo-crite who cunningly manipulated his priestly status to ensnare the unsuspect-ing female believer. According to one song, Father Girard was a "tartuffe," a popular term from Molière's play of the same name. By the eighteenth century, it was commonly used to describe a religious "hypocrite."[53] In Molière's 1664 play, Tartuffe's pious demeanor hides his immoral purposes: to appropriate his patron's wealth and his wife.[54] Although Molière did not call Tartuffe a Jesuit, there were numerous parallels between his portrayal of this "imposter" and late seventeenth-century anti-Jesuit polemics.[55] Like Tartuffe, Father Girard moves into the private world of the Cadières rapidly, promising Catherine that "If you are discreet / I will tell you a secret / that will delight you, my beauty."[56]

Verses, sometimes in the form of dialogues, demonstrated how Father Girard wrapped this secret in the language of Quietism. Perhaps taking their cue from Chaudon, authors emphasized how, over the course of many con-versations, Father Girard overpowered the devout and gullible Catherine by persuading her that "voluptuousness" led to sainthood.[57] In all likelihood, it was

not theological subtleties that attracted writers to Quietism but the phrase "oubliez-vous, laissez-faire," "forget yourself and let yourself go." This pithy expression allowed writers to communicate Father Girard's transgressions—spiritual
incest and heresy—quickly. Not surprisingly, the lyrical, flexible slogan made
its way into nearly a dozen poems and songs.[58] One might imagine that in the
summer and fall of 1731, people in cafés and other gathering places evoked the
expression while telling a crude joke about clerical sexuality.

In the end, seduction was not just about honeyed words and spiritual
promises but about flesh. Chaudon claimed modesty, but polemicists had
no such misgivings and gleefully identified body parts and sexual positions.
For example, in the "Dialogue entre le père Girard et la Dlle. Cadière," when
Catherine expresses horror at his desire, the confessor describes her doubts as
a "sin" and then declares, "To punish this sin / I am[,] my Catherine / showing
you discipline / on your dappled ass / to punish this sin."[59] Another poem, a
"reflection" on clothing, declared that spiritual directors forbade wearing pan-
iers, the side hoops worn beneath gowns. Why? So they could feel their dévotes'
sides, an allusion to Father Girard's close inspection of Catherine's wounded
side.[60] A four-stanza verse noted that Father Girard had kissed his penitent "par
derrière et par devant"—in the back and the front. The reference to "derrière"
was also an allusion to sodomy, a trait often associated with Jesuits. It was a
point of hilarity that Father Girard, unlike many of his Jesuit cohorts, preferred
to "enter" from the front.[61]

A series of thirty-two erotic engravings narrates the Girard/Cadière liaison, using Catherine's version as the "true" story. The first twenty images take
the viewer through the various sites of seduction, beginning with the confessional and moving into Catherine's bedroom, the eventual space of consummation (fig. 11). Seduction and blasphemy coalesce when the Jesuit introduces
Catherine to a host of demons while she is lost in prayer. One plate features
Girard blowing into Catherine's mouth, thus manipulating her trust (fig. 12).
At one point, she kneels before him, her "master," in a worshipful manner,
which allows him to punish and then possess her (fig. 13). In perhaps a nod to
the phrase "par derrière et par devant," the Jesuit also gazes at her buttocks in
worshipful desire after having used a scourge to "punish" her for her sins (fig.
14). These poses mimic what happened in the confessional, thus equating the
confession with the bedchamber. Plate 16, the midpoint of the series, illustrates
Father Girard's final triumph as he holds his erect penis and prepares to pen-
etrate an unconscious Catherine from behind (fig. 15). Was she in a mystical
swoon or in ecstasy? The rest of the engravings narrate how Father Girard gives

FIGURE 11
Standing just outside the confessional booth, Girard and Catherine embrace and are furtively observed, possibly by one of the other *dévotes*. The Jesuit has taken his hat off, signaling the repudiation of his priestly role. The presence of the demon is suggestive of witchcraft and temptation. In *Historische print- en dicht-tafereelen van Jan Baptist Girard, en juffrou Maria Catharina Cadiere*. Courtesy of the Bibliothèque Méjanes, Aix-en-Provence.

FIGURE 12
Using the power of the confessional, as suggested by the booth, Girard blows into Catherine's mouth, an act often associated with bewitchment. From then on, she is possessed both by him and by demons, as suggested, respectively, by the satyr and the floating demon. In *Historische print- en dicht-tafereelen van Jan Baptist Girard, en juffrou Maria Catharina Cadiere*. Courtesy of Bibliothèque Méjanes, Aix-en-Provence.

Catherine an abortifacient and then takes her to Ollioules, yet another closed sacred space transformed into a site of illicit love. The last four plates hastily illustrate Catherine's accusations and imprisonment. The trial itself receives very little attention, suggesting that perhaps the plates were completed sometime in the spring or summer of 1731. The final plate offers the possibility of hope in the form of justice (fig. 16).

Most of the plates feature satyr-demons, symbols of sin and unbridled passion.[62] The satyrs are half human and half animal and thus echo anti-Jesuit rhetoric characterizing the Jesuits as bestial. Did they lead Girard astray or are they his partners in crime? Chasing away the lone angel, the satyr-demons steer Catherine toward temptation and eventually to hell. In keeping with their own lascivious inclinations, the satyrs assist the Jesuit in fulfilling his desires, celebrating his triumph. In classical mythology, satyrs cavort with nymphs, often

FIGURE 13

Father Girard appears to be punishing Catherine for her sins and visions—a prelude to seduction, as suggested by the bed. The expressions on both imply the perversion of penitence for the sake of pleasure. To make sure that Girard can achieve his goals, a satyr prevents anyone from entering the room. In *Historische print- en dicht-tafereelen van Jan Baptist Girard, en juffrou Maria Catharina Cadiere*. Courtesy of Bibliothèque Méjanes, Aix-en-Provence.

FIGURE 14

Father Girard stoops before Catherine's buttocks, pretending to inspect his punishment of her sins and visions. His expression of desire subverts devotion. The satyr celebrates this moment when lust is revealed. In *Historische print- en dicht-tafereelen van Jan Baptist Girard, en juffrou Maria Catharina Cadiere*. Courtesy of Bibliothèque Méjanes, Aix-en-Provence.

spying on them—their voyeurism, as suggested by the magnifying glass, representing another form of titillation. We might ask if the satyrs' gaze and that of the viewer overlap. Interestingly, *Thérèse philosophe* later refers to Dirrag (Girard) as a "satyr" consumed by lust. Perhaps its author was familiar with these plates and further exploited the sexual significance of satyrs.

Father Girard is unquestionably the villain of this visual narrative, but what about Catherine? The plates, such as the one in which Father Girard "punishes" Catherine, suggest ambiguity. At best, her face reflects foolishness, and at worst, acquiescence and even pleasure. Various songs and poems also hint at Catherine's complicity through imagined conversations between the Toulonnaise and the Jesuit. Similarly, an image from a set of four plates, printed in London, shows Catherine wearing a sweet, almost angelic, expression even as Father Girard fondles her breast, reminding her to "oubliez-vous et laissez-faire" (fig. 17).

FIGURE 15

Stripped of his priestly habit, Father Girard prepares to take full possession of Catherine. Demons look on, protecting Father Girard and perhaps verifying sexual consummation with the magnifying glass. In *Historische print- en dicht-tafereelen van Jan Baptist Girard, en juffrou Maria Catharina Cadiere.* Courtesy of Bibliothèque Méjanes, Aix-en-Provence.

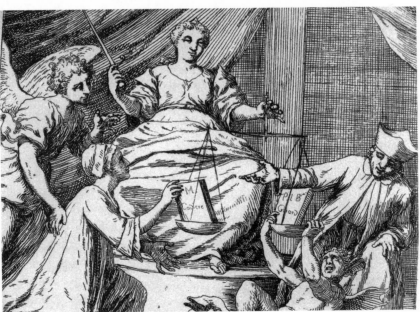

FIGURE 16

Encouraged by an angel, Catherine gently touches a *factum* while kneeling in supplication before Justice, who holds scales. On the other side, egged on by Father Girard (holding his own *mémoire judiciaire*), a demon tugs at the scales. Catherine looks to Justice, but Father Girard has his eyes on the demon. In *Historische print- en dicht-tafereelen van Jan Baptist Girard, en juffrou Maria Catharina Cadiere.* Courtesy of Bibliothèque Méjanes, Aix-en-Provence.

FIGURE 17

Here, Father Girard's features follow conventions of anti-Semitic caricatures, which highlight the Jesuit's status as an outsider within a Christian community. Sacrilege is suggested by the painting of the Madonna and Child above the pair. Catherine's position remains ambiguous. Was the shoe a sign of acquiescence, or was it a symbol of seduction? Plate 1 of "Quatre planches relatives aux rapports qu'aurait eus le Jésuite Jean Baptiste Girard avec Catherine Cadière." Bibliothèque nationale de France, Paris.

While some polemical work hinted at a more complicated relationship between Catherine and her former confessor, poems in the form of fables told the unambiguous story of predatory seduction. Verses such as "The Dove and the Crow" and "The Swallow and the Sparrow" imitated the allegorical style of the seventeenth-century fabulist Jean de La Fontaine (1621–1695), using animals as vehicles to carry moral messages.[63] Within these fables, writers warned readers, especially women, the "feeble sex," about the dangers of deceitful confessors.[64] Although gender-specific, this cautionary message became universal and timeless when encased in a fable. Similarly, an etching depicts Catherine perched like a bird, surrounded by birds of ill omen with Jesuit-like faces, while a doubtful peasant, symbolizing the public, looks on from the lower left (fig. 18).[65]

FIGURE 18

Gazing in a mirror, Catherine is being attacked by a bird (Father Girard) whose wings are part of an ecclesiastical habit. The surrounding Jesuit birds, peacocks and birds of prey, look on with expressions of pride and lust, indicating the complicity of the Jesuit order in Father Girard's crime. Meanwhile, a demon tugs at the string attached to Catherine's left ankle so that he can pull her toward hell. "Catherine Cadière sur un perchoir est embrassée par un oiseau à tête d'homme." Bibliothèque nationale de France, Paris.

This image of Catherine besieged by predatory Jesuits was reinforced by the widespread belief that the Jesuits had tampered with judicial proceedings in Aix. The parlement's activities were the subject of well over thirty songs and poems with titles such as "Vers adressés au parlement d'Aix" and "Calotte sur le parlement d'Aix." Most expressed exasperation and anger at the twelve magistrates who had condemned Catherine while protecting Father Girard. In the end, this intense scrutiny raised questions about judicial process in the Old Regime. Could individuals unconnected to powerful institutions or individuals receive a fair trial? How were clearly biased magistrates to be held accountable?

Identifying specific lawyers and judges represented one method of accountability. Not surprisingly, the prolific Chaudon was the object of various epigrams and odes. Some lauded his defense, but others, such as the "Avis au public," supposedly by the "Girardin" judge Montvalon, attacked his "writings full of lies."[66] Pazery de Thorame, Father Girard's attorney, was also maligned in verse as well as in the pamphlet *Antifactum*.[67] A few authors praised the judges who had sought to convict Father Girard. One *calotte* specifically singled out Bandol, Maliverny, and Gaufridy for their eloquence and honor.[68] Conversely, the two commissioners, Faucon and Charleval, were reviled. One epigram declared of Faucon: "It's not that he is a Jesuit, / But isn't he only, it's said, the hand, / Of a sodomite, to a sodomite."[69]

But it was the parlement's chief magistrate and provincial *intendant* Cardin Le Bret who became the most intense object of disgust and hostility. The short verse "Against M. Le Bret premier president of the parlement of Aix" left readers and listeners with no question about how the author interpreted the judge's unwavering support of Father Girard. Another verse declared that "the people have removed the sweet title of Father," indicating how much this fierce unpopularity was a volte-face for Le Bret.[70] The adjective "sweet" suggested that, before the trial, Le Bret had successfully fulfilled the role of the benevolent, paternal authority.[71] Now, Le Bret had become an implacable authoritarian who had betrayed his paternal responsibilities to his "children," the people of Provence.

These hostile responses to the once-revered Le Bret reflected a widely held belief that there had been a reversal of justice and inversion of law to save Father Girard. Some verses mocked the parlement of Provence, echoing the laughter that erupted around the courthouse the night of October 10. A very widely circulated epigram captured what many saw as the ruling's absurdity:

> Girard, full of infamous ardor,
> Made a virgin into a wife,
> And made her pass for a whore.
> But the Parlement easily,
> Using its sovereign power,
> Made a wife into a virgin.[72]

In order to make the Jesuit confessor innocent, the court had done the impossible. As Catherine lamented in one "prayer," "I find myself guilty and innocent at the same time / Of an inconceivable mix of crimes and virtues."[73]

Descriptions of this inversion of innocence and guilt deployed the binary metaphor of blackening and whitening, *noircir* and *blancher*, a linguistic device that left no room for ambiguity. The "Vers adressés au parlement d'Aix" declared that the "vile troupe of magistrates" had sullied themselves "in order to whiten the blackest of rascals."[74] As a result, the dove (Catherine) had also been blackened, while the crow (Father Girard) had been whitened.[75] Another epigram narrated the tale of "an escapee from Guinea / as black as soot" who, hearing that the parlement had turned Father Girard "white," declared, "I will try his soap."[76] The references to the escaped slave and "blackening" raise the question of racist overtones. Toulon had engaged in the slave trade with the Middle East and Africa, but it remained uninvolved with the rapidly expanding Atlantic slave trade. Although Europeans believed in their superiority over people from Africa and the Americas, the discussion of biological racial difference was still nearly two decades away.[77] We might read the verse of the escaped slave as reflecting a belief in immutable differences written in nature. Just as it was absurd for the parlement to restore Catherine's virginity after her seduction, it was ludicrous to think that the courts could alter a man's color. And yet the parlement of Provence had accomplished the unthinkable by acquitting Father Girard simply "because he was a Jesuit."[78]

According to one sonnet, the parlement was a "tribunal corrupted by the society."[79] Another piece, written as a poster, or *affiche*, declared that there were 10,000 louis d'or missing in the Palais de Justice and asked readers to restore them to the Jesuits' sacristy.[80] The Society had bought de Mons, Parade, Le Bret, Faucon, and d'Argens.[81] "And our abbé Charleval / isn't he yet a cardinal?"[82] Despite this contempt, we should not read these verses as expressions of anxiety about systemic corruption within the judicial process. Indeed, personal connections and monetary compensation were inherent within most Old Regime institutions, since the social and the political, the personal and the public, were intrinsically connected. Rather, the stakes involved the Jesuits' abuse of power.

TRYING THE JESUITS

The majority of songs expressed undisguised hostility toward Jesuits, effectively putting the order itself on trial. Such heated animosity was not simply rooted in local rivalries between religious orders and between magistrates but tied to a far more widespread, long-standing "anti-jesuitism."[83] Themes of the Jesuits' immorality and their methods of infiltration were amply developed in works about Jesuit conspiracies such as *Les Intrigues Secrettes des Jésuites traduites du Monita Secreta*.[84] This preexisting "anti-jesuitism" gave songwriters, versifiers, and pamphleteers a ready arsenal of imagined crimes with which to attack Father Girard and his order. Bestial and demonic allusions signaled that the Jesuits were outsiders within Christendom and human society. In the end, the

Society's achievements concealed a vast conspiracy to usurp power from all legitimate forms of authority—fathers, magistrates, bishops, and ultimately the king himself.

The polemical literature generated during the Cadière affair dehumanized the Society of Jesus, transforming them into the "other." Authors compared the order to predatory animals such as wolves that hid "under the skin of sheep, black rascals."[85] This metaphor was particularly trenchant because "sheep" generally denoted the faithful. There were references to "Indian serpents," commonly called *jésuitiques* in Provence, which attacked men, women, and children.[86] These allusions were powerful because they linked the Jesuits to wild animals that terrorized many parts of rural France and, of course, to the creature associated with the fall of Adam and Eve.[87] Even as humans, the Jesuits were deviants, as seen in the allusion to Faucon and the Jesuits as "sodomites." According to one *calotte*, Father Sabatier deserved to be the "bishop of Sodom," because of his great exploits with "young boys, girls, and women."[88] In the early modern context, sodomy was "second only to bestiality in gravity of sin, incarnated sheer lust, as did all sins against nature."[89] These sexual allusions were less homophobic insults than tirades against moral corruption.

Given their association with serpents and sins, the Jesuits were no strangers to hell. Father Girard, "this accursed Lucifer," inspired two poems alleging his close ties to the underworld: "The Triumphant Entry of Father Girard, Jesuit, into Hell," and its sequel "The Return of Father Girard from Hell to Earth." In the "Triumphant Entry," Pluto, Hell's sovereign, greets Father Girard with fanfare, assuming that the parlement had ordered the Jesuit's execution. In anticipation of Father Girard's arrival, Pluto acknowledges his debt to the Jesuits because without the order, "my empire would be deserted."[90] Demonization automatically made the Jesuits "the troupe of the Devil."[91] They were social pariahs in a Christian world in which a constant battle raged between good and evil, between God and the devil. These characterizations of the Jesuits as a fundamentally un-Christian order gained power within the larger political context of the Jansenist controversies.

JANSENISM

Complaining how Father Girard had been treated "without respect, without regard," a pro-Girard poem explained why: "Do you know what is causing such damnable abuse / It is the Bull *Unigenitus*."[92] Indeed, the Cadière affair provided new labels for identifying a "Jansenist" or a "Molinist," a common eighteenth-century label for the Jesuits that referred to the Jesuit theologian Luis de Molina (1535–1600). "Are you a Cadièriste, are you a Girardiste . . . / La Cadièriste means Jansenist, le Girardiste is Molinist / Voilà the whole order of battle."[93] These poems, images, and pamphlets put the concerns raised by *Unigenitus* within the private world of the confession and the family.

For many eighteenth-century observers, the connection between the Jansenist struggles and the Cadière affair was to be found in the events of Saint-Médard. We might think that miracles and physical contortions automatically linked the *convulsionnaires* and Catherine. However, various polemical literature of the early 1730s juxtaposed Father Girard and François de Pâris. In contrast to the descriptions of Father Girard, François de Pâris was the ideal: the good curé, a figure of sincere piety and selfless charity. A rare pamphlet, *Réflexions simples et naturelles sur monsieur Pâris et sur le père Girard*, suggested that the two men were mirror opposites. Pâris, a "true pastor," was the source of "miracles," while Father Girard, the "mercenary pastor," had committed "enormous crimes."[94] Similarly, another verse stated that "the one perverts / the other edifies / the one is all peace all charity / the other all force and all authority."[95]

Comparisons were made between the false saint and the true saint—a compelling subject, since there was a brief movement to have Pâris beatified.[96] Prints depicting Pâris's life of piety and self-sacrifice, along with a number of biographies, reinforced the notion that the deacon of Saint-Médard had led a saintly, indeed Christlike, life. If we place the erotic engraving series, the *Histoire du père Jean-Baptiste Girard jésuite*, beside engravings of the deacon Pâris, we see the contrast between true and false sanctity. A number of engravings featured the deacon kneeling in intense prayer. In one example, the curtains are drawn around the beds, while several feet away, François de Pâris is bowed down, deep in prayer (fig. 19). With eyes downcast and arms crossed, he gives the impression of a man engaged in meditative prayer, looking inward as he seeks God. This serene devotion matched the austere apostolic life Pâris led in the parish of Saint-Médard.

In contrast to this pure faith directed appropriately toward God, prints of Father Girard reinforce the image of a Jesuit who uses the cover of priesthood to sate his appetites. He adopts a reverential gaze that focuses on Catherine's naked body. At times, his arms are outstretched in a parody of baroque piety, fondling Catherine's breast. Another image depicts Father Girard carrying an icon of two lovers as opposed to the more traditional representations of the Virgin and Child or the Sacred Heart that saints were often seen wearing (fig.

Hæc puerulus Obſervabat.

Monsieur de PARIS encore Enfant, se lève la nuit pour prier à l'insçu de son Precepteur

FIGURE 19

François de Pâris's tutor looks on in awe at the deacon, a young man rapt in prayer. "Monsieur de Pâris encore Enfant, se lève la nuit pour prier à l'insçu de son Precepteur." Courtesy of the Bibliothèque de la Société de Port-Royal, Paris.

20). Thus, the appearance of sanctity cloaks Girard's unruly passion. Moreover, the Jesuits abet this subterfuge by awarding Father Girard the title of "saint."[97]

Did contemporaries see these opposing images of Girard and François de Pâris together? In a letter to the marquis de Caumont, Monsieur d'Anfossy remarked on the libertine images being sold and noted that "it was a pleasant contrast to see being sold, on the one side the life and miracles of M. Paris, and on the other, the infamies attributed to the Bonze." ("Bonze" referred to Japanese or Chinese monks, which d'Anfossy and Caumont used instead of "Jesuit.")[98] Moreover, even if viewers did not see these images together, they may have encountered prints and engravings during the same period. The visual contrast would have been strengthened by comparisons made in various *libelles* circulating both in the capital and in the provinces. Some verses suggested how the Jesuits had subverted the understanding of sainthood: "Abbé

Pâris, in vain, you made miracles. . . . If one lacks the seal of the Society / which will never support the Truth."[99]

Father Girard and the deacon Pâris also encapsulated the difference between those who defended *Unigenitus* and those who fought for the appellant cause. These disparities between Father Girard and the "blessed Pâris" were embedded in a theological worldview to which many diehard Jansenists, including the deacon of Saint-Médard, subscribed. In the years immediately after *Unigenitus*'s promulgation, theologians from the seminary of Saint-Magloire, the hub of Jansenist thought, applied a "figurist" theology to history. This history treated the past and the present as a broader struggle between a small group of persecuted "true" believers and those who had strayed from a pure Christian vision.[100] No individual, however obscure, appeared randomly but instead represented either persecutors of or martyrs to the Truth, *la Vérité*.

FIGURE 21

Is the figure at the bottom left Catherine, her hands clasped either in supplication or prayer, ignored by everyone? Catherine was not a Jansenist, but for Jansenist advocates like the *Nouvelles Ecclésiastiques*, her sufferings at the hand of the Jesuits placed her within a figurist narrative of martyrdom and persecution. "Les Fruits de Constitution *Unigenitus*." Courtesy of the Bibliothèque de la Société de Port-Royal, Paris.

Furthermore, their roles were prefigured by earlier Biblical episodes and individuals. The ideas of Saint-Magloire were spread through sermons, schools, and the *Nouvelles Ecclésiastiques* in the hope of winning over a wider lay public.[101]

A number of poems reflected this figurist point of view, suggesting that followers of the Jansenist cause saw Catherine's story as part of the larger history between good and evil. The Biblical past and the world of France in the 1730s were intertwined. A poem compared 1731 with the "century of Elijah," noting that there had been a three-year drought in the prophet Elijah's time, just like the drought France was undergoing.[102] Within Jansenist figurist thinking, the Jesuits featured heavily and, as we have seen, Jansenists quickly blamed the order for all their troubles: *Unigenitus* and the ongoing oppression of the appellants. The *Réflexions simples et naturelles*, a pamphlet with an obviously Jansenist point of view, was also one of the few pieces that actually described Father Girard as a proponent of the bull.[103]

One etching presented the Cadière trial itself as a chapter within the larger figurist history, in which Father Girard and François de Pâris reflected the ongoing struggle around *la Vérité* (fig. 21).[104] The middle caption in the lower half states, "Remarkable epoch during 1731, making a part of the passion of Jesus Christ that Cusa predicted must happen in the Church between 1700 and 1734." The darkly clad Father Girard is compared to Barabbas, the thief whom Pontius Pilate had pardoned instead of Jesus.[105] In contrast, the "blessed Pâris," dressed in white and crowned with a halo, relives the martyrdom of Christ. These New Testament images are linked to the Old Testament with a line from Isaiah 5: "Woe to those . . . who acquit the guilty for a bribe, and deny justice to the innocent."[106] Pointedly, this scene takes place before the parlement of Aix; the remark about greed reinforces the notions of judicial corruption and the miscarriage of justice. Below this scene, a divided public, epitomized by fighting dogs, looks on; some support Father Girard while others weep for Pâris.

The Jansenist perspective of this etching, with its strong apocalyptic themes, reminds us of the centrality of faith to those involved. The austere Jansenists of Paris might have had little in common with Catherine's *dévotes*, whose religious practices were flamboyant, even excessive. Nevertheless, they both belonged to a community of the faithful for whom it was not simply a question of rejecting miracles as superstition and dismissing Jesuits as symptomatic of a corrupt Church. Taken together, the *convulsionnaire* movement and the Girard/Cadière scandal represented a crisis of faith, as suggested by a poem in the form of a "complaint" delivered by "religion."[107]

THE THREAT OF DESPOTISM

As we saw in the arguments made in various *factums*, Father Girard's crimes were a microcosm of the larger *political* evils the Jesuits represented. The Society of Jesus's conduct during the Cadière trial only compounded the growing belief that the Jesuits were engaged in a far-reaching plot to dominate French subjects. A distillation of the long list of crimes attributed to the Jesuits boiled down to despotism, a crime that would become irrevocably linked to them well into the nineteenth century.[108]

Just as Girard had used the confession to control the Cadière family, the Jesuits had installed *Unigenitus*, "this constitution / that serves our [the Jesuits'] ambition," to empower themselves in France.[109] One *calotte* described how the Jesuits, carrying "Marie Alacoque and Girard" on their standard, punished anyone who dared oppose the bull.[110] Individuals like Jean Soanen were pursued

PUBLIC OPINION

through illegitimate assemblies like the Council of Embrun, "a coup d'état."[111] And others, "Jansenists, Augustinians and Thomists," were subject to garroting, questioning, hanging, impaling, burning, torture, piercing, pillaging, and pulverizing.[112] These violent punishments underscored that Jesuits wielded "despotic authority" and "tyrannical power."[113] Within this framework, the order achieved their ambitions: "through their impious writings / Kings, magistrates, princes / realms and provinces / trembled under their [authority]."[114] Thus, Father Girard's efforts to dominate Catherine were part of a larger Jesuit system.

In the 1730s, the concept of despotism was grounded in the history of ancient Rome, which included Tarquin, the subject of the abbé Caveirac's *Le Nouveau Tarquin*. Known for his "intolerable despotism so sovereignly established," Tarquin had murdered the legitimate king Servillius Tuilius and usurped his throne.[115] In the play, Tarquin, with the assistance of "Scarpinello" (Father Sabatier), satisfies his desire for Lucretia through sorcery and the corruption of laws: "Religion is only purely political, to serve the passions of some and hide the vices of others."[116] Lucretia's lover, Collatinus, sees through such impiety and seeks revenge, for himself and for Rome. Through these connections between the private and the public, *Le Nouveau Tarquin* intimated that Father Girard's seduction of Catherine's soul and his rape of her body symbolized the vulnerability of all French subjects before the ambitious Jesuit order.[117]

Caveirac's interpretation fell in line with anti-Jesuit sentiments that equated Jesuits with usurpation of legitimate authority. Their methods of domination and oppression had even more sinister connotations in this verse: "God keep our kings from a Father Guignard / And our daughters from a Father Girard."[118] Guignard referred to Jean Guignard, a Jesuit executed in 1595 for possessing writings on regicide, a crime associated with the order since the assassination of Henry III (1551–1589) in 1589; according to the marquis d'Argens, Guignard had "solicited and corrupted" Jean Châtel, who tried to kill Henry IV (1553–1610) in 1594.[119] By bringing together Guignard and Girard, these lines put regicide and seduction on equal footing. In a country that saw two kings assassinated within two decades, regicide also evoked alarming images of civil war and instability.[120] Seduction, which represented a social "death" for a woman, brought dishonor and disorder to a family. As we have seen, the family and the monarchy were interlocking categories in early modern political thought, in which the family served as a microcosm of the larger body politic. Thus, the Jesuits' ascendancy over the family signified its supremacy over the crown.

This narrative of Jesuit dominion and usurpation was an image of despotism, both sexually and politically charged. While the term itself would gain greater currency from the 1750s onward, the concept of despotism was already gaining traction. The *philosophe* Montesquieu's novel *The Persian Letters* (1721) was also a treatise on oriental despotism. A veiled critique of the late Louis XIV, Montesquieu uses the seraglio or harem to explore how an individual with limitless power abused his authority to serve his personal desires and uncontrolled passions. Indeed, the lawyer Jean-Baptiste Chaudon suggested Father Girard ruled like an Oriental despot: "It was notorious in Toulon that this chaste Director had made a little seraglio of seven to eight devoted women with stigmata. What a scandal!"[121] Similarly, the *Entrée triomphante du père Girard* applauds Father Girard for surrounding himself with a "seraglio" or harem—the epicenter of Oriental despotism.[122] This conflation of sexual excess and untamed power extended to the Jesuit order: "The Bar moans and Rome thunders / We pawn our liberties our rights," and in the meantime, the Jesuits "debauched children, women, and mistresses" with the approval of the parlement of Provence.[123]

But if poems and *Le Nouveau Tarquin* raised fears about Jesuit subjugation of French subjects, the public that asserted itself during the Cadière affair was hardly acquiescent or easily intimidated. During the trial, the public gained in importance and authority in a manner that mirrored a subtle transformation of Catherine Cadière's own public image. In his *factums*, Jean-Baptiste Chaudon cast Catherine in the role of the ideal eighteenth-century woman, timid and passive. Nevertheless, the twenty-one-year-old Toulonnaise also exercised agency through conscience. During the dramatic confrontation with Father Girard on October 4, Catherine acknowledged that, despite her ecstasies and obsessions, she continued to take communion frequently at her spiritual director's bidding. But she did not do so with "a free conscience."[124]

Catherine's use of the term "free conscience" was at odds with the practices and principles behind Jesuit spiritual direction. In its definition of "conscience," the 1694 *Dictionnaire de l'Académie française* provided a set of commonly used phrases, including "director of conscience." This definition revealed how the implicit understanding of conscience embraced the clergy, who acted as watchdogs over the consciences of the faithful.[125] But now, Catherine's "free" conscience had its own moral compass that essentially voided the hierarchical relationship between spiritual director and penitent.[126] This severing of "conscience" from the priest/penitent relationship followed the Jansenist oppositional model of conscience. Since 1713, Jansenists had "invoked their conscience for discussion and eventually for resistance."[127] When Catherine spoke for herself, her insistence on her conscience was reminiscent of Jansenist resistance to *Unigenitus*.

Both the public and Catherine Cadière suggested a new kind of subject, one who had some autonomy. Theoretically, the public in the Old Regime were passive subjects who owed obedience to powerful persons. The Girard/Cadière affair invoked a new kind of public, one that was self-aware and even active. Like lawyers, polemicists gave the public voice, or "voix publique," credibility and, by extension, a certain authority and autonomy: "If it [the public] was a fearless censor, it was an equitable judge."[128]

THE AFTERMATH

Less than twelve hours after the parlement of Aix had delivered its bewildering verdict, Father Girard left prison by the back door, hoping to escape unnoticed. But "a spy" alerted the waiting crowd, and Girard endured jeers and curses all the way to the Jesuit Church of Saint-Louis.[1] There, he celebrated mass and gave thanks for his "happy deliverance."[2] Outside the church, however, most people were scandalized, seeing his actions as "an insult to the altar."[3] Enthusiastic crowds nearly suffocated Father Nicolas and the Cadière brothers. The star of the moment was Catherine, who left prison "triumphant."[4] Crowds escorted her to her carriage, which took her to her mother at the home of her prosecutor, Antoine Aubin. Outside the house, huge crowds gathered to glimpse this celebrity, who appeared at a window to thank them for their good will.[5]

The dramatically different receptions for Catherine and her former confessor symbolize how the trial created divisions that would persist in the coming days, months, and, indeed, years. In Toulon, jubilation at Catherine's release soon gave way to anger toward the Jesuits, expressed through macabre rituals and violence. Inside the Palais de Justice, the magistrates continued to be at one another's throats. In subsequent months, Cardin Le Bret used his role as the king's *intendant* to punish Catherine's partisans while church authorities in Provence made the trial an excuse to pursue Jansenists. Their actions tried to restore order in *le monde renversé*.

DAYS AFTER

In the weeks after October 10, the Cadière scandal's aftershocks continued to disrupt almost every level of Provençal society. From Provence to Paris, people had hoped that Father Girard would burn at the stake. A series of explosive events in Toulon during October 1731 illustrates that, though people celebrated Catherine's release, they clearly believed that justice had not been done. Within the parlement, the situation was equally volatile. To Cardin Le Bret's dismay, the lower chambers staged a revolt by seeking to prosecute the two commissioners for their activities in Toulon back in February.

Contemptuous of the parlement's authority, the populace of Toulon and Aix-en-Provence mined existing rituals to bring Father Girard and his order to justice. In the nights before October 10, young men in Aix roamed around the Palais de Justice and the prisons housing Girard and Catherine. Eager for the Jesuit's execution, they prepared a barrel of wine and a side of beef to be roasted and distributed to the public. This extravagant gesture was usually reserved for public holidays.[6]

Toulon reverberated with similar emotions. The verdict was announced on a Wednesday, and people spent "all day Thursday in expectation," receiving the news only twenty-four hours later, at six in the evening.[7] The next day, in the *hôtel de ville*, or town hall, the town's bourgeois celebrated by decorating a chair with a carpet and ribbons. The chair, known as a "cadière" in the Provençal dialect, was unoccupied in anticipation of Catherine's triumphant return to Toulon. Outside, a tuna fisherman swore that God would give him the largest fish if the judges pardoned Catherine. And indeed, this "miracle" came to pass when the fisherman caught a tuna "so fat" and "rare," unlike any seen in over fifty years.[8] Was it a miracle, or was it simply a way for the tuna fishermen, or *fermiers des madragues*, to best their rival fishermen by flaunting a giant catch?[9] Crowds gathered to see the beribboned tuna ceremoniously set on a table, but plans to parade it around town were jettisoned when Toulon authorities intervened.

These episodes in Toulon and Aix reveal how people appropriated rituals and economic practices to voice their opinions about the trial. In both cases, these moments of celebration were not so subtle expressions of dissent against authorities. Furthermore, they also reveal how over the course of 1731, the Cadière trial had become intertwined with the civic identity of both Toulon and Aix.

Such amusing episodes were soon replaced by violence that certainly alarmed the authorities. When news of the parlement's *arrêt* arrived in Toulon, "one saw fires of joy in all the streets."[10] While celebratory fires were lit on the Cadières' street, flames thrown into the Jesuit seminary's garden were more sinister. The order's property was saved only when a Jesuit slipped out a small side door and sped to the governor of Toulon. The governor, M. Dupont, brought in troops to disperse the crowds of "500 to 600."[11] In the meantime, the Ursuline convent and Madame Guiol, Father Girard's closest confidante within his circle of *dévotes*, were also at risk. During the first few nights, people surrounded the Guiols' shop and broke windows; fearing for her safety and possibly her life, Madame Guiol left town to wait for tempers to cool.[12]

However, Toulon's deepest hostility was reserved for Father Girard. For three days, the townspeople paraded his effigy through the streets. The figure was covered in an ankle-length soutane, undoubtedly belted according to Jesuit custom. Its head was topped with horns resembling those that "painters gave to characterize the Devil."[13] Sometimes, the effigy was brought before the houses of "Girardins," and an impromptu interrogation was held. Had Girard locked himself up with Catherine? Had he blown into her mouth? After this mock trial, "Father Girard" was condemned to be burned, an event that took place "with grand ceremony" on the aristocratic Champs de Bataille, later known as the Place d'Armes, within sight of the Jesuit seminary.[14] Were these vociferous demonstrations manifestations of pent-up tensions in a town where the Girard/Cadière affair had been the focal point for nearly a year? The destructive fires and riots show the characteristics of mob violence: spontaneity, disorder, and volatility. However, a closer look suggests that the townspeople of Toulon used violence as a vehicle of justice.

While outrageous, the mock "trial" of Father Girard was not unusual in French urban and rural popular culture. During Carnival or Christmas festivities, communities convened mock courts that "presided" over actual cases such as those involving wives who beat and dominated their husbands.[15] Carnival-like trials and festivities provided an outlet for chastising elites guilty of "crimes" such as excessive taxation.[16] Even unusual episodes of violence showed logical patterns reflecting the morals and values of a more stable society. In 1750, nineteen years after the Cadière trial, an aggravated Paris populace responded violently when overzealous officials abducted children in an effort to suppress vagrancy. In a series of riots, the crowd carried out its own form of justice by murdering the constable implicated in these abductions.[17] The populace of Toulon in 1731 thus used certain conventions to make officials hear their voices.

Private letters and official correspondence reveal how people well beyond Toulon also voiced their anger at the Jesuits. When a rumor circulated in Angers, some four hundred miles northwest of Aix, that Étienne-Thomas Cadière and some of his supporters had been executed, the governor intervened to quell a disturbance.[18] In Avignon, crowds chased a Jesuit priest who saved himself by desperately crying, "I am not Father Girard, I am not Father Girard!"[19] Similarly, Édmond Barbier noted that "the good city of Paris, which is Jansenist from head to foot, is strongly irritated against the arrêt, [and] regards it as unjust."[20] Such bitterness was aggravated by misleading rumors that Girard had been found guilty, hanged, and burned.

Can we call these actions "revolutionary"? In a letter full of foreboding, Henri Belsunce wrote to Cardinal Fleury about the "insolent and seditious words against the judges who had not been behind Cadière, against Monsieur le premier président [Cardin Le Bret], against the government, against confession, against religion."[21] Belsunce's response seems somewhat out of proportion. After all, crowds in Toulon, comprising "both sexes," marched through the streets with torches and maintained a chant of "Long live the King and Cadière."[22] Violence in these instances was not about overthrowing a system but about punishment and justice for specific individuals. Nevertheless, Belsunce's somewhat hysterical comments suggest that the intense dissatisfaction signaled a shift. Not only had the public lost respect for figures of authority, but people now openly expressed their contempt.

Turmoil in the streets of Toulon was mirrored in the Palais de Justice in Aix. The rifts exposed within the Grand'Chambre during the summer did not disappear in the days after October 10. The explicit point of contention involved Faucon and Charleval and accusations that they had overstepped their duties in Toulon. These divisions continued to fester when Louis XV and Chancellor d'Aguesseau sought further clarification about the verdict. The magistrates' justification of their votes and the public's response to their accounts clearly indicate that, even two years later, the Cadière affair was neither forgotten nor forgiven.

The accusations against Faucon and Charleval's integrity added another layer to an already tortuous procedure. On October 6, Father Nicolas appeared before the court to deliver a "learned dissertation" on the confessional.[23] In a "strong discourse," Father Nicolas declared that he could not believe that the commissioners still had the right to opine on the affair. He railed against the abbé Charleval for his willingness to sacrifice both the Carmelite friar and the Cadière family "to the humor of the Society and for the consecration of a guilty Jesuit at the expense of innocence."[24] At the end of this diatribe, Father Nicolas bowed and exited, leaving the two commissioners stunned and outraged.[25]

His claims quickly became an instrument with which the pro-Cadière magistrates tried to slow down the trial. On October 9, attorney general Jacques Gaufridy, who had spoken so eloquently on Catherine's behalf in July, insisted that before any other decisions, the charges against Faucon and Charleval necessitated further investigation. When two of the other *gens du roi* suggested that this would create an unwanted public outcry, Gaufridy countered that as "avengers of the public," the *gens du roi* were obligated to pursue the matter.[26]

Despite this request, on October 10 Le Bret went ahead with deliberations on the Cadière affair.[27] But the proceedings were interrupted, not once but twice, by members of the two lower chambers, the Tournelle and the Enquêtes, who insisted that the charges against the commissioners be discussed before the Cadière case. To the astonishment of many, they also demanded that all the parlement's chambers assemble for this hearing.[28] Was this an effort to stall the proceedings further, or was it simply institutional rivalry between the most senior chamber and the other chambers, whose members had lower status than magistrates of the Grand'Chambre? Whatever their motives, Le Bret turned them away, placating them by promising to assemble the chambers on October 11, *after* delivering judgment on the Cadière case.

On October 11, Gaufridy presented Catherine's and Father Nicolas's charges against the commissioners.[29] The "friends of Le Bret and the commissioners," who included Suffren (Faucon's uncle), Piolenc, Valabres, and de Mons, denounced the charges as false and injurious to the two men. Villeneuve attacked Chaudon's writings, arguing that they must be destroyed; not only had they damaged the commissioners' reputations, but they had also harmed the magistracy itself.[30] Not surprisingly, Faucon delivered an impassioned speech, "like a mad man," according to one observer. The attorney general's zealous efforts to examine the commissioners' actions were "a pretext created to stall the judgment of la Cadière, whom he had always appeared to favor." Throughout this heated speech, the commissioner's "eyes appeared to be popping out of his head, and he gesticulated with his hands like a man possessed."[31] In the end, Gaufridy failed to exact official condemnation of the commissioners, because the majority of magistrates rejected the charges. When Gaufridy protested, de

Mons "had the audacity and temerity to tell him that he no longer had a mouth to speak" since the court had decided. The infuriated Gaufridy retorted that it was not he but de Mons who needed to shut up.[32]

At a moment when the parlement of Provence's reputation had been severely damaged, how did the two sides justify their positions? Personal resentments were justified in terms of the "public." Gaufridy said that his duty was to pursue the charges against the two men because the parlement had been charged to punish errant ministers, not just to defend their reputations.[33] The parlement's integrity depended on keeping public trust. However, Faucon's and Charleval's supporters argued that perhaps the "public avengers" had heeded public discourse "prematurely." Consequently, they had exposed the reputations of the magistrates "to their enemies and the caprice of a public," a public a bit too eager to criticize.[34] Their view reflected another image of the public: an unreliable, uncontrollable entity to be treated with skepticism and caution.

Not surprisingly, both commissioners chose to restore their good names by ignoring the public and appealing straight to those in power. The abbé Charleval left for Paris a week later, on October 18, and took up residence at the archbishop of Paris's palace near the cathedral of Notre-Dame; he was forced to adopt a pseudonym—the abbé Tammarlet—because the Paris populace, like the crowds in Aix, held him in contempt.[35] Working with the Jesuits and his colleague, the *procureur-général* Boyer d'Argens, Charleval lobbied Chancellor d'Aguesseau with two objectives in mind: first, to reverse the October 10 *arrêt*, and second, to suppress the accusations against Faucon and himself.[36] Back in Aix, Faucon bombarded the chancellor with a barrage of agitated letters in which he railed against the public, Gaufridy, Jean-Baptiste Chaudon, and another Cadièriste magistrate, Boyer de Bandol. The aggrieved commissioner lamented that "all of Europe regards me as a liar, attributing the most unfair motives to me."[37]

For Chancellor Henri d'Aguesseau, the persistent lobbying by the Provençal magistrates, combined with the embarrassing *arrêt* of October 10, must have been an added headache amid a larger political crisis unfolding at precisely the same time. Historically, d'Aguesseau had enjoyed strong ties to the parlement of Paris, but, as chancellor and Cardinal Fleury's appointee, he was expected to negotiate with the judicial courts on the Crown's behalf.[38] His loyalties were certainly tested in 1731, when the parlement as well as the Parisian Order of Barristers engaged in combat against ultramontane bishops. The parlement maintained its right to limit clerical abuse, while the episcopal powers staunchly argued that religious affairs were no business of the secular courts.

The rhetoric grew more inflamed in 1731 during the "affaire des avocats," which raised the question of secular intervention in ecclesiastical matters. The Jansenist lawyer François de Maraimberg wrote an incendiary *mémoire*—signed by thirty-nine other lawyers—that asserted parlementary right to intervene in clerical affairs. It stated that "all laws are contracts [*conventions*] between those who govern and those who are governed."[39] The language of contract held both sides accountable; moreover, it implicitly placed those in positions of authority on an equal footing with subordinates. The exasperated d'Aguesseau remarked, "here we are again in Poland where the king is only the head of the Republic!"[40]

Was the Cadière affair just an annoyance, or did it, in fact, compound the problems faced by a besieged royal ministry in late 1731? One may argue for the latter position. As we saw, the pro-Cadière magistrates railed against clerical abuse, arguing that the parlement was vital in limiting ecclesiastical overreach. Furthermore, some of these judges, such as Gaufridy, already had a record of opposing *Unigenitus* and clashing with ultramontane bishops like La Tour du Pin-Montauban. The anti-Jesuitism of Gaufridy and likeminded magistrates' attacks against clerical authority symbolized an affront, in one way or another, to all forms of authority in an Old Regime that God had sanctified. To the commissioners' satisfaction, the Crown seemed to punish these challenges by issuing an *arrêt du conseil* on March 27, 1732; the edict invalidated the deliberations of the Tournelle and Enquêtes, whose activities revealed "irregularity" and "indecency."[41]

But the *arrêt* of October 10 remained standing. Placating the Jesuits and satisfying Faucon and Charleval was perhaps not worth the risk of inviting public outrage at a particularly unstable moment. And the mood of the French capital was decidedly mutinous, especially since the population resented ultramontane bishops' effort to enforce *Unigenitus*.[42] On another occasion, d'Aguesseau privately commented that "the King does not rule over the opinions of men: he judges individuals, and the public judges him."[43] In other words, even the king could not ignore public opinion.

But perhaps d'Aguesseau himself did not necessarily credit Father Girard's innocence, especially after he read the *motifs* written by both sides explaining their conclusions.[44] According to a letter written in Marseille on November 10, 1731, "the king was surprised by the *arrêt*, and the diversity of opinions was so extraordinary that His Majesty wishes to see an account of the opinions and the entire procedure."[45] Faucon's and Le Bret's reflections on the affair remained in manuscript form.[46] Le Bret affirmed his belief that ecclesiastical judges, not the Grand'Chambre, should have heard the case. In Faucon's opinion, the

Cadière trial represented a violation of procedure and law, for which he blamed "the 100 infidel lawyers," referring no doubt to Chaudon.[47] Unfortunately for d'Aguesseau, Maliverny's anti-Girard and Montvalon's pro-Girard motivations or *motifs* quickly went into print, keeping interest in the Cadière affair alive two years later.

When the pro-Cadière judges released their *Motifs des juges du parlement de Provence* as a printed pamphlet in February 1733, people "ran like fire" to obtain a copy.[48] Mathieu Marais gushed that Maliverny's *motifs* were "penetrating, ingenious, subtle."[49] In thirty-one pages, Maliverny presented evidence explaining why the twelve judges believed that Father Girard, a "criminal," deserved execution. "The first crime, and the source of all that Justice had to pursue during this great Trial, is a sacrilegious abuse of all that is sacred in religion in favor of deceit that one cannot punish enough."[50] The pamphlet denounced the behavior of Toulon's ecclesiastical officials toward Catherine; it noted how the procedure had been manipulated in Girard's favor. The ten judges who voted for Catherine had had to overcome adversities in order to arrive at "a judgment that Religion, public order, the interest of truth, and Justice demand."[51]

No doubt goaded by the success of the *Motifs*, the judges who had sided with Father Girard soon produced their own pamphlet. The principal author was André de Barrigue de Montvalon, one of the Jesuit's most avid supporters in the Grand'Chambre.[52] This treatise became a pamphlet with different titles, including *Motifs des juges qui ont mis le père Jean-Baptiste Girard hors de cour et de procès* and *Lettres écrites d'Aix sur le procez du père Girard et de la Cadière*. In the series of "letters" to d'Aguesseau, Montvalon argued that Father Girard was "a pious monk, simple in his morals, a slave of the good opinion he had of his penitent, [and] victim of her bad faith."[53] In contrast, Catherine was a compulsive liar, fickle and craving attention—"a spirit capable of pushing crime to its extremes."[54] Montvalon also defended Toulon's *officialité* and the commissioners: "There perhaps isn't any magistrate in the realm who would resort to this kind of threat against a girl who so visibly counterfeited being imbecilic."[55]

Arguments such as these apparently did not help Montvalon's case, and the magistrate adopted another tactic. A few months later, a third edition of Maliverny's *Motifs* appeared, with critical notes taken from the "letters written in Aix, using the motives of the judges with the contrary opinion." These annotations suggest Montvalon's frustration with public rancor against the Jesuits and the pro-Girard judges. Indeed, the revised pamphlet began on the hopeful note that perhaps the public would change its mind about the Cadière affair.[56]

But Montvalon's strategy failed miserably. According to Marais, a colporteur at the doors of the Tuileries, perhaps desperate to sell the revamped *Motifs*, described his wares as the *motifs* of Father Girard, "accused of having performed miracles."[57]

A RETURN TO ORDER

Dueling *motifs* aside, the Cadière affair was not simply a war of words; it affected Cadière supporters in very tangible, detrimental ways. As Provence's *intendant*, Cardin Le Bret was responsible for restoring public order. To punish potential sedition, he used the resources available to him as *intendant*—such as armed soldiers brought in from Marseille and the *lettre de cachet* allowing him to arrest individuals without due process.[58] In a long account sent to Fleury in early May 1732, Le Bret revealed how he interpreted the Cadière trial as a crisis, a subversion of royal authority, which he blamed on the Jansenists. Le Bret's actions in many ways contradict the reputation for moderation he had enjoyed since becoming *intendant* in 1703.[59] According to one observer, the *intendant* "was furious for being hooted and whistled at. He for whom one readily would have erected a statue last year."[60]

Almost immediately after October 10, Le Bret went into action and conducted a series of arrests using the *lettre de cachet*. Information gathered in the streets, shops, and even elite private homes apparently yielded a plot in which fifty men were poised for insurrection had Catherine not been freed. His clerk Bouteille reported that in Aix, a young naval ensign, "J. B. Chaumont," had been heard to say that his sword was ready to defend Catherine and Father Nicolas.[61] Chaumont's superior sent him to the galleys while Perrin, a member of the king's cavalry, was "simply put in prison with the threat of being broken."[62]

Perrin and Chaumont pointed to a larger group with links to other parts of Provence. Apparently, one Charbonnier, "a bourgeois from Aix," known for speaking warmly in Catherine's defense, had heard of this conspiracy being organized in the shop of a café owner named Beaudin.[63] Beaudin's fate remains unclear, but Charbonnier turned into a key informant, perhaps because his wife and five children were reduced to begging.[64] The head of the Cadière faction in Marseille was Caire, who, according to one correspondent, was an "honest man, a rich trader from Marseille and aged more than forty-five years old."[65] Caire apparently traveled to Aix, where he was seen glaring at Father Girard; he had also been known to speak with the Cadières. The authorities sent Caire to the Château de Saint-Jean by the port of Marseille, while Charbonnier was briefly placed in the citadel of Saint-Tropez.[66] A letter dated May 10, 1733, noted that Caire was still in prison—in an *oubliette* whose only point of entry was a trapdoor on the ceiling. Ironically, although the *oubliette* was designed to vanquish an individual into oblivion, Caire's incarceration was meant to serve as an "example."[67]

In addition to armed insurrection, sedition also included *mauvais discours*, subversive words in satire and verse. The *intendant* identified one "Sieur Marin," who purportedly distributed such material and who "for a long time has played a role in ruining the children of families and attracting all slanders and who never stopped railing against the Jesuits and judges on whom the Cadières could not depend." Autheman, a prosecutor tied to the financial Cours des comptes, also had the temerity to put together collections of satirical verses for distribution.[68] Then there was Sieur Larmeni, a notary from Aix, who also sold inflammatory writings and may have had close connections to Father Nicolas; in addition, he regularly sent letters from Aix to Marseille that were read at the Café de la Prost, a hotbed of opposition.[69] Larmeni was imprisoned in the infamous Château d'If located on an island two miles off Marseille. Eventually, he was released on condition that he leave the province; in the meantime, officials searched Larmeni's house for papers.[70]

The papers in question belonged to the eighteen-year-old abbé Jean Novi de Caveirac (1713–1782), whose "bad character would have merited a graver punishment [than imprisonment] given his spirit and his very dangerous heart."[71] Contemporary accounts indicate that Caveirac, although a "gentleman" and the son of a high-ranking administrator in Nîmes, was a drifter. During the Cadière scandal, he was a regular at Beaudin's café in Aix; in Marseille, he "frequented the café known as the Prost."[72] The young abbé was apparently influenced by anti-Jesuit *rieurs*, or "jokers." As a result, "Caveirac decided to be against them [the Jesuits], and wrote, without [any] mission, extrajudicial factums in Cadière's favor to amuse the jokers."[73] As we saw earlier, he also authored the *Nouveau Tarquin*, poems, and possibly the *Antifactum critique-comique du père Girard*; Caveirac was thought to have assisted Chaudon in drafting some of the *factums* for Catherine.[74] The young abbé was also a friend of Larmeni's, going so far as to give the notary money at his arrest, only to find himself out of funds at the time of his own arrest. Although Caveirac initially escaped apprehension in Aix, thanks to friends who hid him in the country outside Marseille, he was apprehended at the end of October. However, to Le Bret's chagrin, Caveirac's family got the spirited young man out of the Château Saint-Jean in January 1731.

Conspiracies and seditious writings did not just operate in the public world of cafés but thrived in private family circles, where the province's elite women played a prominent role. Madame de Galice, wife of the "Cadièriste" magistrate, tolerated and indeed encouraged anti-Jesuit rhetoric; she was heard to express anger at her brother, M. de Gueydan, one of the five *gens du roi* who favored Father Girard.[75] It appears that lawyers and magistrates also met at the homes of Madame de Valbelle and Madame de Simiane, the granddaughter of Madame de Sévigné. A wealthy widow, Madame de Valbelle seems to have contributed generous sums to make sure that pro-Cadière *libelles* were printed and circulated in Geneva, Holland, and Paris.[76] Nor did these women escape Le Bret's anger. For example, the *intendant* sent the opinionated Madame de Volomne packing to the countryside. On her departure, the countess angrily told him: "I'm leaving, Monsieur, but I will be back one day, but you Monsieur, you will leave, and you will never return."[77]

Despite this ominous pronouncement, Le Bret persevered. Respected lawyers and magistrates also faced retribution for backing Catherine Cadière. Le Bret targeted Jean-Baptiste Chaudon, whose *mémoires judiciaires* had circulated vicious images of Father Girard. Moreover, the *intendant* had allies in the ultramontane clergy.[78] The bishop of Marseille wrote to Cardinal Fleury that Chaudon's "wretched writings" were the source of all the "crimes" connected to the Cadière affair.[79] And the bishop of Toulon felt personally aggrieved: "The lawyer Chaudon thought he had the right to dishonor me throughout France, and if I dare say in all the world (because in which part of the world haven't his scandalous writings penetrated?)."[80] On October 20, 1731, ten days after the parlement had censored Chaudon's *factums*, the bishop of Sisteron, the former Jesuit Pierre-François Lafitau, issued a withering pastoral edict condemning Chaudon's writings. In early November, the *Dénonciation des factums de M. Chaudon* also joined the condemnation.[81]

Chaudon's *factums* were viewed as crimes against "religion." Combined with Catherine's Lenten recital, they were "injurious to God and to Religion, their propositions respectively false, rash, contrary to good morals, a derision, an abuse, and sacrilege against the sacraments, the Church's ceremonies and all that our Mysteries regard as most holy."[82] According to Henri Belsunce, Catherine's graphic Lenten memoir, together with Chaudon's briefs, had made the Church vulnerable to "libertines and heretics" who seized upon the trial as an opportunity "to authorize vice and insult our holy religion."[83] The bishop probably had in mind Parisian salons and drawing rooms where elite men and women amused themselves by making "a quantity of scandalous and often impious pleasantries."[84] Thanks to Chaudon, confessors had become a subject of hatred, as had the Jesuits, a "body so dear to the Church."[85]

Chaudon did not accept such scathing criticism quietly. Writing to d'Aguesseau, he complained that the bishops of Marseille and Sisteron were seeking to obtain a *lettre de cachet* against him.[86] He countered their accusations of gross impiety by stating that "the dishonor to religion is therefore not the crimes of my writing; it is in Father Girard's conduct, and that of his defenders."[87] Chaudon had sacrificed his own interests, those of his family, and his own health for a cause that was the cause of "all the lawyers in his realm."[88] He had fulfilled his duties with "the courage and integrity that are always the most essential qualities, which produce this noble liberty of speech so necessary to the defender of great causes, and above all, of criminals against powerful and official persons."[89] These high-minded principles probably further irritated d'Aguesseau, who had spent recent months trying to contain similar assertions by obstreperous Parisian lawyers. Rumors circulated that Chaudon was headed for the prison of Tarascon, south of Avignon.[90] In the end, however, Chaudon appears to have escaped any real punishment.[91]

As the leading magistrate of the parlement of Provence, Le Bret was painfully aware that his own house was in complete disarray. He noted how Maliverny, author of the pro-Cadière *Motifs*, had attacked the proceedings being held behind closed doors. He and his colleague, St. Jean, had shown clear preference for Catherine during the interrogations. However, Le Bret admitted that Maliverny had not done anything really wrong other than vote for Father Girard's death. Maliverny's punishment could be limited to a *"memoire* of reproaches" and the denial of honoraria. Le Bret also expressed reluctance to punish St. Jean since he had young children.[92] Despite the fact that Boyer de Bandol had advocated convening the assembled chambers, Le Bret did not blame him: "He [Boyer de Bandol] is a zealous friend and sometimes too zealous."[93] In other words, the man was easily influenced, a pawn of more persuasive men like Gaufridy.[94]

Le Bret directed his wrath at others who worked closely with Jacques-Joseph Gaufridy, whom, as we shall see, Le Bret regarded as the true problem in the upper chambers. He focused on Joseph-Alexandre de Besieux and the marquis de Bruée, who had attacked Faucon and Charleval, and then demanded that all the chambers assemble to deliberate the matter. Both magistrates, who belonged to the parlement's lower chambers, were handed *lettres de cachet* sending them into exile.[95] In the case of Besieux, Le Bret justified this action because Besieux "had prided himself on being a Jansenist for some years."[96]

More troubling to Le Bret was the counselor's influence over other members of the Chambres des Enquêtes: "It is important not to leave the direction of these young people in the hands of a President capable of preferring the counsels of an impassioned lawyer like Audibert to those of his family, full of people who served the king with distinction."[97] Pierre Audibert had ties with Cadière supporters in Marseille and Toulon and a decided predilection for "all the writings the Jansenist party produces."[98]

Two men in particular ignited Le Bret's wrath: the attorney general Gaufridy and the magistrate Jean-Louis-Hyacinthe Esmivi de Moissac, whose father had died during the trial. In his eyes, these two had spearheaded a "cabal" that had compromised judicial procedure and roused popular animosity against Girard. Le Bret bitingly described the judge Esmivi de Moissac as having a "violent character" and prescribed permanent exile to his country estate or the sale of his office unless Moissac yielded to the king's wishes.[99] Le Bret expressed unremitting hostility toward Gaufridy, and his personal antagonism appears to have momentarily gotten the better of him. Early pages of his narrative accused Gaufridy of writing an anonymous anti-Girard pamphlet, *Anatomie de l'arrest rendu par le parlement de Provence*. But several pages later, the *intendant* stated that, based on conversations with other magistrates, Moissac was the author.[100]

Both magistrates also had ties to the Jansenist opposition to *Unigenitus*, which Le Bret regarded as an affront to royal authority. He believed that Moissac had connections to the *Nouvelles Ecclésiastiques*.[101] But it was Gaufridy who had worked most assiduously to advance the Jansenist cause; after all, his opposition to the "constitution" *Unigenitus* went back fifteen years. Le Bret caustically noted how the "praise" the attorney general received from certain colleagues in Paris had "encouraged" him to take up *causes célèbres* like the Cadière affair in order "to flatter" the Jansenists. Gaufridy's "declared aversion" to the Jesuits had profoundly disturbed tranquility and peace.[102] Le Bret must have known that these accusations would resonate with d'Aguesseau. After having spent some months in Paris at the end of 1731, the *intendant* no doubt had a clear picture of how much his interpretation of Gaufridy's anti-Jesuit sentiments coincided with the chancellor's own struggles against opponents of *Unigenitus*.

How did officials link the Cadière affair to the larger threats posed by Jansenism? For certain bishops, Jansenism was a doctrinal pathology, and they used the Cadière affair as an excuse to eradicate heresy in the region. According to Henri Belsunce, "a famous Jansenist" had assured someone that within "three or four years, there would be no other religion than that of the Fathers of the Oratory," referring to the order's affiliation with Jansenist teachings in Provence.[103] Just weeks after the Cadière verdict, Belsunce launched a mission, a religious campaign, for the "conversion of souls."[104] In January 1732, he organized processions in Marseille; he and the cleric Bredenne took to the pulpit, denouncing Jansenist theology as well as the Oratorians.[105] The bishop also visited the hilly town of Allauch, about seven miles northeast of Marseille. He gathered the population of Allauch to warn them of the dangers of Jansenism preached by the Oratorian fathers, whose retreat was the nearby Notre-Dame-des-Anges.[106] As always, Le Tour du Pin-Montauban followed Belsunce's lead and tried to shut down the Oratorian college of Toulon, on the grounds of their dubious morals and doctrine.[107]

While acknowledging the threat of Jansenism to doctrinal orthodoxy, Le Bret viewed Jansenism through a decidedly more political lens. Le Bret's sources stated that in private conversations, Moissac supposedly had said that the king allowed himself to be conducted by a teacher "and that all of his subjects should be Ravaillacs" who would assassinate Cardinal Fleury.[108] Evoking the regicide Ravaillac, who had murdered Henry IV in 1610, was treasonous. Moissac's purported remarks were essentially an attack on royal authority—Fleury was, after all, the king's minister. Moreover, they effectively gave the king's subjects permission to question that authority.

However, Gaufridy's treachery went much further, because it was connected to a larger effort to undermine the king. The attorney general's "friends" in Paris supposedly advised him "to renew the agitation of spirits."[109] Specifically, these connections led Gaufridy to try to galvanize his peers against the April 3, 1730, *lit de justice*, a royal session that essentially forced the parlement of Paris to accept *Unigenitus* as a law of the state. According to Le Bret, Gaufridy persuaded Boyer de Bandol to remonstrate against the royal *arrêt*, although it had been registered already.[110] In defying the king's *arrêt* about *Unigenitus*, Gaufridy went a step further than simply supporting the parlements' right to limit episcopal authority.[111] Gaufridy and his supporters, like Boyer de Bandol, challenged the king's authority. According to Le Bret, the attorney general needed to remember that "the king is our master, that to him alone belongs the governing of the state, that those who act in a contrary way to what his justice and prudence resolves on, move away from the obedience that all his subjects owe him."[112]

By punishing magistrates, lawyers, Oratorians, and polemicists, Le Bret, Belsunce, and La Tour du Pin-Montauban reaffirmed both royal and ecclesiastical authority. Nevertheless, the extreme nature of their efforts—ordering imprisonment and exile—shows the depths of their anxiety. In their eyes, the

Girard/Cadière trial had destabilized Provençal society profoundly. The scandal had undermined the principles of obedience and deference to authority—the cornerstone of early modern French society—because it had made those in positions of power objects of contempt. Their suppression of words and individuals harshly reminded the public who was in charge.

The persecution of Catherine's supporters ended in late 1734, when Cardin Le Bret died. In 1826, an Aixeois lawyer and historian, Prosper Cabasse, included an account of Le Bret's demise, suggesting how the Cadière affair had, indeed, been the death of the *intendant* and *premier président*. One of Le Bret's nemeses had been Pauline de Grignan, marquise de Simiane. A close associate of Gaufridy's, the marquise had been outspoken in her belief that Father Girard was guilty, and according to Cabasse, Le Bret had obtained a *lettre de cachet* against her. Fortunately, the marquise had a powerful ally in Charlotte Aglaé d'Orléans, daughter of the king's cousin, the duc d'Orléans. In October 1734, at a gathering in which all three were present, Charlotte upbraided Le Bret for trying to destroy her "dear mother," Madame de Simiane, and showed him letters as evidence. In a state of shock, Le Bret passed away a few hours later, "the same day that he had signed the *arrêt* for Father Girard and la Cadière three years ago."[113] While most evidence suggests that this compelling vignette is apocryphal, it became a persistent legend. Regardless of its veracity, this story strongly suggests how personal the scandal had become to the exhausted, embittered Le Bret, once so admired. Indeed, the persecutions against the "Cadièristes" stopped almost immediately after Le Bret's successor, Jean-Baptiste des Gallois de La Tour, took his place.[114]

How were the principals of the trial—Girard, Nicolas, Catherine and her family—affected by the publicity and persecution? In October 1731, Father Girard quickly left Aix after people discovered that he had said mass in the Jesuit church. He avoided imprisonment, which was required until the Toulon *officialité* had pronounced its sentence. Girard made his way to Lyon, where he tried unsuccessfully to regain his position as director.[115] By year's end, he found himself in Viviers, where, ironically, the abbé François Gastaud, Chaudon's collaborator, lived in exile until his death in 1733.[116] Although the bishop, François de Villeneuve (1683–1766), prevented the Jansenist Gastaud from receiving last rites, he welcomed the Jesuit with open arms, ready to give him "marks of my confidence and esteem."[117] Girard stayed in Viviers, and the bishop comforted this man who was now in "feeble health."[118]

In March 1732, Father Girard returned to his birthplace, Dôle, where he died on July 4, 1733. Although he may have lived out his final months quietly, if not perhaps in peace, Girard was a constant topic of conversation, especially when Toulon's *officialité* exonerated him of all wrongdoing.[119] Even his death became a scandal when the prefect of Dôle's Jesuit college wrote to Father Tribolet in Nancy, describing how Father Girard had died like a saint. Soon after, a printed version of this letter surfaced, complete with annotations mocking Father Girard and the Jesuits. Remarking on the prefect's observation that the chapel was full of women who came to pay their respects, a comment noted, "Always the women for Father Girard in death or in life."[120] In September, Paris police tried to prevent the circulation of this letter, which was being sold sub rosa in places such as the rues Saint-Antoine and Saint-Séverin.[121] Even after death, Father Girard remained an object of debate and vicious mockery.

Like Father Girard, Father Nicolas did not remain long in Aix. In May 1732, he returned to Avignon, where he had debated successfully against the Jesuits a few years earlier.[122] Now, however, the Society of Jesus had the upper hand and was determined that this Carmelite friar who had dishonored the order should be punished. According to one observer, the Jesuits persuaded the papal vice legate to act on their behalf. The superior of Avignon's Carmelite order was ordered to tell Father Nicolas to leave the province. Ostracized by his own community, the friar left Avignon and essentially vanished, the rest of his life undocumented. In the meantime, the bishop of Toulon punished the Carmelites in Toulon by forbidding them to sing the Te Deum when one of their order was appointed cardinal.[123]

What of the Cadière family? Although Catherine was released on October 11, the authorities by no means forgot her. On Holy Friday 1733, an officer, accompanied by thirteen men, arrived at the Cadière household at six in the morning.[124] They threatened Elisabeth Pomet with imprisonment if she did not disclose her daughter's whereabouts. The soldiers proceeded to take all papers, including the business documents of the oldest Cadière son, Laurent. Soon after, Laurent wrote to Cardinal Fleury complaining about the ruin of his business, the mysterious confiscation of papers, and a *libelle* circulating in Aix that maligned the Cadière family. His meeting with Le Bret in July had disastrous results. On August 30, Laurent was arrested in the street on his way to mass and placed in the citadel of Saint-Tropez, where he remained for almost two years. Even after his release in 1735, Laurent was not allowed to return to Toulon.

Catherine's fate is murky. Clearly, Elisabeth was in Toulon in the spring of 1733, but the location of the other three children remains a mystery. Mathieu Marais wrote on October 28 that Catherine was in Nice; three days later, he noted, "La Cadière, whom one says was in Nice, has returned to Toulon."[125] But there was no record of her arrival there, where she was a beloved celebrity. The consensus was that Catherine went into hiding, probably in response to ongoing arrests elsewhere in Provence. According to one story, Catherine fell ill but was so well hidden that no one knew her whereabouts. A young woman named Rose, thought to have tended the sick woman, was arrested and closely interrogated for a year, with no result. In Marseille, some were detained and questioned when it was rumored that Catherine had been seen in town.[126] Another rumor held that the Jesuits were willing to go to any length to catch and punish her.[127] What if the Jesuits did, in fact, capture Catherine (and the equally elusive Étienne-Thomas and François)? Perhaps she spent the rest of her life in a remote prison.

After a year of relentless publicity and scrutiny, the earth seems to have swallowed up this daughter of an obscure bourgeois family. Did deaths, disappearances, and detention signal the true end of the Cadière affair? Could things return to the way they were before a twenty-year-old woman instigated one of the most infamous trials in eighteenth-century France?

EPILOGUE

In 1739, Charles de Brosses (1707–1777), count of Tournay, magistrate and man of letters, crossed Provence en route to Italy. He relished the beautiful countryside of Ollioules, rich with pomegranates, oranges, and lemons: "I am grateful to *la Cadière* for having chosen this town to perform her miracles." The Dijon magistrate then visited the Jesuit seminary in Toulon. Out of "politeness," de Brosses felt he must extend the same courtesy to Father Girard, since he had visited the Cadière home.[1]

Why would an erudite scholar trouble to commemorate a trial nearly a decade old? Perhaps it was a joke. It might also have been the influence of his fellow Dijonnais Jean Bouhier, with whom Mathieu Marais had exchanged gossip on the Cadière affair in 1731.[2] But de Brosses's remarks also show that both Cardin Le Bret and Henri Belsunce's efforts to suppress the Girard/Cadière scandal had failed. This notorious *cause célèbre* enhanced the black legend of the Jesuits, who became associated with all forms of political crimes—notably, despotism. Over the course of the eighteenth century, the Girard/Cadière affair cleaved to a deeper disaffection with the clergy. For intellectuals and men of letters, the case epitomized the superstition and ignorance inherent in Christianity.

In the three decades after the Girard/Cadière affair, accusations against Father Girard and the Jesuits continued to evolve as regicide and despotism became staple components of a growing list of Jesuit "crimes." In 1757, an unstable servant, Robert-François Damiens, unsuccessfully attempted to assassinate Louis XV with a dull blade. Although there was no concrete proof that the Jesuits had orchestrated Damiens's attack, there seemed, at least to Édmond Barbier, a Jansenist conspiracy to blame the Jesuit order.[3] Jansenists tapped into the regicides of Henry III and Henry IV, histories with tenuous links to the Jesuits.[4] Three years later, two leading Jansenist thinkers, Christophe Coudrette (1701–1774) and Louis-Adrien Le Paige, wrote a "history" of the Jesuits asserting that the Society "exclusively inclines to arrogate itself into a monarchy or rather a universal despotism . . . to render itself the sovereign and despotic arbiter of all the dignities and riches of the Christian world."[5]

This rhetoric came to a head in the early 1760s, when the Jesuit order— not just one individual—found itself on trial. In 1760, the banking house of Lioncy and Gouffre sued the Society for bankrupting them due to financial mismanagement by Father Antoine de La Valette (1708–1767), who headed the Jesuit mission in the West Indies.[6] When the courts ruled for the bankers and their creditors, the Jesuits developed temporary amnesia and appealed to the parlement of Paris, although there was no love lost between the order and the parlement. But the Jesuits thought they could find more allies in the Grand'Chambre, much as they had done thirty years before in Provence.[7] The parlement of Paris conducted an investigation of the Jesuits' constitutions, which quickly transformed into a challenge to the order's very legitimacy on French soil. In an effort to save the Jesuits and pacify the Paris magistrates, Louis XV issued an edict on March 8, 1762, reaffirming the Jesuits' religious functions while establishing French control over the order.[8] Jansenist lawyers and magistrates moved to counter the king's edict and sought support from provincial parlements, including that of Provence.

If some members of the parlement in Aix had figuratively tried the Jesuit order in 1731, they now did so literally. Thirty-one years later, familiar names resurfaced: Boyer d'Argens (or the baron d'Éguilles), Montvalon, Galice, Ripert de Montclar. Some of the same people, such as the eighty-four-year-old de Mons, were present. Boyer d'Éguilles was the son of Boyer d'Argens, "so famous in the affair of Father Girard, during which he had served the Jesuits as a good valet."[9] While most sons seemed to have followed fathers in supporting or opposing the Jesuits, there was one notable exception. In 1731, Pierre-François Ripert de Montclar had voted in Father Girard's favor. His son, Jean-Pierre-François, now spearheaded the charge against the Jesuits.

The trial in Aix began on March 6, 1762, and almost immediately went against the Jesuits when the prosecutor-general Jean-Pierre-François Ripert de Montclar demanded an investigation into the Jesuits' constitutions. Three months later, on June 3 and 4, he delivered a three-hundred-page report, a *compte rendu*, that immediately circulated in print. It appeared that Ripert de Montclar had majority backing for his demands: to lodge an *appel comme d'abus* against the Jesuit constitutions and to close the order's schools and seminaries. However, with Boyer d'Éguilles at the helm, magistrates loyal to the Jesuits fought back. Like his father Boyer d'Argens, Boyer d'Éguilles incurred the hatred of Aix's populace, whose animosity toward Jesuits seems to have been undiminished since the turbulent days of October 1731. Over the next six months, "the most violent debates" erupted as each side defended their cause.[10] The octogenarian Montvalon well may have felt he was reliving the infamous trial of three decades earlier. According to one rumor, despite his age, he plunged into the fray, calling Ripert de Montclar a liar; Montvalon's two sons leapt to their father's defense.[11]

If the quarrels within the Palais de Justice on the Place des Prêcheurs smacked of *déjà vu*, Ripert de Montclar's arguments then revived the spirit of Blaise Pascal *and* the accusations against Father Girard. Ripert de Montclar vigorously denounced Jesuit casuistry, claiming that, though secular courts punished crimes such as adultery and murder, the Jesuits' flexible approach to sin left the guilty free and unrepentant.[12] Through laxity, the Jesuits spread their "spirit of domination" over families, the young, and ultimately, France itself.[13] Can we doubt that Ripert de Montclar's references to "devoted penitents" and Quietism intentionally conjured up Catherine Cadière and Jean-Baptiste Girard?[14] Moreover, the most important accusation—"despotism"—captured the spirit of Father Girard's hold over Catherine: "The government of the Society is despotic, no subject is assured of his state; there are no intermediaries . . . the despot is the Legislature and Judge, he does not adjust to any rule, his will decides all."[15] Fundamentally, Jesuit governance was antithetical to "the Maxims of the Gallican Church, directly opposed to the true spirit of religion, inadmissible in all of civil society."[16]

After such arguments, the king was significantly more reluctant to support the Jesuits publicly than he had been in 1731. Moreover, the king's hand was decided when two confidential *mémoires* written by Boyer d'Éguilles began circulating in manuscript and then in print. These inflammatory documents, in which he and his cohorts planned a "secession" from the parlement, led to his condemnation by *all* parlements of the realm. On December 23, 1762, Louis XV announced that "the two memoirs of M. d'Éguilles had made no impression on his mind, and . . . that his Majesty was very satisfied with the fidelity, the zeal and the conduct of his Parlement of Aix."[17] Events then moved quickly as a substantial number of d'Éguilles supporters disavowed the *mémoires*.

On January 28, five months after the parlement of Paris, the parlement of Provence accepted Ripert de Montclar's conclusions to suppress the Jesuit order. Similar *arrêts* were issued by other parlements, including those of Toulouse, Grenoble, and Dijon. At the end of November 1764, Louis XV delivered a royal edict expelling the Society of Jesus from France. The order's supporters faced a similar reversal of fortune. Pro-Jesuit magistrates of Provence were punished, much as Le Bret had reprimanded pro-Cadière judges in 1732. Two who suffered severely were Boyer d'Éguilles, banned from the kingdom in perpetuity, and the abbé de Montvalon, son of the magistrate Montvalon, who was banned from Provence.

To say that the Cadière trial brought about the expulsion of the Jesuits from France would be an overstatement. Widespread publicity of the affair undoubtedly strengthened a negative image of the Jesuits. Yet as the Jansenist *libelliste* Nicolas Jouin noted in a 1750 compilation of famous court cases involving Jesuits, the story of Father Girard was only one of "100,000" like it, and "one cannot hear the tale without horror and without shuddering."[18] Where Chaudon and the pro-Cadière magistrates argued for the parlement's right to try an individual Jesuit, by the 1760s, the parlements claimed Gallican prerogative to suppress the Jesuits altogether.

In 1765, Jean Le Rond d'Alembert, co-editor of the *Encyclopédie*, published an account of these events, *On the Destruction of the Jesuits in France;* he credited "philosophy" for bringing down the Jesuits. In this instance, philosophy referred to the Enlightenment and denoted secular values in all areas of life, including politics *and* religion. For proponents such as Voltaire and Diderot, traditional religious practices and institutions were roots of injustice in the Old Regime.[19] Narrating the Jesuits' expulsion, d'Alembert targeted both Jansenists and Jesuits. He ridiculed the abbé Caveirac, the author of *Le Nouveau Tarquin*, who "had started in the service of the Jansenists, and through writing against Father Girard in the ridiculous Cadière affair. Since that time, God enlightened him, and Caveirac became an apologist for a good cause, the Jesuits and St.

Bartholomew."[20] This referred to Caveirac's spirited defense of the 1572 Saint Bartholomew's Day massacre of the Huguenots. For d'Alembert, the Girard/ Cadière affair symbolized a faith at odds with reason and nature.

Indeed, the Girard/Cadière affair became a vehicle for attacking Christian beliefs as well as the clergy, notably in 1748, when *Thérèse philosophe* was published. To consider how the Cadière affair made its way into this lubricious popular novel, we return to the question of authorship. Édmond Barbier wrongly assumed that Denis Diderot was arrested because the police suspected that he had written this lewd novel. However, many scholars take the word of the libertine marquis de Sade (1740–1814), a native of Provence, who attributed the novel to the marquis d'Argens—son of the prosecutor Boyer d'Argens and brother of Boyer d'Éguilles.[21] The unruly, libertine marquis seemed fairly obsessed with the Girard/Cadière affair, including it in the *Lettres juives* (1736–37) and the *Lettres cabalistiques* (1737–38).[22] In conjunction with the marquis's memoirs, the novel's details—such as the Quietist mantra "oubliez-vous, laissez-faire," and his musings on pleasure—all point to him as the likely author.

The novel bridged the gap between legal *factums*—the world of the marquis's father and brother—and Enlightenment philosophy, to which d'Argens also belonged. Like Chaudon's *factums, Thérèse philosophe* exposed clerical power and hypocrisy by mocking spiritual incest.[23] But Chaudon's purpose had been to punish Father Girard in order to restore Christian virtue. The novel turns Christian morality on its head.

In establishing the opposition between Christian ethics and nature, d'Argens rearranges the relationship between body and spirit. Within a Christian framework of sin and salvation, the body tempts the individual and therefore jeopardizes the soul's efforts to reach God and achieve salvation. In *Thérèse philosophe*, the sinful body now becomes an amoral machine.[24] According to Father Dirrag, "The mechanism is infallible, my dear girl [Éradice]: we feel, and we receive our ideas of physical good and evil as well as moral good and evil . . . only through our senses."[25] Father Dirrag advances a materialist philosophy in which matter—in this case, the body—determines ideas and morals. Significantly, Thérèse's intellectual development as a female *philosophe* comes from her sexual awakening.[26] Here, then, d'Argens radically reimagines the most controversial—and most unknown—part of the Cadière affair. Instead of restating an anti-Jesuit or anticlerical position, the novel presents a radical inversion of Christianity itself.

For many, the Girard/Cadière affair raised fundamental concerns about the place of the sacred in French society. What constituted authentic, acceptable expressions of faith? How did an individual reconcile spiritual interiority with social expectations? Were there limits to the role of the priest in spiritual life? Significantly, these questions were not only asked by skeptics such as Enlightenment *philosophes*. Individuals and communities grappled with these questions, not with any intent of unmasking Christianity, but precisely because their faith, as well as their priests, were central to their lives. The Cadière trial showed how religious disaffection was not simply a critique from outside but a crisis *within* the "community of believers."

In addition, the Girard/Cadière affair raised more systemic concerns about the religious principles underpinning French society and politics. Kingship, paternal power, and clerical authority claimed legitimacy because they were divinely ordained. On the surface, people involved in the Cadière trial subscribed to these ideals of authority, hierarchy, and obedience. At the same time, they invited the public to interrogate the actions of clerics and magistrates—of religious and secular authorities—which invariably undermined those ideals. Keeping in mind this connection, the attacks on Father Girard and the Jesuits, which endured for decades, point to a process of "desacralization" that effectively dislodged the sacred as an organizing principle.[27]

The Cadière story endured well into the next century, retold in a nexus of anticlericalism and the new psychiatry.[28] During the nineteenth century, historian Jules Michelet argued that Jesuit priests like Father Girard manipulated vulnerable *dévotes* like Catherine Cadière to enslave the French nation through superstition and ignorance. The Jesuits were an impediment to progress and to the values of the French Revolution. Just as the Cadière trial in the eighteenth century had been caught up in the complex political web of Jansenism, so in later eras it became attached, indirectly, to political conflicts between Catholic conservatism and republicanism.[29] Michelet's detailed account of the scandal also suggests that Catherine's convulsions and visions signaled her revolt against Girard's abuse.[30] This interpretation marked a broader intellectual shift that categorized witchcraft and excessive religious experiences as forms of hysteria.[31] The language of science replaced supernatural explanations.

By the late twentieth century, fiction and scientific literature made Catherine a sexually starved creature who could not live with her shame and guilt.[32] In Provence, the scandal still resonates in local history, commemorated in exhibits on the Old Regime.[33] Later generations still ask "did they or didn't they?" Catherine and Father Girard continue to carry, and reflect, the disquiet of changing times.

Notes

AAE	Archives du Ministère aux Affaires étrangères, Paris
ADBR	Archives départementales des Bouches-du-Rhône, Aix-en-Provence
AM Toulon	Archives municipales, Toulon
Arbaud	Musée Paul Arbaud, Aix-en-Provence
BA, AB	Bibliothèque de l'Arsenal, Archives de la Bastille, Paris
BM Dijon	Bibliothèque municipale, Dijon
BnF, MS Fr.	Bibliothèque nationale de France, Paris, Manuscrits français
Ceccano	Bibliothèque municipale d'Avignon, Mediathèque Ceccano, Avignon
Lagoubran	Bibliothèque municipale, Lagoubran, Toulon
Méjanes	Bibliothèque Méjanes, Aix-en Provence
NE	*Nouvelles Ecclésiastiques*

In the notes, I have chosen not to list every *factum* that appeared during the trial.
Instead, I cite the *Suite des procédures de Catherine Cadière, contre le révérende père Girard, contenant la réponse au mémoire instructif de ce jésuite* (La Haye: Henri Scheurleer, 1731), as well as the three main comprehensive collections containing all the *mémoires judiciaires*, abbreviated as follows:

Recueil général *Recueil général des pièces concernant le procez entre la demoiselle Cadière de la ville de Toulon. Et le père Girard, jésuite, recteur du séminaire royal de la marine de ladite ville.* 2 vols. N.p., 1731.

Recueil général (Aix) *Recueil général des pièces contenues au procez du père Jean-Baptiste Girard, jésuite, recteur du séminaire de Toulon, et de demoiselle Catherine Cadière, querellante.* 5 vols. Aix: Joseph David, 1731.

Recueil général (La Haye) *Recueil général des pièces concernant le procez entre la demoiselle Cadière, de la ville de Toulon; et le père Girard, jésuite.* 8 vols. La Haye: Swart, 1731.

Unless otherwise indicated, all translations are my own.

INTRODUCTION

1. Barbier, *Chronique de la régence*, 4:377.
2. As cited in Bonnefon, "Diderot prisonnier à Vincennes," 223.
3. Police records make no mention of the novel. See ibid., 208–9.
4. Barbier, *Chronique de la régence*, 4:377.
5. [De Boyer, marquis d'Argens], *Thérèse philosophe*, 3:71.
6. Ibid.
7. Translation taken from Darnton, *Forbidden Best-Sellers*, 255.
8. Ibid., 259.
9. Ibid., 260.
10. Ibid., 262.
11. On the *Encyclopédie*, see Jones, *Great Nation*, 171–77.
12. Darnton, *Forbidden Best-Sellers*, 90.
13. Goulemot, *Forbidden Texts*.
14. [De Boyer, marquis d'Argens], *Thérèse philosophe*, 111.
15. Jean-Baptiste Chaudon, *Mémoire instructif pour demoiselle Catherine Cadière de la ville de Toulon . . .*, in *Recueil général* (La Haye), 1:18.
16. De Boyer, marquis d'Argens, *Mémoires*, 297–98, 302.
17. Kreiser, "Devils of Toulon."
18. The two major works on Jansenism are Van Kley, *Religious Origins of the French Revolution*, and Maire, *De la cause de Dieu*.
19. These "republican" ideas were articulated by the French theologian Édmond Richer. See Préclin, *Les Jansénistes du XVIIIe siècle*.
20. Maire, *Les Convulsionnaires de Saint-Médard*; Kreiser, *Miracles, Convulsions, and Ecclesiastical Politics*.
21. Fabre and Maire, *Les Antijésuites*.

22. Pavone, *Wily Jesuits and the Monita Secreta*.
23. Van Kley, "Religious Origins of the French Revolution, 1590–1791," 126.
24. Barbier, *Chronique de la régence*, 3:106.
25. Jean-Baptiste Chaudon, *Réponse au sécond mémoire instructif du père Jean-Baptiste Girard, pour demoiselle Catherine Cadière*, in *Recueil général*, 2:1.
26. Baker, *Inventing the French Revolution*, 170. For Baker's complete argument, see 168–72.
27. De Voyer, marquis d'Argenson, *Mémoires*, 3:338–39.
28. Darnton, *Forbidden Best-Sellers*, 90.
29. Lanson, *Voltaire*, 48.
30. Kaiser, "Public Sphere," 419. See also Kaiser, "Money, Despotism, and Public Opinion"; Campbell, *Power and Politics*; and Bell, *Lawyers and Citizens*.
31. Farge, *Subversive Words*.
32. See Perovic, *Sacred and Secular Agency*, 5.

CHAPTER 1

1. Lamotte, "Le Fait divers dans la ville."
2. Michelet, *La Sorcière*, 2:118–19.
3. Smollett, *Travels through France and Italy*, 79–80.
4. Nugent, *Grand Tour*, 4:145. See also Mead, *Grand Tour*, 239–45.
5. A. Young, *Arthur Young's Travels in France*, 263.
6. Smollett, *Travels through France and Italy*, 104.
7. The marriage took place on November 1. "Baptêmes, Mariages, et Decès du 1 janvier au 31 décembre 1689," AM Toulon, MS GG 81, armoire 16.

8. Delayen, *La Sainte de M. de Toulon*, 13.

9. Hardwick, *Practice of Patriarchy*, 52.

10. From Jean-Joseph Julien, *Nouveau commentaire sur les statuts de Provence* [1778], as cited in Fauve-Chamoux, "To Remarry or Not," 432. See also Collomp, "Alliance et filiation," and Collomp, *La Maison du père*.

11. Hardwick, *Family Business*, 52. Throughout this book, Catherine's mother will be referred to as "Elisabeth Pomet."

12. On the streets of Toulon, see Masse, *Toulon pas à pas*.

13. Michelet, *La Sorcière*, 2:118.

14. Jean-Baptiste Chaudon, *Mémoire instructif pour demoiselle Catherine Cadière de la ville de Toulon . . .* , in *Recueil général* (La Haye), 1:6.

15. For accounts of the Grand Hiver, see Lachiver, *Les Années de misère*, 268–301; Monahan, *Year of Sorrows*, 71–73.

16. Lachiver, *Les Années de misère*, 343–44.

17. As cited in Laforêt, "L'Hiver 1709," 73.

18. On the siege of Toulon, see Vergé-Franceschi, *Toulon: Port Royal, 1481–1789*, 123–30; see also Paoletti, "Prince Eugene of Savoi."

19. Michelet, *La Sorcière*, 2:120.

20. De Boyer, marquis d'Argens, *Mémoires*, 282.

21. On the birth of Catherine's sister, see "Baptêmes, Mariages, et Decès du 1 janvier au 31 décembre 1690," AM Toulon, MS GG 82, armoire 16; on her father's death, see "Baptêmes, Mariages, et Decès du 1 janvier au 31 décembre 1710," AM Toulon, MS GG 103, armoire 16.

22. Agulhon, *Histoire de Toulon*, 114.

23. Catherine Cadière, *Justification de damoiselle Catherine Cadière contenant un récit fidèle de tout ce qui s'est passé entre cette damoiselle et le p. Jean-Baptiste Girard*, in *Recueil général* (La Haye), 1:4.

24. Chaudon, *Mémoire instructif pour demoiselle Catherine Cadière*, 6.

25. Bourgarel, *Mémoire instructif pour Messire François Cadière, prêtre de la ville de Toulon, appelant du decret d'assigné contre lui rendu le 23 février dernier . . . contre monsieur le procureur général du Roy*, in *Recueil général* (La Haye), 4:6.

26. Bergin, *Church, Society, and Religious Change*, 108–9.

27. Cadière, *Justification de damoiselle Catherine Cadière*, 5.

28. On the Sisters of Charity, see E. Rapley, *The Dévotes*, 83–100; see also Agulhon, *Histoire de Toulon*, 135–36.

29. Chaudon, *Mémoire instructif pour demoiselle Catherine Cadière*, 7.

30. See Vovelle, *Piété baroque et déchristianisation*. See also Jones, *Great Nation*, 94–95. For the importance of visual culture in the Catholic Reformation, see Hsia, *World of Catholic Renewal*, 152–64.

31. Jones, *Great Nation*, 94; see also Loupès, *La Vie religieuse en France*, 17–26.

32. Agulhon, *Pénitents et Francs-Maçons*, 23; Agulhon, *Histoire de Toulon*, 20. See also Phillips, *Church and Culture*, 20.

33. Agulhon, *Pénitents et Francs-Maçons*, 89.

34. Bergin, *Church, Society, and Religious Change*, 366.

35. Cadière, *Justification de damoiselle Catherine Cadière*, 5; Delayen, *La Sainte de M. de Toulon*, 17.

36. Jones, "Plague and Its Metaphors in Early Modern France," 99.
37. Gaffarel, *La Peste de 1720*; Constantin, *Toulon, entre peste et choléra*; Vergé-Franceschi, *Toulon: Port Royal*, 136–52; Bertrand, "La Peste en Provence aux temps modernes," 401–12. On the plague in Marseille, see Takeda, *Between Crown and Commerce*, 106–57.
38. D'Antrechaux, *Relation de la peste dont la ville de Toulon fut affligée en 1721*, 83.
39. Ibid., 46, 338–39.
40. Ibid., 263.
41. Ibid., 130–34.
42. Maurice de Toulon, *Traité de la peste*, 2–3.
43. Jones, *Great Nation*, 91–92. For more detailed discussion of Belsunce during the plague, see Takeda, *Between Crown and Commerce*, 168–75.
44. Gaffarel, *La Peste de 1720*, 522–24.
45. Jonas, *France and the Cult of the Sacred Heart*, 9–53.
46. Belsunce, *Lettre de M. l'évêque de Marseille à la très-honorée soeur Marie-Agnès de Greard*, 12; *La Vie de la très honorée soeur Anne-Magdelaine Rémuzat*, 139. See also Takeda, *Between Crown and Commerce*, 171–73.
47. D'Antrechaux, *Relation de la peste*, 208; Gaffarel, *La peste de 1720*, 522–24.
48. D'Antrechaux, *Relation de la peste*, 334.
49. Playstowe, *The gentleman's guide*, 144.
50. Ibid., 179–80. On foreigners' views on French penal practices, see Lough, *France on the Eve of Revolution*, 188–209.
51. On Toulon's elites, see Vergé-Franceschi, *Toulon: Port Royal*, 130–34.

52. D'Antrechaux, *Relation de la peste*, 80; Vergé-Franceschi, *Toulon: Port Royal*, 143–45.
53. Michelet, *La Sorcière*, 2:21; Crook, *Toulon in War and Revolution*, 11; Agulhon, *Histoire de Toulon*, 132–33.
54. Agulhon, *Histoire de Toulon*, 133; Loupès, *La Vie religieuse en France*, 66.
55. Agulhon, *Histoire de Toulon*, 133; Vergé-Franceschi, *Toulon: Port Royal*, 227.
56. Crook, *Toulon in War and Revolution*, 11.
57. Vergé-Franceschi, *Toulon: Port Royal*, 119.
58. McManners, *Clerical Establishment*, 62.
59. On the Capuchins' popularity, see Dompnier, "Ordres, diffusion des dévotions et sensibilités religieuses," 21–59.
60. Hogue-Poullet, "Oratoriens et Jésuites à Toulon."
61. Vergé-Franceschi, *Toulon: Port Royal*, 105.
62. Fabre and Maire, *Les Antijésuites*.
63. Saint-Simon, *Memoirs*, 2:157–58.
64. McManners, *Clerical Establishment*, 40–41.
65. On seventeenth-century Jansenism, see Sedgwick, *Jansenism in Seventeenth-Century France*; Kostroun, *Feminism, Absolutism, and Jansenism*.
66. Van Kley, "Jansenism and the International Suppression of the Jesuits," 306.
67. Strayer, *Suffering Saints*, 20.
68. Van Kley, "Jansenism and the International Suppression of the Jesuits," 305.
69. [Annat], *Le Libelle intitulé "Théologie morale des Jésuites,"* 3–4.

70. Phillips, *Church and Culture*, 103–4.

71. For discussions of *Unigenitus*, see Préclin, *Les Jansénistes du XVIIIe siècle*; Kreiser, *Miracles, Convulsions, and Ecclesiastical Politics*, 10–26.

72. Bergin, *Politics of Religion in Early Modern France*, 289.

73. Ardoin, *La Bulle "Unigenitus"*; Takeda, *Between Crown and Commerce*, 162–68, 175–79; Froeschlé-Chopard, "Le Jansénisme dans les bibliothèques des couvents," 57–79; Vovelle, *Piété baroque et déchristianisation*, 458–537. On Jansenism and the Toulon Dominicans, see Froeschlé-Chopard, "La Bibliothèque des dominicains," 16–24.

74. Ardoin, *La Bulle "Unigenitus,"* 1:103–4, 107–11, 178–80.

75. Strayer, *Suffering Saints*, 57. On these divisions within Toulon, see Agulhon, *Histoire de Toulon*, 136–39.

76. De Boyer, marquis d'Argens, *Mémoires*, 282; [de Boyer, marquis d'Argens], *Thérèse philosophe*, 3:74.

77. Chaudon, *Mémoire instructif pour demoiselle Catherine Cadière*, 7.

78. *Vie de la Vénérée soeur Anne-Madeleine Rémuzat*, 173–74.

79. [Pagi], *Histoire du procez entre demoiselle Cadière . . . et le père Girard jésuite, recteur du séminaire royal de Toulon, de l'autre*, in *Recueil général* (La Haye), 1:4.

CHAPTER 2

1. Diefendorf, *From Penitence to Charity*, 65–71.

2. *Recueil de lettres du p. Girard et de la demoiselle Cadière*, 67.

3. McManners, *Religion of the People*, 246.

4. Ibid., 251.

5. Although almost always clerics, spiritual directors were not necessarily priests.

6. Bernos, "Des Sources maltraitées pour l'époque moderne."

7. Bilinkoff, *Related Lives*, 16–17.

8. De Sales, *Introduction to a Devout Life*, 12.

9. Sluhovsky, "Discernment of Difference," 187. See also Bilinkoff, *Related Lives*, 2–3, 18–20.

10. Ignatius of Loyola, *Personal Writings*, 283.

11. Kostroun, *Feminism, Absolutism, and Jansenism*; Sedgwick, *Travails of Conscience*, 126–27.

12. B. Pascal, *The Provincial Letters*, 374–76. See also Jonsen and Toulmin, *Abuse of Casuistry*, 229–49.

13. For discussion of the connection made between Jesuits and moral laxity, see Gay, *Morales en conflit*, 171–202. See also Gay, "La Jésuite improbable: Remarques sur la mise en place du mythe du Jésuite corrupteur de la morale en France à l'époque moderne," in *Les Antijésuites*, 305–27.

14. André de Barrigue, sieur de Montvalon, "Histoire du père Girard de la Cadière tirée de la procédure," Arbaud, MS MQ 365, fols. 1–2.

15. Ibid., fol. 3.

16. Ibid., fol. 2.

17. *Procédure sur laquelle le père Jean-Baptiste Girard . . . ont été jugé*, 20.

18. Claude Pazery de Thorame, *Mémoire instructif pour le père Jean-Baptiste Girard, jésuite, recteur du séminaire royal de la marine de la ville de Toulon*, in *Recueil général*, 1:2.

19. John 19:5.

20. [Chiron de Boismorand], *Résultat des mémoires de la demoiselle*

Cadière et adhérans. Contre le père
Girard jésuite, in Recueil général (La
Haye), 6:9.

21. Catherine Cadière, Justification de
damoiselle Catherine Cadière, contentant un récit fidèle de tout ce qui
s'est passé entre le père Jean-Baptiste
Girard, recteur du séminaire de la
marine des jésuites de Toulon, . . . et
elle, in Recueil général, 1:2.

22. Bourgarel, Mémoire instructif pour
messire François Cadière, prêtre de la
ville de Toulon . . . contre monsieur le
procureur général du roy, in Recueil
général, 1:3.

23. Cadière, Justification de damoiselle
Catherine Cadière, 2.

24. Ibid.

25. Jean-Baptiste Chaudon, Observations
sur les réponses du père Girard,
jésuite, et de la demoiselle Cadière,
in Recueil général (Aix), 2:368–69.
Delayen, La Sainte de M. de Toulon,
30.

26. Manning, "Confessor and His
Spiritual Child," 109.

27. As cited in Bilinkoff, Related Lives, 88.

28. Ibid.

29. Ibid., 27–31, 96–110.

30. Hsia, World of Catholic Renewal,
138–48.

31. Ibid., 105–6; Sluhovsky,
"Discernment of Difference," 183; on
Teresa of Avila's influence in France,
see Diefendorf, From Penitence to
Charity, 95–96.

32. Pazery de Thorame, Mémoire
instructif pour le père Jean-Baptiste
Girard, 3. See also [André de
Barrigue de Montvalon], Lettres
écrites d'Aix sur le procez du père
Girard et de la Cadière, 1.

33. Quotations cited in Gasquet, La
Vénérable Anne-Madeleine Rémuzat,

142, 145. The majority of these letters
were destroyed during the French
Revolution.

34. "Commencement du Caresme
ou mémoire des faveurs dont j'ay
joui par la grande miséricorde du
Seigneur pendant tous les cours de
ce mois passé l'an 1730," BnF, MS Fr.
23861, fol. 59. A printed copy of the
mémoire was attached to Girard's
first legal brief. Pazery de Thorame,
Mémoire instructif pour le père Jean-
Baptiste Girard, 40.

35. "Commencement du Caresme," fol.
61.

36. Claude Pazery de Thorame, Second
mémoire pour le père Girard jésuite,
servant de réponse au nouveau mémoire de la Cadière, et à ceux de ses
frères, in Recueil général (La Haye),
7:38.

37. Ibid., 42.

38. Procédure sur laquelle le père Jean-
Baptiste Girard . . . ont été jugé, 28.

39. Ferber, Demonic Possession and
Exorcism, 114. See also Sluhovsky,
Believe Not Every Spirit, 13–32,
137–65.

40. "Commencement du Caresme," fol.
61. See also [Pagi], Histoire du procez
entre demoiselle Cadière, in Recueil
général, 1:6.

41. For a more detailed discussion of
discernment, see Sluhovsky, Believe
Not Every Spirit, 169–205.

42. Timmermans, L'Accès des femmes à
la culture, 620–59.

43. Languet de Gergy, La Vie de la
vénérable mère Marguerite-Marie.
Jansenist and anti-Jesuit polemicists
used the hagiography to taunt the
prelate. See Extrait d'une lettre de
Monseigneur l'évêque d'Auxerre. In
1730, Languet was awarded the title

archbishop of Sens. See also Van
Kley, *Religious Origins of the French
Revolution*, 115–18.

44. *NE,* January 1, 1730, 1.

45. Barbier, *Chronique de la régence,*
2:100.

46. Jean-Baptiste Chaudon, *Mémoire
instructif pour demoiselle Catherine
Cadière de la ville de Toulon . . .*, in
Recueil général (La Haye), 1:30.

CHAPTER 3

1. De Boyer, marquis d'Argens,
Mémoires, 283.

2. Catherine Cadière, *Justification
de damoiselle Catherine Cadière
contenant un récit fidèle de tout ce
qui s'est passé entre cette damoiselle et
le p. Jean-Baptiste Girard*, in *Recueil
général* (La Haye), 1:10.

3. Ibid., 15.

4. Jean-Baptiste Chaudon, *Mémoire
instructif pour demoiselle Catherine
Cadière de la ville de Toulon . . .*, in
Recueil général, 1:7.

5. Ibid.

6. Ibid.

7. Michelet, *La Sorcière*, 2:146–47.

8. Ibid., 147.

9. Choudhury, *Convents and Nuns in
French Politics and Culture.*

10. Sluhovsky, "Devil in the Convent,"
1385.

11. Ibid., 1379–80. On the Grandier
affair, see R. Rapley, *Case of
Witchcraft.*

12. Chaudon, *Mémoire instructif pour
demoiselle Catherine Cadière*, 9.

13. Jean-Baptiste Chaudon, *Analyse des
témoins produits par le promoteur en
l'officialité de Toulon, querellante en
inceste spirituel and autres crimes*, in
Recueil général (La Haye), 5:50.

14. These events are in Chaudon,
*Mémoire instructif pour demoiselle
Catherine Cadière*, 9.

15. Claude Pazery de Thorame, *Mémoire
instructif pour le père Jean-Baptiste
Girard, jésuite, recteur du séminaire
royal de la marine de la ville de
Toulon*, in *Recueil général*, 1:9.

16. Chaudon, *Mémoire instructif pour
demoiselle Catherine Cadière*, 10.

17. Pazery de Thorame, *Mémoire
instructif pour le père Jean-Baptiste
Girard*, 8.

18. Louis-Pierre de La Tour du Pin-
Montauban, *Mémoire des faits qui
se sont passez sous les yeux de m.
l'évêque de Toulon, lors de l'origine
de l'affaire du père Girard jésuite, et
de la Cadière*, in *Recueil général* (La
Haye), 6:1.

19. Ibid., 2.

20. Chaudon, *Mémoire instructif pour
demoiselle Catherine Cadière*, 10.

21. Jean-Jacques Pascal, *Mémoire instructif pour le père Nicolas de Saint
Joseph, prieur des carmes déchaussés
. . . contre le père Jean-Baptiste
Girard*, in *Recueil général* (La Haye),
5:81.

22. [Pagi], *Histoire du procez entre demoiselle Cadière . . . et le père Girard
jésuite, recteur du séminaire royal de
Toulon, de l'autre*, in *Recueil général*
(La Haye), 1:10–14.

23. Sluhovsky, "Discernment of
Difference," 182–83, 187.

24. *Recueil des lettres du père Girard et
de la demoiselle Cadière*, 24.

25. Ibid., 34.

26. Ibid., 31.

27. Ibid., 43, 46.

28. Ibid., 25.

29. Ibid., 26–27.

30. Ibid., 60.

31. Bilinkoff, *Related Lives*, 85–90.
32. Claude Pazery de Thorame, *Dénonciation des factums de M. Chaudon, avocat de la Dlle. Cadière*, in *Recueil général* (La Haye), 8:30–36.
33. *Recueil des lettres du père Girard et de la demoiselle Cadière*, 39.
34. Ibid., 47, 83.
35. Ibid., 65.
36. Ibid., 24–25, 31, 44, 51, 79.
37. Ibid., 110–11.
38. Chaudon, *Mémoire instructif pour demoiselle Catherine Cadière*, 30.
39. Claude Pazery de Thorame, *Sécond mémoire pour le père Girard jésuite, servant de réponse au nouveau mémoire de la Cadière, et à ceux de ses frères*, in *Recueil général* (La Haye), 7:179.
40. J.-J. Pascal, *Mémoire instructif pour le père Nicolas de Saint Joseph*, 5–6.
41. Pazery de Thorame, *Mémoire instructif pour le père Jean-Baptiste Girard*, 11.
42. Ardoin, *La Bulle "Unigenitus,"* 1:45, 61.
43. J.-J. Pascal, *Mémoire instructif pour le père Nicolas de Saint Joseph*, 8.
44. Ibid., 9–10.
45. Ibid., 10.
46. Cadière, *Justification de damoiselle Catherine Cadière*, 16.
47. R. Rapley, *Case of Witchcraft*, 31.
48. De Boer, *Conquest of the Soul*, 97–111; Briggs, *Communities of Belief*, 280; Bernos, *Les Sacrements dans la France*, 57–71, 153–63.
49. Bossy, "Social History of Confession," 29.
50. A letter dated November 1731 notes that Gastaud was exiled for having helped Chaudon compose the *Justification*. BnF, MS Fr. 23860, fol. 175.
51. Ravel, "Husband-Killer, Christian Heroine, Victim," 130.
52. Cadière, *Justification de damoiselle Catherine Cadière*, 6.
53. *The Life of St. Teresa of Jesus, of the Order of Our Lady of Carmel*, trans. David Lewis, http://www.gutenberg.org/dirs/etext05/8trsa10h.htm#prologue, accessed May 27, 2011.
54. Cadière, *Justification de damoiselle Catherine Cadière*, 7.
55. Ibid., 8.
56. Ibid., 9.
57. Ibid., 11.
58. Ibid.
59. Ibid., 12.
60. Ibid.
61. Ibid., 14.
62. For the attribution to Pagi, see Henri-Joseph Thomassin de Mazaugues to Joseph Seytres, the marquis de Caumont, July 2, 1731, Ceccano, MS 2371, fol. 63; see also frontispiece, Méjanes, MS D 2357.
63. [Pagi], *Histoire du procez entre demoiselle Cadière*, 5.
64. Claude Pazery de Thorame, *Réponse à tous les factums faits contre le père Girard*, in *Recueil général* (La Haye), 8:49; Pazery de Thorame, *Mémoire instructif pour le père Jean-Baptiste Girard*, 2.
65. Pazery de Thorame, *Mémoire instructif pour le père Jean-Baptiste Girard*, 3.
66. Bruneau, *Women Mystics Confront the Modern World*; Randall, "'Loosening the Stays,'" 15–22. See also Timmermans, *L'Accès des femmes à la culture*, 547–67. Goldsmith, *Publishing Women's Life Stories*, 73–74.
67. *La Vie de la très honorée Soeur Anne-Magdelaine Rémuzat*, 126–27.

Goldsmith, *Publishing Women's Life Stories*, 72–73.

68. Translation taken from Randall, "'Loosening the Stays,'" 19. See also Bergin, *Church, Society, and Religious Change*, 330–31.

69. [Pagi], *Histoire du procez entre demoiselle Cadière*, 4.

70. Pazery de Thorame, *Mémoire instructif pour le père Jean-Baptiste Girard*, 3–4.

71. Ibid., 10.

72. Ibid.

73. Ibid., 11.

74. "Lettre du père Girard à un jésuite de ses amis. A Lyons le 17 novembre 1731," BnF, MS Fr. 23861, fol. 171.

CHAPTER 4

1. Marais, *Journal et mémoires*, 4:201.

2. [Pagi], *Histoire du procez entre demoiselle Cadière . . . et le père Girard jésuite, recteur du séminaire royal de Toulon, de l'autre*, in *Recueil général* (La Haye), 1:13.

3. For a discussion of exorcism, see Sluhovsky, *Believe Not Every Spirit*, 61–93.

4. Ibid., 88–89.

5. Ibid., 66.

6. Ibid., 75.

7. Briggs, *Witches and Neighbors*, 203.

8. Ferber, *Demonic Possession and Exorcism*, 63–69, 150–51; Sluhovsky, *Believe Not Every Spirit*, 267.

9. Claude Pazery de Thorame, *Mémoire instructif pour le père Jean-Baptiste Girard, jésuite, recteur du séminaire royal de la marine de la ville de Toulon*, in *Recueil général*, 1:12; Louis-Pierre de La Tour du Pin-Montauban, *Mémoire des faits qui se sont passez sous les yeux de m.*

l'évêque de Toulon, lors de l'origine de l'affaire du père Girard jésuite, et de la Cadière, in *Recueil général* (La Haye), 6:7–10.

10. [Chiron de Boismorand], *Résultat des mémoires de la demoiselle Cadière et adhérans. Contre le père Girard jésuite*, in *Recueil général* (La Haye), 6:17.

11. Jean-Jacques Pascal, *Mémoire instructif pour le père Nicolas de Saint Joseph, prieur des carmes déchaussés . . . contre le père Jean-Baptiste Girard*, in *Recueil général* (La Haye), 5:5.

12. Ibid., 11–12.

13. Jean-Baptiste Chaudon, *Mémoire instructif pour demoiselle Catherine Cadière de la ville de Toulon . . .* , in *Recueil général*, 1:11.

14. Pazery de Thorame, *Mémoire instructif pour le père Jean-Baptiste Girard*, 13.

15. Ibid., 14–15.

16. J.-J. Pascal, *Mémoire instructif pour le père Nicolas de Saint Joseph*, 16.

17. Pazery de Thorame, *Mémoire instructif pour le père Jean-Baptiste Girard*, 15.

18. Michelet, *La Sorcière*, 2:115. For songs, see, for example, "Chanson sur l'air du pendu" and "Brevet pour le Pere Sabatier," BnF, MS Fr. 23859, fols. 1, 60.

19. "Verbal d'Accredit fait à la maison de Catherine Cadière, contentant ses interrogats et réponses du 18 nov. 1730," in *Procédure sur laquelle le père Jean-Baptiste Girard, jésuite, Catherine Cadière, le père Estienne-Thomas Cadière dominicain, Mre. François Cadière Prêtre, et le père Nicholas de S. Joseph carme déchaussé on été jugez par arrêt du*

parlement de Provence, du 10 octobre 1731, ADBR, MS Theta 11.

20. Chaudon, *Mémoire instructif pour demoiselle Catherine Cadière*, 12.

21. See Desan and Merrick, *Family, Gender, and Law in Early Modern France*; Hanley, "Social Sites of Political Practice," 27–52; Maza, *Private Lives and Public Affairs*; Hardwick, *Family Business*; Root, *Peasants and King in Burgundy*; Lanza, *From Wives to Widows*.

22. McManners, *Clerical Establishment*.

23. The deposition is contained in Chaudon, *Mémoire instructif pour demoiselle Catherine Cadière*, 12–15.

24. Catherine Cadière, *Justification de damoiselle Catherine Cadière contentant un récit fidèle de tout ce qui s'est passé entre le père Jean-Baptiste Girard, recteur du séminaire de la marine des jésuites de Toulon, et elle*, in *Recueil général*, 1:6.

25. The four pamphlets were *Premiers Actes et contrat protestifs de la demoiselle Cadière*; *Recueil des premières requestes de la demoiselle Cadière, du père Étienne-Thomas Cadière, Jacobin, et du père Nicolas de Saint Joseph*; *Requestes incidents de la demoiselle Cadière. Et du père Estienne-Thomas Cadière, jacobin*; *Acte protestatif et interpellatif, fait par la demoiselle Cadière à la dame supérieure du second monastère de la Visitation de la ville d'Aix*, in vol. 1 of *Recueil général*.

26. Jean-Baptiste Chaudon, *Mémoire instructif des objets proposez contre les témoins, pour demoiselle Catherine Cadière, contre le père Jean-Baptiste Girard, jésuite*, in vol. 2 of *Recueil général* (Aix); Jean-Baptiste Chaudon, *Analyse des témoins produits par le*

promoteur en l'officialité de Toulon, querellante en inceste spirituel and autres crimes, in vol. 5 of *Recueil général* (La Haye).

27. "Acte Protestatif de mlle. Catherine Cadière signifié au père Girard, le quinzième mars," in *Premiers Actes et contrat protestifs de la demoiselle Cadière*, 3.

28. "Lettre de M. Le Bret à m. le comte de St. Florentin, datée à Aix, le 7 décembre 1730," BnF, MS Fr. 23861, fols. 91–94. Le Bret had already written to Saint-Florentin on November 20.

29. Chaudon, *Mémoire instructif pour demoiselle Catherine Cadière*, 15.

30. The women were confined by early December. "Lettre de M. Le Bret. Le comte de Saint-Florentin, le 10 février 1731," BnF, MS Fr. 23861, fol. 109.

31. Richer, *Causes célèbres et intéressantes*, 358.

32. Chaudon, *Analyse des témoins*, 6.

33. Jean-Baptiste Chaudon, *Réponse au mémoire instructif du père J.B. Girard, jésuite pour demoiselle Catherine Cadière, de la ville de Toulon, appellante à minima de décret assigné rendu par messieurs les commissaires du parlement*, in *Recueil général* (Aix), 2:158.

34. Chaudon, *Analyse des témoins*, 18.

35. Ibid., 5.

36. Ibid., 8.

37. "Copie de la lettre de la soeur de Cogolin religieuse à Ste. Ursule, à la soeur Beaussier la cadette religieuse à Ollioules du 28 janvier 1731," BnF, MS Fr. 23861, fol. 103.

38. Chaudon, *Mémoire instructif des objets proposez contre les témoins*, 185.

39. "Information recolemens et confrontations. Information prise par Nous
Joseph Martely Chautard, Conseiller
du Roy, Lieutenant-Général-
Criminel en la sénéchaussée de
cette ville de Toulon, conjointement
avec M. Larmodieu, prêtre docteur
en sainte théologie, chanoine en
l'Église Cathedrale dudidt Toulon,"
in *Procédure sur laquelle le père Jean-
Baptiste Girard . . . ont été jugé,* 29–30.
40. "Acte Protestatif de mlle. Catherine
Cadière signifié au père Girard, le
quinzième mars," 3.
41. Ibid., 2.
42. Richer, *Causes célèbres et intéressantes,* 362; *NE,* March 20, 1731, 53.
43. Elisabeth Pomet wrote to
d'Aguesseau on December 10, 1730,
and then on February 4, February
11, and February 14, fols. 95, 105–108,
111. She wrote to Fleury on March 21,
1731, fols. 117–118. All letters are in
BnF, MS Fr. 23861.
44. *NE,* March 20, 1731, 54–55.
45. "Arrêt du Conseil qui enlève à
l'official et la sénéchaussée de Toulon
et renvoie à la Grande-Chambre
le procès criminel de Catherine
Cadière contre le père Jean-Baptiste
Girard, recteur du séminaire des
aumôniers de la marine à Toulon, 16
janvier 1731," ADBR, MS B 3405, fols.
93–95. The actual patent letters were
released on January 25, the same day
that Catherine filed her complaint
before the *baillage* about the slowness of the proceedings.
46. De Boyer, marquis d'Argens,
Mémoires, 294.
47. François Cadière received a *décret
d'assigné.* For an explanation of these
writs, see *The case of Mrs. Mary
Catharine Cadiere.*

48. Catherine Cadière, *Justification
de damoiselle Catherine Cadière
contenant un récit fidèle de tout ce
qui s'est passé entre cette damoiselle et
le p. Jean-Baptiste Girard,* in *Recueil
général* (La Haye), 1:21.
49. Ibid.
50. Jean-Baptiste Chaudon,
"Recollement de la demoiselle
Cadière" (Aix: René Adibert, [1731]),
in *Recueil général,* 1:1–2.
51. *NE,* May 29, 1731, 105.
52. Chaudon, *Mémoire instructif pour
demoiselle Catherine Cadière,* 16.
53. Cadière, *Justification de damoiselle
Catherine Cadière,* in *Recueil général,* 1:7.
54. Ibid., 8.
55. "Requeste de demoiselle Elisabeau
Pomet Mère de Catherine Cadière à
nosseigneurs du parlement," BnF, MS
Fr. 10980, fol. 206.
56. See *Premiers Actes et contrats protestifs de la demoiselle Cadière.* See also
*Recueil des premières requestes de la
demoiselle Cadière.*
57. *Acte protestatif et interpellatif, fait
par la demoiselle Cadière, à la dame
supérieure du second monastère de la
Visitation,* 71.
58. Chaudon, *Mémoire instructif pour
demoiselle Catherine Cadière,* 18.
59. On the *appel comme d'abus,* see
Cagnac, *De l'appel comme d'abus;*
Généstal, *Les Origines de l'appel
comme d'abus.*
60. For discussions of Fleury's policies
against the Jansenists, see Campbell,
Power and Politics, 237–74;
Chaunu, Foisil, and Noirfontaine,
Le Basculement religieux de Paris,
190–240; Jones, *Great Nation,*
99–110; Van Kley, *Religious Origins
of the French Revolution,* 122–28.

61. Flammermont, *Remontrances du Parlement de Paris au XVIIIe siècle*, 267.

62. [Catherine Cadière and Aubin], "A nosseigneurs de parlement," in *Recueil des premières requestes de la demoiselle Cadière*, 10–12.

63. Chaudon, *Mémoire instructif pour demoiselle Catherine Cadière*, 21.

64. *NE*, May 29, 1731, 205–6; Richer, *Causes célèbres et intéressantes*, 408.

65. *NE*, June 16, 1731, 117; Richer, *Causes célèbres et intéressantes*, 413.

66. "Lettre de la dlle. Cadière à M. Le Chancellier à Aix, le 2 mai 1731," fol. 135. For other letters to d'Aguesseau dated April 13, April 27, and May 6, 22, and 21 of that year, see fols. 119–120, 127, and 137–141. Letters in BnF, MS Fr. 23861.

67. *NE*, May 29, 1731, 206.

68. Campbell, *Power and Politics*, 122.

69. Richer, *Causes célèbres et intéressantes*, 414; on d'Aguesseau's alteration, see Campbell, *Power and Politics*, 124–25.

70. For a copy of d'Aguesseau's letter, see *NE*, August 18, 1731, 161. On the king's *arrêt*, see "Arrêt du Conseil ordonnant que le procès criminel de Catherine Cadière contre le père Girard soit continué par-devant la grandchambre, 11 juin 1731," ADBR, MS B 3405, fols. 724–728.

71. *Recueil des premières requestes de la demoiselle Cadière*. . . .

72. [Nicolas de St. Joseph and Jean-Jacques Pascal], "A nosseigneurs de parlement," in ibid., 1.

73. Marquis de Caumont to d'Anfossy, May 23, 1731, Ceccano, MS 6807, fol. 222.

74. *NE*, June 18, 1731, 118; Delayen, *La Sainte de M. de Toulon*, 121–22.

75. Delayen, *La Sainte de M. de Toulon*, 111–21.

76. Maza, *Private Lives and Public Affairs*, 12, 38. See also Maza, "Tribunal de la Nation."

77. The page count is based on briefs that were printed on pocket-sized pages as opposed to the larger folio editions. See Chaudon, *Mémoire instructif pour demoiselle Catherine Cadière*, 2.

78. Thomassin de Mazaugues to the marquis de Caumont, December 29, 1730, Ceccano, MS 2372, fol. 38. In the letter to Caumont, Mazaugues notes that at this point, forty-five witnesses had given their depositions; in his January 20 letter to Marais, Bouhier also noted forty witnesses, suggesting that Mazaugues was sharing similar information with his various correspondents in France. On Bouhier's relationships with magistrates in Provence and with Caumont, see Broglie, *Les Portefeuilles du président Bouhier*, 292–328.

79. *Madame de Sévigné, de sa famille et de ses amis*, 11:56.

80. Marais, *Journal et mémoires*, 201.

81. Barbier, *Chronique de la régence*, 2:180.

82. For the reference to different places where the *factums* were sold, see "Du 10 et 11 février 1731," BA, AB, MS 10161, fol. 99. For references to "nouvellistes," see ibid., fols. 154, 195–196. On police spies, see Farge, *Subversive Words*, 18–26; Graham, "Crimes of Opinion," 79–103; and Walton, *Policing Public Opinion*, 17–37. On the *nouvellistes*, see Funck-Brentano, *Les Nouvellistes*.

83. BA, AB, MS 11263, fol. 208.

84. Farge, *Subversive Words*, 129.
85. For a recent discussion of "the public," especially as it pertains to Jürgen Habermas's concept of the public sphere, see Kaiser, "Public Sphere," 409–28. Quotation taken from ibid., 420.
86. Chaudon, *Mémoire instructif pour demoiselle Catherine Cadière*, 1.
87. Melton, *Rise of the Public in Enlightenment Europe*, 50–53.
88. On the Council of Embrun, see Maire, *De la cause de Dieu*, 372–81; Merrick, *Desacralization of the French Monarchy*, 53–54.
89. On Embrun, see *Suite des Nouvelles Ecclésiastiques*, June 3, 1728, 49–51.
90. Farge, *Subversive Words*, 36–48.
91. Maire, *Les Convulsionnaires de Saint-Médard*; Kreiser, *Miracles, Convulsions, and Ecclesiastical Politics*. On Lorme, see Marais, *Journal et mémoires*, 4:303.
92. Melton, *Rise of the Public in Enlightenment Europe*, 50–52; Van Kley, *Religious Origins of the French Revolution*, 95.
93. Maire, *Les Convulsionnaires de Saint-Médard*, 153–79.
94. *NE*, March 20, 1731, 53.
95. The *Gazette d'Amsterdam*, one of the most important political papers of the eighteenth century, had extensive coverage on the affair starting in July of 1731. Sixteen other articles, ending December 25, 1731, followed the *Gazette*'s first reference to the Cadière affair.
96. Hanley, "Social Sites of Political Practice," 33–36; Maza, *Private Lives and Public Affairs*, 33–38.
97. *Recueil des factums pour et contre l'affaire du p. Girard*, Méjanes, MS 1632 (1497). The comments about the

judge are found on the inside front cover.
98. Ravel, *Would-Be Commoner*.
99. Marais, *Journal et mémoires*, 4:301.
100. Ibid., 255.
101. Thomassin de Mazaugues to the marquis de Caumont, June 18, July 2, July 6, and July 18, 1731, Ceccano, MS 2372, fols. 61, 63, 65, and 68.
102. *Madame de Sévigné, de sa famille et de ses amis*, 84.
103. Thomassin de Mazaugues to the marquis de Caumont, December 19, 1731, Ceccano, MS 2372, fol. 86.
104. See, for example, *A compleat translation of the whole case of Mary Catherine Cadiere*; *Factum oder Vertheidigungs-Schrifft Marien Catharinen Cadiere*.
105. Marais, *Journal et mémoires*, 301.
106. Bell, *Lawyers and Citizens*, 75–76, 85–87.
107. On the *causes célèbres* compilations, see Maza, *Private Lives and Public Affairs*, 24–25.
108. Ibid., 130.

CHAPTER 5

1. Chaudon's piece *Précis des charges, pour demoiselle Catherine Cadière, de la ville de Toulon* was followed by Pazery de Thorame's *Brève réponse à tous les factums faits contre le père Girard*, which then elicited an *observation* from Chaudon. See vol. 2 of *Recueil général*.
2. Jean-Baptiste Chaudon, *Réponse au mémoire instructif du père Jean-Baptiste Girard, jésuite. Pour la demoiselle Catherine Cadière de la ville de Toulon*, in *Suite des procédures de Catherine Cadière*, 64.

3. Chaudon, letter to Cardinal Fleury, February 27, 1732, AAE, MS 1735, fol. 100.

4. *NE*, June 16, 1731, 117.

5. Marquis de Caumont to d'Anfossy, June 20, 1731, Ceccano, MS 6807, fol. 227.

6. Thomassin de Mazaugues to the marquis de Caumont, July 2, 1731, Ceccano, MS 2372, fol. 63.

7. "D'Aix, 7 mai 1731," BnF, MS Fr. 23860, fol. 12.

8. Chaudon, *Réponse au mémoire instructif du père Jean-Baptiste Girard*, 64.

9. Ibid., 63.

10. Ibid., 70, 74.

11. Ferber, *Demonic Possession and Exorcism*, 70–88; Walker and Dickerman, "Notorious Woman"; Marshman, "Exorcism as Empowerment."

12. Jean-Baptiste Chaudon, *Mémoire instructif pour demoiselle Catherine Cadière de la ville de Toulon . . .*, in *Recueil général*, 1:32.

13. Ibid., 1:17.

14. Claude Pazery de Thorame, *Sécond mémoire pour le père Girard jésuite, servant de réponse au nouveau mémoire de la Cadière, et à ceux de ces frères*, in *Recueil général* (La Haye), 7:92.

15. Claude Pazery de Thorame, *Mémoire instructif pour le père Jean-Baptiste Girard, jésuite, recteur du séminaire royal de la marine de la ville de Toulon*, in *Recueil général*, 1:19.

16. De Boyer, marquis d'Argens, *Mémoires*, 293.

17. McManners, *Religion of the People*, 224–31; Bever, "Witchcraft Prosecutions and the Decline of Magic," 263–93.

18. Mollenauer, *Strange Revelations*, 130.

19. The classic argument regarding the growing division between elite and popular culture remains Burke, *Popular Culture in Early Modern Europe*. For counterarguments, see Briggs, *Communities of Belief*. For a recent reevaluation of Burke's thesis, see Smith, *Monsters of the Gévaudan*.

20. Jean-Baptiste Chaudon, *Parallèle des sentimens du p. Girard avec ceux de Molinos*, in *Recueil général* (La Haye), 8:2.

21. Sluhovsky, *Believe Not Every Spirit*, 100–101.

22. Armogathe, *Le Quiétisme*, 26–39; Broekhuysen, "Quietist Movement," 139–43.

23. On Marseille, see *NE*, June 16, 1731, 120; on the Rhodez affair, see *NE*, September 14, 1932, 177–78. See also Coleman, *Virtues of Abandon*, 101–5.

24. Chaudon, *Réponse au mémoire instructif du père Jean-Baptiste Girard*, 55.

25. Jean-Baptiste Chaudon, *Précis des charges, pour demoiselle Catherine Cadière, de la ville de Toulon*, in *Recueil général* (La Haye), 5:17.

26. Ibid., 27.

27. Ibid., 74.

28. Codified under Justinian in the sixth century, "spiritual incest" outlawed sexual relations between those linked in a spiritual association, like confessors and penitents, and baptismal kinship, like godparents and their godchildren. Haas, "Boccaccio, Baptismal Kinship, and Spiritual Incest."

29. Chaudon, *Mémoire instructif pour demoiselle Catherine Cadière*, 8, 39.

30. Chaudon, *Réponse au mémoire instructif du père J.B. Girard*, 92.

31. Chaudon, *Réponse de la demoiselle Cadière, à la séconde partie du sécond mémoire du père Girard*, in *Recueil général* (La Haye), 7:63.

32. Chaudon, *Réponse au mémoire instructif du père J.B. Girard*, 107.

33. Ibid., 108.

34. Chaudon, *Mémoire instructif pour demoiselle Catherine Cadière*, 46.

35. Armstrong-Partida, "Priestly Wives," 166–214.

36. Riddle, *Contraception and Abortion*, 110–14, 153.

37. Chaudon, *Réponse de la demoiselle Cadière, à la séconde partie du sécond mémoire du père Girard*, 88.

38. Chaudon, *Réponse au mémoire instructif du père J.B. Girard*, 138.

39. Ibid., 142.

40. Jean-Louis Fouque, *Réflexions sur la recrimination en prétendu complot imputé au père Estienne Thomas, prêtre*, in *Recueil général* (La Haye), 5:12.

41. Chaudon, *Réponse au mémoire instructif du père J.B. Girard*, 148.

42. "Simplicité," *Dictionnaire de l'Académie française*, 1st and 4th editions (1694, 1762).

43. Jean-Louis Fouque, *Réponse au sécond mémoire imprimé sous le nom du p. Girard, jésuite. Pour le P. Estienne-Thomas Cadière, prêtre, religieux de l'ordre de Saint Dominique*, in *Recueil général* (La Haye), 8:110.

44. *NE*, March 20, 1731, 53.

45. On references to Lafitau and Vayrac, respectively, see marquis de Caumont to d'Anfossy, August 20, 1730, and October 1, 1731, Ceccano, MS 6807, fols. 249, 262. Pagi shared the piece with Thomassin de Mazaugues. Thomassin de Mazaugues to the marquis de Caumont, July 2, 1731, Ceccano, MS 2371, fol. 63.

46. Pazery de Thorame, *Mémoire instructif pour le père Jean-Baptiste Girard*, 19.

47. Ibid., 21, 25.

48. Ibid., 24.

49. Pazery de Thorame, *Second mémoire pour le père Girard*, 106.

50. Ibid., 104; [Chiron de Boismorand], *Résultat des mémoires de la demoiselle Cadière et adhérans. Contre le père Girard jésuite*, in *Recueil général* (La Haye), 1:119.

51. Pazery de Thorame, *Second mémoire pour le père Girard*, 100–101.

52. Marais, *Journal et mémoires*, 4:239, 259.

53. Pazery de Thorame, *Réponse à tous les factums*, 55.

54. Pazery de Thorame, *Mémoire instructif pour le père Jean-Baptiste Girard*, 30.

55. Pazery de Thorame, *Second mémoire pour le père Girard*, 126.

56. Ibid., 27.

57. Ibid., 43.

58. Pazery de Thorame, *Mémoire instructif pour le père Jean-Baptiste Girard*, 20.

59. Pazery de Thorame, *Second mémoire pour le père Girard*, 82–87.

60. Ibid., 87.

61. Ibid., 46.

62. The Jansenists criticized the Jesuits for using theater as a pedagogical tool in their colleges: "Indecent and facetious dances, masquerades, disguises of one sex for another, discourses and songs in which intemperance is canonized: what lessons for youth and the Public!" *NE*, October 20, 1736, 168.

63. Scott, "Actress and Utopian Theatre Reform," 18–27; Berlanstein, *Daughters of Eve*, 33–83.

64. [Pagi], *Histoire du procez entre demoiselle Cadière . . . et le père Girard jésuite, recteur du séminaire royal de Toulon, de l'autre*, in *Recueil général* (La Haye), 1:13. *Dénonciation des factums de M. Chaudon, avocat de la Dlle. Cadière*, in *Recueil général* (La Haye), 8:20.

65. Pazery de Thorame, *Second mémoire pour le père Girard*, 6.

66. Claude Pazery de Thorame, *Démonstration des impostures sacrileges des accusateurs du père Girard, jésuite, et de l'innocence de ce père*, in *Recueil général* (La Haye), 8:7. Much of the *Démonstration* was devoted to exposing the Lenten journal as a fraud.

67. Pazery de Thorame, *Second mémoire pour le père Girard*, 37–38.

68. Pazery de Thorame, *Démonstration des impostures sacrileges*, 8.

69. Claude Pazery de Thorame, *Réponse à tous les factums faits contre le père Girard*, in *Recueil général* (La Haye), 8:79.

70. Pazery de Thorame, *Second mémoire pour le père Girard*, 67.

71. Ibid., 158, 181; [Chiron de Boismorand], *Résultat des mémoires de la demoiselle Cadière et adhérans*, 11, 52.

72. [Pagi], *Histoire du procez entre demoiselle Cadière*, 13.

73. Pazery de Thorame, *Second mémoire pour le père Girard*, 191.

74. Pazery de Thorame, *Démonstration des impostures sacrileges*, 16.

75. Pazery de Thorame, *Second mémoire pour le père Girard*, 172.

76. Pazery de Thorame, *Réponse à tous les factums*, 62.

77. Pazery de Thorame, *Second mémoire pour le père Girard*, 201.

78. *Lettres écrites d'Aix, pendant le procez du père Girard*, 4.

79. Pazery de Thorame, *Démonstration des impostures sacrileges*, 8.

80. Caumont to d'Anfossy, July 13, 1731, Ceccano, MS 6807, fol. 238.

81. Bourgarel, *Mémoire instructif pour messire François Cadière, prêtre de la ville de Toulon . . . contre monsieur le procureur général du roy*, in *Recueil général*, 1:6.

82. Pazery de Thorame, *Second mémoire pour le père Girard*, 82–87. See also Froeschlé-Chopard, "La Bibliothèque des dominicains," 3–34.

83. Fouque devoted four pages connecting Surin's writings and Catherine's various states of ecstasy and possession. Fouque, *Réponse au second mémoire imprimé sous le nom du p. Girard, jésuite*, 105–10.

84. Jean-Jacques Pascal, *Mémoire instructif pour le père Nicolas de Saint Joseph, prieur des carmes déchaussés . . . contre le père Jean-Baptiste Girard*, in *Recueil général* (La Haye), 5:71.

85. Ibid., 42, 71.

86. Marquis de Caumont to d'Anfossy, May 23, 1731, Ceccano, MS 6807, fol. 22.

87. D'Anfossy to the marquis de Caumont, October 5, 1731, Ceccano, MS 2277, fol. 239; Bouhier, *Lettres de Mathieu Marais*, 193. On Aubry and Cochin, see Bell, *Lawyers and Citizens*, 73, 85, 93.

88. J.-J. Pascal, *Mémoire instructif pour le père Nicolas de Saint Joseph*, 1.

89. Ibid., 110.

90. Ibid., 25.

91. Ibid., 15, 81.

92. Van Kley, *Religious Origins of the French Revolution*, 114–22.

93. Fouque, *Réponse au sécond mémoire imprimé sous le nom du p. Girard, jésuite*, 89, 135.

94. Bourgarel, *Mémoire instructif pour messire François Cadière*, 36.

95. Ibid., 7.

96. Bourgarel, *Sécond mémoire pour messire Cadière, prestre*, 73.

97. Bourgarel, *Mémoire instructif pour messire François Cadière*, 55.

98. De Boyer, marquis d'Argens, *Mémoires*, 297–98.

99. Merrick, "Patriarchalism and Constitutionalism," 321.

100. Chaudon, *Mémoire instructif pour demoiselle Catherine Cadière*, 57.

101. Pazery de Thorame, *Démonstration des impostures sacrileges*, 11.

102. [Chiron de Boismorand], *Résultat des mémoires de la demoiselle Cadière et adhérans*, 66.

103. J.-J. Pascal, *Mémoire instructif pour le père Nicolas de Saint Joseph*, 145–46.

104. "Réflexion sur la relation de l'affaire de Mademoiselle Cadière," Bibliothèque nationale de France, Clairambault, MS 569, fol. 139.

105. *Réflexions sur les mémoires du p. Jean-Baptiste Girard, jésuite et de Catherine Cadière, et ses co-accusez*, in *Recueil général* (La Haye), 6:38.

106. Bourgarel, *Sécond mémoire pour messire Cadière, prestre*, 50.

CHAPTER 6

1. Jean-Jacques Pascal, *Mémoire instructif pour le père Nicolas de Saint Joseph, prieur des carmes déchaussés . . . contre le père Jean-Baptiste Girard*, in *Recueil général* (La Haye), 5:168.

2. Black, "France in 1730," 56.

3. Playstowe, *The gentleman's guide*, 140; see also Fairchilds, *Poverty and Charity in Aix-en-Provence*, 3–13.

4. Playstowe, *The gentleman's guide*, 141.

5. On Provence's relations with the Crown, see Blaufarb, *Politics of Fiscal Privilege*, 25–26.

6. Kettering, *Judicial Politics*, 41. On the *parlements*, see Mousnier, *Institutions of France*, 2:255–63, 302–11.

7. Kettering, *Judicial Politics*, 32–33; Beik, *Social and Cultural History of Early Modern France*, 136.

8. De Brosses, *Lettres familières écrites d'Italie*, 1:27.

9. BnF, MS Fr. 23860, fol. 19.

10. Richer, *Causes célèbres et intéressantes*, 410–11. Kettering, *Judicial Politics*, 36.

11. "Troisième Remarque," BnF, MS Fr. 10980, fol. 105. Lécrivain, "Les Jésuites et le Parlement d'Aix au XVIIIe siècle," in *Le Parlement de Provence*, 176.

12. "Lettre de la dlle. Cadière à M. le chancellier, avec un acte signifié au M. le Procureur-Général," Aix, April 13, 1731, BnF, MS Fr. 23861, fol. 120.

13. Gaufridy's father, Jean-François Gaufridy (1622–1689), served as a counselor for the parlement and wrote a two-volume history of Provence. Kettering, *Judicial Politics*, 209–10. See also "Éloge de Monsieur de Gaufridi," in vol. 1 of Gaufridy, *Histoire de Provence*.

14. "Lettre de M. de Gaufridy, au sujet de l'affaire de la dlle. Cadière du 15 avril 1731," BnF, MS Fr. 23861, fol. 122.

15. Ibid.

16. Ibid., fols. 121–122.
17. "Mémoire sur le procès du p. Girard et de la Cadière," AAE, MS 1735, fol. 158.
18. *NE*, August 18, 1731, 161.
19. Thomassin de Mazaugues to the marquis de Caumont, July 20, 1731, Ceccano, MS 2372, fol. 69.
20. Untitled, Méjanes, MS 927, fol. 8.
21. Richer, *Causes célèbres et intéressantes*, 422; the segment of Gaufridy's speech pertaining to procedure is found on 421–24. A full summary of this speech may be found in Méjanes, MS 927, 9 pages.
22. Richer, *Causes célèbres et intéressantes*, 424.
23. "Conclusions de Messieurs les gens du roy, portées par m. l'avocat général de Gaufridi de Trez, sur l'appel comme d'abus, et la cassation de la procedure," in *Procédure sur laquelle le père Jean-Baptiste Girard . . . ont été jugé*, 370.
24. *Suite de les Nouvelles Ecclésiastiques*, August 18, 1731, 161.
25. "Lettre à Aix, le premier août 1731," BnF, MS Fr. 23860, fols. 29–33.
26. Richer, *Causes célèbres et intéressantes*, 429–30; *NE*, August 18, 1731, 162.
27. "Lettre à Aix, le premier août 1731," BnF, MS Fr. 23860, fol. 30. Richer, *Causes célèbres et intéressantes*, 428–29.
28. Richer, *Causes célèbres et intéressantes*, 430–32.
29. Cubells, *La Provence des lumières*, and Bohanan, *Old and New Nobility*.
30. *Madame de Sévigné, de sa famille et de ses amis*, 11:149. See Cubells, *La Provence des lumières*, 67–79.
31. Méchin, *L'Enseignement en Provence*, 2:225; Cubells, *La Provence des lumières*, 250.
32. "Mémoire sur le procès du p. Girard et de la Cadière," AAE, MS 1735, fol. 187.
33. On Gaufridy's opposition to *Unigenitus* in this period, see Ardoin, *La Bulle "Unigenitus,"* 1:40, 106, 114–16. For an account of Gaufridy's deathbed, see *NE*, July 3, 1741, 106.
34. Merrick, *Desacralization of the French Monarchy*, 76.
35. Collins, *State in Early Modern France*, 101.
36. Van Kley, *Religious Origins of the French Revolution*, 73.
37. Cubells, *La Provence des lumières*, 267.
38. On the parlement of Aix's opposition to *Unigenitus*, see Ardoin, *La Bulle "Unigenitus"*; Cabasse, *Essais historiques sur le parlement de Provence*, 3:136–37. On the parlement of Paris's discussion, see Van Kley, *Religious Origins of the French Revolution*, 74.
39. Ardoin, *La Bulle "Unigenitus,"* 1:109–16; Cabasse, *Essais historiques sur le parlement de Provence*, 3:154–55.
40. "A M. l'abbé Gastaud, avocat au parlement de Provence. Il le consulte sur le prochain concile d'Embrun," in *Lettres de messire Jean Soanen évêque de Senez*, 1:505–12. *Suite de les Nouvelles Ecclésiastiques*, June 3, 1728, 49–51.
41. *Défense du discours de monsieur de Gaufridy*, 63.
42. Ibid., 65.
43. Ibid., 50.
44. Ardoin, *La Bulle "Unigenitus,"* 2:25; Marais, *Journal et mémoires*, 4:516.
45. On *Pastoralis officii*, see Cubells, *La Provence des lumières*, 276.
46. Ibid., 281.

47. Bossuet, *Politics Drawn from the Very Words of Holy Scripture*, 61.

48. "A Aix, le premier aoust 1731," BnF, MS Fr. 23860, fol. 31.

49. *NE*, August 18, 1731, 162; names are found in Méchin, *L'Enseignement en Provence*, 2:334.

50. *NE*, August 18, 1731, 162.

51. "A Aix, le premier aoust 1731," BnF, MS Fr. 23860, fol. 31.

52. Ibid.

53. Marais, *Journal et mémoires*, 271.

54. "A Aix le 3 août 1731," BnF, MS Fr. 23860, fols. 35–36.

55. *Procédure sur laquelle le père Jean-Baptiste Girard . . . ont été jugé*, 372.

56. Ibid. "D'Aix le 12 septembre 1731," BnF, MS Fr. 23860, fol. 64.

57. "15 septembre 1731," BnF, MS Fr. 23860, fol. 65.

58. *Correspondance littéraire et anécdotique*, 2:89.

59. Méjanes, MS F1095, vol. 3, fol. 67.

60. BnF, MS Fr. 23860, fol. 64; Richer, *Causes célèbres et intéressantes*, 452.

61. In the Bibliothèque Méjanes, the two versions of "Rélation ou journal de ce qui s'est passé dans l'interieur de la grand chambre depuis que le procès de la Cadière et du p. Girard a été mis sur le Bureau" are located in MS F1095, vol. 3, fols. 69–192 and MS 928, fols. 72–101. See also AM Toulon, FF 640. These accounts are not identical, a likely outcome of transcription and abridgment. Nevertheless, their structure, details, and sympathies line up.

62. "15 septembre 1731," BnF, MS Fr. 23860, fol. 65.

63. *Procédure sur laquelle le père Jean-Baptiste Girard . . . ont été jugé*, 221.

64. Richer, *Causes célèbres et intéressantes*, 461–62.

65. BnF, MS Fr. 23860, fol. 72. The term "inflexible" was applied to the pro-Cadière St. Jean.

66. Méjanes, MS F1095, vol. 3, fol. 86.

67. Ibid., fol. 89.

68. Ibid., fol. 92.

69. Ibid., fol. 97.

70. BnF, MS Fr. 23860, fol. 85.

71. Méjanes, MS F1095, vol. 3, fol. 109.

72. BnF, MS Fr. 23860, fol. 93; Richer, *Causes célèbres et intéressantes*, 463.

73. Richer, *Causes célèbres et intéressantes*, 463.

74. *NE*, December 3, 1731, 234.

75. BnF, MS Fr. 23860, fol. 95.

76. Méjanes, MS F1095, vol. 3, fols. 110, 114.

77. Ibid., fols. 114, 116.

78. BnF, MS Fr. 23860, fol. 95.

79. Richer, *Causes célèbres et intéressantes*, 474; Méjanes, MS F1095, vol. 3, fol. 140.

80. Richer, *Causes célèbres et intéressantes*, 474.

81. Ibid., 477.

82. *NE*, December 5, 1731, 235.

83. Ibid.

84. Méjanes, MS F1095, vol. 3, fol. 141.

85. Ibid., fol. 145.

86. *NE*, December 5, 1731, 235.

87. Richer, *Causes célèbres et intéressantes*, 482.

88. *NE*, December 5, 1731.

89. Baker, *Inventing the French Revolution*, 168; Bell, *Lawyers and Citizens*, 105.

90. BnF, MS Fr. 23860, fol. 121.

91. Méjanes, MS F1095, vol. 3, fol. 172.

92. Ibid.

CHAPTER 7

1. "Epigramme," Lagoubran, MS 48 (R. 1362), fols. 281–282.

2. Robert Darnton uses this phrase in *Poetry and the Police*, 15–21.
3. Darnton, "Blogging Now and Then."
4. On the continued importance of manuscripts in the eighteenth century, see Moureau, *De Bonne Main*.
5. Darnton, "Early Information Society," 4.
6. Duccini, "Regard sur la littérature pamphlétaire," 313–14.
7. "Libelle," *Dictionnaire de l'Académie française*, first edition (1694).
8. Maire, *De la cause de Dieu*, 203–34.
9. Maza, *Private Lives and Public Affairs*, 188–90.
10. D'Anfossy to the marquis de Caumont, August 10, 1731, Ceccano, MS 2277, fol. 223. On Beaucaire's reputation for licentiousness, see *La Foire de Beaucaire*. For a more complete discussion of these images, see Lamotte, "L'Affaire Girard-Cadière," 1:436–75.
11. Wachenheim, "Le 'péril de séduction,'" 37–38.
12. The thirty-two plates are located in the following collection: [Gissey de Bordelet], *Histoire du père Jean-Baptiste Girard jésuite . . .*, available in the Bibliothèque nationale, Paris. A copy of the *Historische print- en dicht-tafereelen van Jan Baptist Girard, en juffrou Maria Catharina Cadiere* may be found at the Bibliothèque Méjanes in Aix-en-Provence.
13. Haydon, "Anti-Catholicism and Obscene Literature," 202–18. Jeremy Jingle, *Spiritual fornication*. Jingle's name was clearly a pseudonym.
14. In 2012, under the direction of Henri Duranton, the Université Jean Monnet, Saint-Étienne, published a digital collection of eighteenth-century satirical poems; a number of them feature the Girard/Cadière affair. See http://satires18.univ-st-etienne.fr / présentation.
15. Barbier, *Chronique de la régence*, 2:180.
16. "Chanson," fol. 11; "Sonnet," fol. 20; and "Chanson sur l'air des pendus," fol. 75, are all in BnF, MS Fr. 23589. See also "Réplique a l'abbé de Boismorand auteur du résultat en faveur du père Girard," BnF, MS Fr. 23589, fol. 4.
17. For example, there were numerous "Epigrammes sur le p. Girard," as well as "Chanson sur le p. Girard." See "Girard/Cadière," BM Dijon, MS 1125 (174), fols. 56, 59, 60–62, 65, 78, 83, 85–92, and 98.
18. Darnton, *Poetry and the Police*, 11, 76.
19. Most *brevets* were in manuscript form.
20. "Calotte pour Dlle. Bertot et Robert," BnF, MS Fr. 23589, fol. 152; "Calotte pour l'abbé de Valbanette," BnF, MS Fr. 23589, fol. 151. This volume at the Bibliothèque nationale contains more than twenty *calottes* targeting individuals by name (as well as pro-Girard judges). For another extensive collection of these *calottes*, see Arbaud, MS MQ 366.
21. Marais, *Journal et mémoires*, 4:311. On the *sarcelades*, see Choudhury, "Unlikely Pair," 543–70. On the *régiment de la calotte*, see Hennet, *Le Régiment de la calotte*, 40. See also de Baecque, "Les Éclats du rire," 477–511.
22. *L'Entrée triomphante du père Girard*.
23. Marquis de Caumont to monsieur d'Anfossy, December 12,

1731, Ceccano, MS 6807, fol. 281. Autreau's play was performed at the Théâtre français on November 23, 1731. See Schwartz, "Jacques Autreau," 526–28.

24. "Parodie d'une scène de la tragédie d'Iphigénie de Racine. Dialogue, entre les Cadières et le marquis de Senas," Lagoubran, MS 48 (R. 1362), fols. 271–274. See also Méjanes, MS F1095, vol. 2, fols. 299–301. "Minos et Rhadamante," Lagoubran, MS 48 (R. 1362), fols. 334–73.

25. Goodman, Republic of Letters, 146–47.

26. English anti-Jesuitism was triggered by the Popish Plot of 1678, which claimed that the Jesuits were going to assassinate Charles II. See Pillorget, "Le Complot papiste."

27. The Wanton Jesuit: or, Innocence seduced.

28. Fielding, The Debauchees; on this episode, see Cross, History of Henry Fielding, 1:125–30. The relevant Grub Street articles may be found in Paulson and Lockwood, Henry Fielding, 47, 56.

29. Wells, "Some Notes on the Early Eighteenth-Century Pantomime," 603–4.

30. "Vers sur l'affaire de Mademoiselle Cadière," BnF, MS Fr. 23859, fols. 24–25.

31. Copie de la lettre de mademoiselle Agnès, pensionnaire au couvent d'Ollioules, adressée à m. l'avocat Chaudon, du premier juillet 1731, in vol. 1 of Recueil général.

32. Quéniart, L'Imprimerie et la libraire à Rouen au XVIIIe siècle, 214.

33. Mémoires pour servir à l'histoire de la calotte, 131; see Hennet, Le Régiment de la calotte, 1–7.

34. Choudhury, "Unlikely Pair," 550–51.

35. Belsunce, Lettre de M. l'évêque de Marseille à la très-honorée soeur Marie-Agnès de Greard.

36. "Lettre de M. l'évêque de Marseille à m. le cardinal de Fleury," BnF, MS Fr. 10980, fol. 68.

37. Belsunce, Lettre de M. l'évêque de Marseille à la très-honorée soeur Marie-Agnès de Greard, 2.

38. Barbier, Chronique de la régence, 2:180–81.

39. Lamotte, "Le P. Girard et la Cadière," 435.

40. Recueil Clairambault-Maurepas. See Darnton, Poetry and the Police, 31–32. Grasland and Keilhauer, "'La Rage de collection,'" 458–86.

41. Marais, Journal et mémoires, 4:251.

42. Marquis de Caumont to monsieur d'Anfossy, August 15, 1731, Ceccano, MS 6807, fol. 247.

43. Bouhier, Lettres de Mathieu Marais, 209, 230.

44. BnF, MS Fr. 23859, fols. 92–95.

45. Du Plessis, Mémoires du maréchal duc de Richelieu, 1:318. Stéphane Lamotte's extensive research suggests that the only physical objects that have survived are ribbons "à la Cadière." Lamotte, "L'Affaire Girard-Cadière," 2:568–69.

46. A copy of "Au Parlement d'Aix" is located in BnF, MS Fr. 23859, fol. 27. For the police copy referring to the broadsheet, see BA, AB, MS 3307, fol. 144.

47. Birn, Royal Censorship of Books.

48. Copie de l'arrest de la cour du parlement de Provence, in Recueil général (La Haye), 8:10–11.

49. BA, AB, MS 11229, fol. 101. On the search for printers responsible for copying factums from the Cadière

affair, see Barbier, *Chronique de la régence*, 2:197.

50. Farge, *Subversive Words*, 59–77.

51. Ibid., 71.

52. "Le monde renversé," BnF, MS Fr. 23859, fol. 15. "The World Turned Upside Down" refers to a popular English Civil War song. See Hill, *World Turned Upside Down*.

53. Howarth, "Theme of Tartuffe."

54. "Chanson," BnF, MS Fr. 23859, fol. 98. The first edition of the *Dictionnaire de l'Académie française* (1694) indicates that the play's title had become a common epithet for religious hypocrites.

55. Calder, "Molière, le Tartuffe, and Anti-Jesuit Propaganda," 303–23.

56. "Chanson," BnF, MS Fr. 23859, fol. 12.

57. "Chanson sur l'aire de la marche faniffaire," BnF, MS Fr. 23859, fol. 1. See also "Chanson sur le père Girard," BM Dijon, MS 1125 (174), fol. 85. The same song in which Father Girard promises Catherine that she will become a saint is titled "Oubliez-Vous et laissez-faire," *Recueil Clairambault-Maurepas*, 5:279–81.

58. "Oubliez-Vous et laissez-faire," *Recueil Clairambault-Maurepas*, 5:279–81. For other examples, see BnF, MS Fr. 23859, fols. 2, 20, 57, 85, 96, and 172.

59. "Dialogue entre le père Girard et la dlle. Cadière, sur l'air ne m'entendez vous pas," BnF, MS Fr. 23859, fol. 29. Another example of an "exchange" between the supposed lovers was the "Entretien de Mlle. Cadière avec son directeur de l'arrivée des ses juges. Sur l'air des cantiques de Saint Eustache," ibid., fol. 34. For examples of how the letters were reformulated

into verse, see "Explication de la lettre du 22 juillet du P. Girard à la dlle. Cadiere sur l'air que je regrete mon amant," ibid., fols. 66–67; another copy, entitled "Chanson sur le p. Girard sur l'air que je regrete mon amant," is at BM Dijon, MS 1125 (174), fol. 78–80.

60. "Autre Réflection sur l'habillement des dévotes sur l'air du mirliton," BnF, MS Fr. 23859, fol. 34.

61. "Quatrain," BnF, MS Fr. 23859, fol. 2.

62. Waddington, *Aretino's Satyr*, 14–15; Kulick, "How the Devil Got His Hooves and Horns."

63. "La Colombe et le corbeau," BnF, MS Fr. 23859, fols. 18–19; *Recueil Clairambault-Maurepas*, 5:276–79, and "L'Hirondelle et le moineau," BnF, MS Fr. 23859, fol. 10. Wadsworth, "Art of Allegory in La Fontaine's Fables."

64. "La Colombe et le corbeau," *Recueil Clairambault-Maurepas*, 5:279.

65. The original scheme of this image dates back to the sixteenth century and is a moral critique of the seduction of women. Lamotte, "L'Iconographie dans l'affaire Girard-Cadière," 97–99; Duprat, *Histoire de France par la caricature*, 31.

66. "Avis au public," BnF, MS Fr. 23859, fol. 96. Pieces favorable to Chaudon include "Chanson," ibid., fol. 3; "Chaudon, avocat au parlement d'Aix adressé ces vers à la dlle. Cadière," ibid., fol. 86; "Ode sur le factum de M. Chaudon," Lagoubran, MS 48 (R. 1362), fols. 22–23; "Ode," in *Recueil de diverses pièces nouvelles en prose et en vers pour et contre la Cadière*, Méjanes, MS D2357, 10–13.

67. *Antifactum criti-comique du père Girard, ou réponse anticipée aux*

écrits que M. Pazery donnera un jour au public avec l'aide du Ciel, in vol. 8 of *Recueil général* (La Haye). "Placet ou requeste de la brigade a Momus," BnF, MS Fr. 23859, fol. 139.

68. "Arrest [*sic*] du régiment de la calotte confirmative de celuy qui a été rendu par le parlement d'Aix en faveur du p. Girard," BnF, MS Fr. 23859, fols. 178–180.

69. "Epigramme á Mr. de Faucon," Lagoubran, MS 48 (R. 1362), fol. 254.

70. "Vers," BnF, MS Fr. 23859, fol. 5; "Contre Mr. le Bret PP. du parlement d'Aix," BnF, MS Fr. 23859, fol. 23.

71. Merrick, "Patriarchalism and Constitutionalism"; Tuttle, "Celebrating the *Père de Famille*."

72. *Recueil Clairambault-Maurepas*, 5:289.

73. "Prière et lamentation de Mlle. Cadière Sonnet," BnF, MS Fr. 23859, fol. 57; see also "Calotte sur le Parlement de Aix, Le Dos à Dos du Parlement d'Aix," BnF, MS Fr. 23859, fol. 181.

74. "Vers adressé au parlement d'Aix," BnF, MS Fr. 23589, fol. 72.

75. "Epigramme," *Recueil Clairambault-Maurepas*, 5:290.

76. "Epigramme," BnF, MS Fr. 23589, fol. 17.

77. Hudson, "'From Nation to Race'"; Curran, "Rethinking Race History."

78. *Anatomie de l'arrest rendu*, 14.

79. "Sonnet sur le Parlement d'Aix," BnF, MS 23589, fol. 27.

80. "Affiche," Lagoubran, MS 48 (R. 1362), fols. 307–308.

81. "Chanson, sur l'air sans mon as," BnF, MS 23589, fol. 31; "Sur Messieurs de Mons et de Parade," BnF, MS 23589, fol. 102; "Calotte pour M. Dansouts," BnF, MS 23589, fol.

169; "Brevet pour M. l'avocat de Gueydan," Arbaud, MS MQ 366, piece no. 9.

82. BnF, MS 23589, "Chanson," fol. 3. "Brevet pour m. l'abbé de Charleval," Arbaud, MS MQ 366, piece no. 7.

83. Fabre and Maire, *Les Antijésuites*.

84. *Les Intrigues Secrettes des Jésuites traduites du Monita Secreta*, in Bibliothèque Mazarine, *Jésuitisme*, A 16 000, vol. 1, fols. 325–349. See also Pavone, *Wily Jesuits and the Monita Secreta*.

85. "Le Mouton, l'Agnelle et les chats, fable," BnF, MS 23589, fol. 70.

86. "Avis au public," BnF, MS 23589, fol. 20; see also Lagoubran, MS 48 (R. 1362), fols. 83–83.

87. Smith, *Monsters of the Gévaudan*.

88. "Brevet pour le p. Sabatier," BnF, MS Fr. 23589, fol. 60.

89. Hurteau, "Catholic Moral Discourse on Male Sodomy," 10. See also Trumbach, "Transformation of Sodomy," 832–47.

90. *L'Entrée triomphante du père Girard*, 4.

91. "Désespoir du pere Girard," BnF, MS Fr. 23589, fol. 61.

92. "Épigramme," Lagoubran, MS 48 (R. 1362), fol. 384.

93. "Prophète de Nostrodamus," BnF, MS Fr. 23859, fol. 45.

94. *Réflexions simples et naturelles sur monsieur Pâris et sur le père Girard*, 5. This rare pamphlet is in Méjanes, MS 1497.

95. "Pâris et Girard," BnF, MS Fr. 23859, fol. 87.

96. Gouzi, "L'Image du diacre Pâris," 29–58; Gouzi, *L'Art et le jansénisme*, 147–233.

97. "Le Monde renversé," BnF, MS Fr. 23859, fol. 15; "Epigramme sur les

miracles du p. Girard et de M. Pâris," BM Dijon, MS 1125 (174), fol. 53.

98. D'Anfossy to the marquis de Caumont, August 10, 1731, Ceccano 2277, fol. 223.

99. "Ambigue Girardique," BnF, MS Fr. 23859, fol. 93.

100. On figurism, see Maire, *De la cause de Dieu*, 163–81.

101. Michel, *Jansénisme et Paris*, 384–445; Cottret, *Jansénisme et Lumières*, 253–63; Garrioch, *Formation of the Parisian Bourgeoisie*, 42–62, 86–102. See also Caen-Lyon, *La Boîte à Perrette*.

102. "Désespoir. Elegie en lamentation," BnF, MS Fr. 23589, fol. 105.

103. *Réflexions simples et naturelles*, 4.

104. While the Bibliothèque nationale's copy of this image is entitled "Girar [*sic*] délivré ainsi que Barabbas" the same image at the Bibliothèque de la Société de Port-Royal in Paris is called "The Fruits of the Constitution *Unigenitus*." BNF Hennin, vol. 94, 8216; Bibliothèque de la Société de Port-Royal, 146. The handwriting at the bottom resembles that found in engravings by Bernard Picart. On Picart, see Wachenheim, "Bernard Picart graveur des jansénistes," 333–56.

105. Another mention of Barabbas is found in "Épigramme," BnF, MS Fr. 23589, fol. 42.

106. Isaiah 5:23.

107. "Plainte de la religion sur le bruit que l'affaire du père Girard, et de la soeur Cadiere a fait par tout le monde," BnF, MS Fr. 23589, fols. 40–41.

108. Merrick, "Patriarchalism and Constitutionalism," 321. Mentions of *Unigenitus* and the Council of

Embrun are in "Poème," BnF, MS Fr. 23589, fol. 56; "Ambigue Girardique," ibid., fol. 92; "Calotte sur le Parlement de Aix, Le Dos á Dos du Parlement d'Aix," ibid., fol. 180.

109. "Chanson sur l'air des pendus," BM Dijon, MS 1125 (174), fol. 99.

110. "Edit portant création d'une chambre ardente dans le régiment de la calotte," [1731], in "Recueil de pièces tant en vers, qu'en prose concernant le régiment de la calottes non imprimées, année 1730 à 1743," vol. 2, BnF, MS Fr. 12655, fol. 154.

111. Ibid., fol. 153.

112. Ibid., fols. 152, 155.

113. Ibid., fol. 151; "Ode sur le pére Girard," BnF, MS Fr. 23589, fol. 136.

114. "Autre réponse à l'ode apologétique," BnF, MS Fr. 23589, fol. 8. Another poem depicted two Jesuits who openly state, "our profound politics / which destroys religion / makes us master of this empire." "Lettre anecdote du R. P. Tartuffe au R. P. Cassar supérieur des missions apostoliques," ibid., fol. 176.

115. "J'ay préferé Tarquin à tout autre à cause de son orgeuil et de son usurpation à la souveraineté." *Le Nouveau Tarquin, comédie en trois actes*, in *Recueil général* (La Haye), 1:3, 22.

116. Ibid., 16.

117. *Les Véritables sentimens de mademoiselle Cadière*, in *Recueil général* (La Haye), 1:7.

118. "Vers," BNF, MS Fr. 23589, fol. 1731. Mathieu Marais felt compelled to send the verse to Jean Bouhier in Dijon. Marais, *Journal et mémoire*, 27.

119. Nelson, *Jesuits and the Monarch*, 47–53. De Boyer, marquis d'Argens, *Lettres juives*, 5:67.

120. Henry IV (1553–1610) was assassinated by François Ravaillac in 1610.
121. Jean-Baptiste Chaudon, *Mémoire instructif pour demoiselle Catherine Cadière de la ville de Toulon . . .* , in *Recueil général*, 1:50.
122. *L'Entrée triomphante du père Girard*, 9.
123. "Chanson sur l'air de Diable malicieux et fin," BnF, MS Fr. 23589, fol. 37.
124. "Confrontation mutuelle dans la grand-chambre du p. Jean-Baptiste Girard, et la D. Catherine Cadière. Du 4 octobre 1731," in *Procédure sur laquelle le père Jean-Baptiste Girard . . . ont été jugé*, 399.
125. "Conscience," *Dictionnaire de l'Académie française*, 1st and 4th editions (1694, 1762).
126. Sluhovsky, "Discernment of Difference," 188.
127. Cottret, *Jansénisme et Lumières*, 183.
128. "Réplique a l'abbé de Boismorand auteur du résultat en faveur du père Girard," BNF, MS Fr. 23589, fol. 4.

CHAPTER 8

1. "De Marseille le 14 octobre 1731," BnF, MS Fr. 23680, fol. 135.
2. "D'Aix le 15 octobre 1731," BnF, MS Fr. 23680, fol. 139.
3. "De Marseille le 14 octobre 1731," BnF, MS Fr. 23680, fol. 135.
4. Ibid.
5. "D'Aix le 5 octobre," BnF, MS Fr. 23860, fol. 139.
6. "De Marseille, le 14 octobre 1731," BnF, MS Fr. 23860, fol. 135.
7. "De Toulon le 14 octobre 1731," BnF, MS Fr. 23860, fol. 128.
8. For descriptions of both Toulon incidents, see "Extrait d'une lettre de Toulon du 13 octobre 1731," BnF, MS Fr. 10980, fol. 43; "De Toulon le 14 octobre 1731," fol. 129, and "A Toulon 13 octobre 1731," fol. 133, in BnF, MS Fr. 23860.
9. Buti, "Résonances urbaines de conflits de pêche en Provence," 439–57.
10. "A Toulon le 13 octobre 1731," BnF, MS Fr. 23860, fol. 133.
11. Ibid.
12. On Madame Guiol's predicament, see "A Toulon 13 octobre 1731," BnF, MS Fr. 23860, fol. 133, and "De Toulon le 14 octobre 1731," fols. 128–129.
13. "Copie d'une letter de Toulon du 26 octobre 1731," BnF, MS Fr. 23860, fol. 131.
14. Cook, *Toulon in War and Revolution*, 10.
15. Davis, *Society and Culture in Early Modern France*, 98–100.
16. Le Roy Ladurie, *Carnival in Romans*.
17. Farge and Revel, *Vanishing Children of Paris*.
18. "Copie d'une lettre d'Angers du 12 octobre 1731," BnF, MS Fr. 23860, fol. 131.
19. "De Marseille, le 22 octobre 1731," BnF, MS Fr. 23860, fol. 149.
20. Barbier, *Chronique de la régence*, 2:202–3.
21. "Lettre de Mr. l'évêque de Marseille à Mr. le cardinal de Fleury," BnF, MS Fr. 10980, fols. 67, 71.
22. "Extrait d'une lettre de Toulon du 13 octobre 1731," BnF, MS Fr. 10980, fol. 42.
23. "Recueil de plusieurs actes lettres et autres pièces fugitives concernant l'affaire de la Cadière et du père Girard contenant une relation de tout ce qui s'est passé de plus secret dans les chambres du parlement de

Provence au subject de la même affaire," Méjanes, MS F1095, vol. 2, fol. 130. On Father Nicolas's speech, see "D'Aix le 6 octobre 1731," BnF, MS Fr. 23860, fol. 105.

24. On the speech, see Méjanes, MS F1095, vol. 3, fols. 130–131; quotation taken from BnF, MS Fr. 23860, fol. 105.

25. Méjanes, MS F1095, vol. 3, fol. 131.

26. "D'Aix le 9 octobre 1731," BnF, MS Fr. 23860, fol. 115.

27. "Registre de la Grand-Chambre," BnF, MS Fr. 10980, fol. 106.

28. While the Grand'Chambre and the Chambre de La Tournelle were immersed in civic and criminal cases, the Chambre des Enquêtes was concerned with fiscal affairs.

29. For the official record of this meeting, see "Délibération de Mrs. De la Tournelle et des Enquêtes, assemblée des chambres, au sujet de l'incrimination de Mrs. de Faucon et de Charleval dans leurs interrogatoires d'attenuation," Méjanes, MS 843.

30. Méjanes, MS F1095, vol. 2, fols. 180–181.

31. Ibid., fol. 182.

32. Ibid., fol. 186.

33. Ibid., fol. 178.

34. Ibid., 185.

35. Richer, *Causes célèbres et intéressantes*, 552–53.

36. "A Aix 19 novembre 1731," BnF, MS Fr. 23680, fol. 173.

37. "Quatrième lettre . . . à M. le chancelier," Méjanes, MS 928, fol. 7.

38. On d'Aguesseau, see Storex, *Le Chancelier Henri François d'Aguesseau*, 274–76.

39. Bell, *Lawyers and Citizens*, 92.

40. As quoted in Campbell, *Power and Politics*, 220.

41. Richer, *Causes célèbres et intéressantes*, 557, 561.

42. Van Kley, *Religious Origins of the French Revolution*, 180–90. Barbier repeatedly observed that the "people" of Paris were avid Jansenists whose zeal had been "ignited by a number of priests." Barbier, *Chronique de la régence*, 3:106.

43. Quotation from Bell, *Lawyers and Citizens*, 4.

44. Richer, *Causes célèbres et intéressantes*, 557.

45. "A Marseille le 10 novembre 1731," BnF, MS Fr. 23860, fol. 168; see also Bouhier, *Lettres de Mathieu Marais*, 292. Given the timetable, it is likely that d'Aguesseau's request to the pro-Cadière judges was made in late 1731, and the date of this letter, which was included at the beginning of the *Motifs des juges du parlement de Provence*, was a misprint.

46. "Motif de M. de Faucon, commissaire de procedure," 12 folio pages; "Motifs envoyés a M. le chancelier par m. le premier président," 25 folio pages, Méjanes, MS 928.

47. "Petites circonstances des jugemens," Méjanes, MS 928, fol. 20.

48. Marais, *Journal et mémoires*, 4:468. Boyer de Bandol also appears to have submitted a similar document to d'Aguesseau, which no longer survives. Reference to his motives is made in a letter he wrote to Cardinal Fleury on January 11, 1731. AAE, MS 1735, fol. 26.

49. Marais, *Journal et mémoires*, 469.

50. *Motifs des juges du parlement de Provence, qui ont été d'avis de condamner le p. Jean-Baptiste Girard, envoyez à M. le Chancelier le 31 décembre 1731*, in *Recueil général*, 2:1.

Certain pieces were added by the owner, as suggested by the handwritten additions to the table of contents.

51. Ibid., 2.

52. Maliverny's defense of the pro-Cadière judges appears to have been written toward the end of December 1732 or early 1733. See [Maliverny], *Motifs des juges du parlement de Provence, qui ont été d'avis de condamner le p. Jean-Baptiste Girard* in vol. 2 of *Recueil général*. Montvalon probably based his justification on a detailed "history" of the case he had sent to Le Bret in February 1732. "Histoire du père Girard et de la Cadière, divisé en deux parties." Arbaud, MS MQ 365.

53. [André de Barrigue de Montvalon], *Lettres écrites d'Aix sur le procez du père Girard et de la Cadière*, 1.

54. Ibid., 28.

55. Ibid., 20.

56. *Motifs des juges du parlement de Provence . . . troisième édition. Avec des notes critiques tirées de la procedure et les lettres écrites* (n.p., 1733), 1.

57. Marais, *Journal et mémoires*, 489.

58. "Mémoire sur l'affaire du père Girard et de la Cadière," May 3, 1732, AAE, MS 1735, fols. 153–155.

59. Ardoin, *La Bulle "Unigenitus,"* 1:38–39.

60. "Extrait d'une lettre de Marseille, 21 decembre 1731," BnF, MS Fr. 23860, fol. 177.

61. AAE, MS 1735, fols. 175–176.

62. Ibid., fols. 185–186.

63. "Extrait d'une lettre de Marseille, 21 décembre 1731," BnF, MS Fr. 23860, fol. 177.

64. Ibid.; "Extrait d'une lettre de Marseille du janvier 1732, " BnF, MS Fr. 23860, 181; AAE, MS 1735, fol. 186.

65. "De Marseille, le 14 octobre 1731," BnF, MS Fr. 23860, fol. 135.

66. AAE, MS 1735, fols. 185–186.

67. "De Marseille, le 10 may 1731," BnF, MS Fr. 23860, fol. 196.

68. AAE, MS 1735, fols. 53, 182. On Autheman and Caveirac's address, see *Suite des Nouvelles Ecclésiastiques,* April 20, 1732, 78–79.

69. AAE, MS 1735, fols. 182–183; "De Marseille, le 14 octobre 1731," BnF, MS Fr. 23860, fol. 136.

70. "De Marseille, le 14 octobre 1731," BnF, MS Fr. 23860, fol. 196.

71. AAE, MS 1735, fol. 187.

72. AAE, MS 1735, fol. 182; "De Marseille, le 14 octobre 1731," BnF, MS Fr. 23860, fol. 138; "De Marseille, le 31 octobre 1731," ibid., fol. 163.

73. Duclos, *Voyage en Italie,* 170.

74. Thomassin de Mazaugues to the marquis de Caumont, August 24, 1731, Ceccano, MS 2372, fol. 75.

75. AAE, MS 1735, fol. 177.

76. Ibid., fol. 188.

77. "15 janvier [1732] de Marseille," BnF, MS Fr. 23860, fol. 185.

78. On Le Bret's discussion on Chaudon, see AAE, MS 1735, fols. 151–152.

79. "Lettre de M. l'évêque de Marseille à m. le cardinal de Fleury," BnF, MS Fr. 10980, fol. 69.

80. "Mandement de M. l'évêque de Sisteron contre les ouvrages de l'avocat Chaudon," BnF, MS Fr. 10980, fol. 72; AAE, MS 1735, fol. 342.

81. Thomassin de Mazaugues to the marquis de Caumont, "6 novembre 1731," Ceccano, MS 2372, fol. 83. *Dénonciation des factums de M. Chaudon, avocat de la Dlle. Cadière,* in *Recueil général* (La Haye).

82. "Mandement de Mr. l'évêque de Sisteron contre les ouvrages de l'avocat Chaudon," BnF, MS Fr. 10980, fols 73–74.
83. Belsunce, *Lettre de M. l'évêque de Marseille à la très-honorée soeur Marie-Agnes de Greard*, 3.
84. Ibid.
85. "Mandement de Mr. l'évêque de Sisteron contre les ouvrages de l'avocat Chaudon," BnF, MS Fr. 10980, fol. 73.
86. AAE, MS 1735, fol. 95.
87. Ibid., fol. 96.
88. Ibid., fol. 104.
89. Ibid., fol. 105.
90. "A Marseille, le 23 octobre, 1731," BnF, MS Fr. 23860, fol. 152.
91. "De Marseille," BnF, MS Fr. 23860, fol. 184.
92. AAE, MS 1735, fol. 169.
93. Ibid., fol. 167.
94. The governess for Boyer de Bandol's son revealed that Gaufridy had visited the *président* at his country home in Valbrillant. Ibid., fol. 161.
95. Richer, *Causes célèbres et intéressantes*, 554.
96. AAE, MS 1735, fol. 167.
97. Ibid., fol. 168.
98. Ibid., fol. 184.
99. Ibid., fol. 175.
100. Ibid., fols. 161, 171.
101. Ibid., fol. 187.
102. Ibid., fol. 162.
103. "Copie de la lettre par M. l'évêque de Viviers à m. l'abbé d'Oppéde, aumônier au roy," BnF, MS Fr. 10980, fol. 68.
104. "15 janvier [1732] de Marseille," BnF, MS Fr. 23860, fol. 185. A similar mission was launched in Aix in 1733. *Relation de la mission faite à Aix en Provence.*
105. *Suite des Nouvelles Ecclésiastiques*, April 14, 1732, 74; "De Marseille," BnF, MS Fr. 23860, fols. 183–184.
106. "A Marseille, le 9 février 1732," BnF, MS Fr. 23860, fol. 189.
107. *Suite des Nouvelles Ecclésiastiques*, November 24, 1732, 227.
108. AAE, MS 1735, fol. 171.
109. Ibid., fol. 164.
110. Ibid., fol. 161.
111. "Remontrances sur l'arrêt du conseil du 30 juillet évoquant l'appel comme d'abus interjeté contre une ordonnance de l'archevêque de Paris," in Flammermont, *Remontrances du parlement de Paris au XVIIIe siècle*, 1:273.
112. AAE, MS 1735, fol. 163.
113. Cabasse, *Essais historiques sur le parlement de Provence*, 3:282.
114. Richer, *Causes célèbres et intéressantes*, 539.
115. Ibid., 497; Marais, *Journal et mémoires*, 311.
116. On Gastaud's death, see *Suite des Nouvelles Ecclésiastiques*, April 14, 1732, 73.
117. Richer, *Causes célèbres et intéressantes*, 499; "Copie d'une lettre du M. l'évêque Viviers au p. Girard jésuite du 14 Novembre 1731," BnF, MS Fr. 23860, fol. 169; Marais, *Journal et mémoires*, 326; *Relation historique, très-curieuse et très intéressante, de la vie et de la mort de Messire Jean-André Audibert*, 43.
118. "Copie de la lettre par M. l'évêque de Viviers à m. l'abbé d'Oppéde, aumônier au roy," BnF, MS Fr. 10980, fol. 63.
119. BA, AB, MS 10161, fol. 154.
120. *Éloges funèbre du rr. Pp. Girard, par les rr. Pp. jésuites de Dôle avec les d'un j. de Paris*, in *Recueil général*, 2:2.

121. BA, AB, MS 10164, fols. 135, 143.
122. On Father Nicolas's departure from Aix, see "De Marseille le 14 octobre 1731," BnF, MS Fr. 23860, fol. 137; on the friar's fate after, see "A Avignon, le 17 may 1732," ibid., fols. 194–195.
123. "A Aix, le 24 octobre 1731," BnF, MS Fr. 23860, fol. 155.
124. Richer, *Causes célèbres et intéressantes*, 533–37.
125. Marais, *Journal et mémoires*, 313.
126. Richer, *Causes célèbres et intéressantes*, 538.
127. BA, AB, MS 10164, fol. 28.

EPILOGUE

1. De Brosses, *Lettres familières écrites d'Italie*, 1:43.
2. Ibid., xlviii–xlix.
3. Barbier, *Chronique de la régence*, 7:497. Van Kley, *Damiens Affair*.
4. Van Kley, *Damiens Affair*, 86, 296–97.
5. Van Kley, *Jansenists and the Expulsion of the Jesuits*, 35.
6. Ibid., 90–107.
7. Ibid., 97.
8. Ibid., 173.
9. *Relation de ce qui s'est passé au parlement d'Aix dans l'affaire des jésuites*, 2.
10. Ibid., 24.
11. Van Kley, *Jansenists and the Expulsion of the Jesuits*, 196.
12. *Compte rendu des constitutions des jésuites, par M. Jean-Pierre-François de Ripert de Montclar*, 171.
13. Ibid., 16.
14. *Plaidoyer de M. de Ripert de Monclar*, 172; *Compte rendu des constitutions*, 82. The accusation of Quietism was notably absent in the Parisian *procureur-général* La

Chatolais's *compte rendu* delivered six months earlier.
15. *Plaidoyer de M. de Ripert de Monclar*, 112.
16. Ibid., 10.
17. Van Kley, *Jansenists and the Expulsion of the Jesuits*, 198; quotation taken from 200–201.
18. [Jouin], *Procès contre les Jésuites pour servir de suite aux causes célèbres*, 203.
19. In 1762, Voltaire defended the Protestant Calas family in Toulouse from false accusations regarding the death of the younger son, Marc-Antoine. See Bien, *Calas Affair*. Although he never devoted a work exclusively to the Cadière affair, Voltaire referenced the trial in fifteen works. Lamotte, "Voltaire, le jésuite et la pénitente."
20. D'Alembert, *Sur la destruction des jésuites en France*, 2:109.
21. On the debates regarding the authorship of *Thérèse philosophe*, see Lamotte, "L'Affaire Girard-Cadière," 2:616–20; Moreau, "preface," *Thérèse philosophe*, 14–27.
22. Domenech, "L'Image du père Girard," 41–53.
23. Chammas, "Le clergé et l'inceste spirituel," 687–704.
24. Jacobs, "Materialist World of Pornography," 201.
25. Translation taken from Darnton, *Forbidden Best-Sellers*, 93; see Darnton's analysis of the novel, 89–114.
26. Brown, "Female *Philosophe* in the Closet," 92–116.
27. Merrick, *Desacralization of the French Monarchy*.
28. For a more extensive discussion of the Girard/Cadière affair in

nineteenth-century France, see
Lamotte, "L'Affaire Girard-Cadière,"
2:641–59.

29. DeToledo, Palmerola, and
Lowe, "Sexual Molestation and
Psychogenic Seizures"; Guignard-
Vanuxem and Fleur, L'Odeur du
bûcher. On the affair in current fic-
tion, see Lamotte, "L'Affaire Girard-
Cadière," 2:660–67.

30. On Michelet, see Moody, "French
Anticlericalism"; Chase, "Jules
Michelet and the Nineteenth-
Century Concept of Insanity," 740.

31. Céard, "Démonologie et démonopathies au temps de Charcot," 337–43;
Sentuc, "Mysticisme hystérique." The
latter examines the convulsionnaires.

32. Goldstein, "Hysteria Diagnosis,"
209–39; Harris, "The 'Unconscious'
and Catholicism in France," 331–54.

33. The Archives départementales des
Bouches-du-Rhône in Aix-en-
Provence featured the trial in an
exhibit on criminality in the fall of
2004: Crimes et châtiments à Aix-en-
Provence: Une Chronique judiciaire
17e–20e siècles.

Bibliography

PRIMARY SOURCES

Manuscripts

Archives départementales des Bouches-du-Rhône, Aix-en-Provence (ADBR)
  B 3405: Royal patent letters and decrees
  B 5600: Parlementary *arrêt*
  Theta 11: Documents pertaining to Girard/Cadière trial

Archives du Ministère aux Affaires étrangères, Paris (AAE)
  1735 *mémoire* and documents, Provence, 1732

Archives municipales, Toulon (AM Toulon)
  GG 81, 82, 102, 103, 640, *Procès Girard-Cadière*: Largely marriage, birth, and death records

Bibliothèque de la Société de Port-Royal, Paris
  146: "Les Fruits de Constitution *Unigenitus*"
  1095: Image of François de Pâris in prayer

Bibliothèque Méjanes, Aix-en-Provence (Méjanes)
  843: MS deliberation of lower chambers on Faucon and Charleval
  999–1000 (927–928): MS *relation* and printed materials pertaining to Grand'Chambre proceedings
  D 2357: Printed material
  F1095, vols. 1–4: Letters, narratives, and songs pertaining to Girard/Cadière trial
  1632 (1497): *Mémoires judiciaires* with annotations, and pamphlet comparing François de Pâris and Jean-Baptiste Girard

Bibliothèque municipale d'Avignon, Mediathèque Ceccano, Avignon (Ceccano)
  2371, 2372, 6807: Correspondence between marquis de Caumont, Monsieur d'Anfossy, and Thomassin de Mazaugues

Bibliothèque municipale, Dijon (BM Dijon)
  1125 (174): Transcribed songs, letters, and *mémoires judiciaires* as well as a joint image of Catherine

Cadière and Jean-Baptiste
Girard

Bibliothèque municipale, dépôt
Lagoubran, Toulon (Lagoubran)
48: Transcribed *Recueil des poésies
sur l'affaire du père Girard,
jésuite avec la demoiselle
Catherine Cadière, le père
Cadière dominicain, l'abbé
Cadière et le père Nicolas Carme
déchaussé,* 1731

Bibliothèque nationale de France, Paris
(BnF)
Bibliothèque de l'Arsenal
Archives de la Bastille (BA,
AB), 10161
Collection Clairambault
569: "Réflexion sur la relation
de l'affaire de Mademoiselle
Cadiere"
Manuscrits français (MS Fr.)
Volumes 10980, 12655, 23589,
23860, 23861: Correspondence,
narratives, and poems related
to the trial

Musée Paul Arbaud, Aix-en-Provence
(Arbaud)
1878 A: Letters
C.C. I 96: Portraits
M 124: Portraits of Girard/Cadière
MD 76–77: Two MS volumes con-
taining verses and pamphlets
MQ 366: Montvalon's manuscript
history of the trial sent to Le
Bret
Port III, IX: Portraits of magistrates

Other Primary Sources

d'Alembert, Jean Le Rond. *Sur la destruction des jésuites en France.* 1765. In
Oeuvres complètes de d'Alembert. 5
vols. Geneva: Slatkine Reprints, 1967.

*Anatomie de l'arrêt rendu par le parlement
de Provence.* [Marseille, 1731?].
[Annat, François]. *Le Libelle intitulé
"Théologie morale des Jésuites," con-
tredit et convaincu en tous ses chefs
par un P. théologien de la Compagnie
de Jésus.* [Cahors], 1644.
Antrechaux, Jean d'. *Relation de la peste
dont la ville de Toulon fut affligée en
1721, avec des observations pour la
posterité.* Paris: Frères Estienne, 1756.
Argenson, Charles-Marc-René de Voyer
de Paulmy, marquis d'. *Mémoires et
journal inédit du marquis d'Argenson,
ministre des affaires étrangères sous
Louis XV.* 5 vols. Paris, 1857. Reprint,
Nedeln: Kraus, 1979.
Barbier, Édmond-Jean-François.
*Chronique de la régence et du
règne de Louis XV (1718–1763), ou
Journal de Barbier.* 8 vols. Paris:
Charpentier, 1857–66.
[de Barrigue, André, de Montvalon].
*Lettres écrites d'Aix sur le procez du
père Girard et de la Cadière, tirées de
la procédure pour servir de réponse
aux Motifs.* Aix: René Adibert,
[1733].
Belsunce de Castelmoron, Henri-
François-Xavier. *Lettre de M. l'évêque
de Marseille à la très-honorée soeur
Marie-Agnès de Greard.* Marseille:
Brebion, 1732.
Bossuet, Jacques-Bénigne. *Politics
Drawn from the Very Words of
Holy Scripture.* Translated and
edited by Patrick Riley. Cambridge:
Cambridge University Press, 1990.
Bouhier, Jean. *Lettres de Mathieu
Marais (1730–1732).* Vol. 4 of
*Correspondance littéraire du
président Bouhier,* edited by Henri
Duranton. Saint-Étienne: Université
de Saint-Étienne, 1984.

de Boyer, Jean Baptiste, marquis d'Argens. *Mémoires du marquis d'Argens: Contenant le récit des aventures de sa jeunesse, des anecdotes et des observations sur plusieurs événemens du règne de Louis XV, et des personnes de ce temps.* Edited by Jacques Peuchet. Paris: F. Buisson, 1807.

[———]. *Thérèse philosophe ou Mémoires pour servir à l'histoire du P. Dirrag, et de Mademoiselle Éradice.* In *Oeuvres anonymes du XVIIIe siècle.* 3 vols. Paris: Fayard, 1986.

Broglie, Emmanuel. *Les Portefeuilles du président Bouhier. Extraits et fragments de correspondances littéraires (1715–1746).* Paris: Hachette, 1896.

de Brosses, Charles. *Lettres familières écrites d'Italie en 1739 et 1740.* Edited by R. Colomb. 2 vols. Paris: P. Didier, 1869.

Buti, Gilbert. "Résonances urbaines de conflits de pêche en Provence (XVIIe–XIX siècles)." *Provence historique* 50, no. 202 (2000): 439–57.

The case of Mrs. Mary Catharine Cadiere, against the Jesuit Father John Baptist Girard. In a memorial presented to the Parliament of Aix. . . . With a preface by the publisher, Containing a short and plain Account of the Rules of proceeding according to the Laws and Customs of France in Cases of this Nature. The sixth edition corrected. London, [1732].

A compleat translation of the whole case of Mary Catherine Cadiere, against the Jesuite Father John Baptist Girard, in a memorial, presented to the Parliament of Aix, in which the Jesuit is accused of seducing her. London: J. Millan, 1732.

Compte rendu des constitutions des jésuites, par M. Jean-Pierre-François de Ripert de Montclar, procureur-général du roy au parlement de Provence, les 28 mai, 3 & 4 juin 1762, 1762.

Défense du discours de monsieur de Gaufridy, avocat général du parlement d'Aix du 22 mai dernier . . . addressée aux RR. PP. jésuites. N.p., 1716.

Duclos, Charles. *Voyage en Italie, ou considérations sur l'italie, par feu M. Duclos, historiographe de France, secrétaire perpétuel de l'Académie Françoise, etc.* Maastricht: J. P. Roux, 1793.

Du Plessis, Louis-François-Armand de Vignerot. *Mémoires du maréchal duc de Richelieu,* ed. Fs. Barrière. 2 vols. Paris: Firmin-Didot, 1858.

L'Entrée triomphante du père Girard, jésuite, aux enfers, suivie de son retour sur la terre. Les ides d'octobre 1731. Rome: Les Frères Gherardi, [1731].

Extrait d'une lettre de Monseigneur l'évêque d'Auxerre au sujet de la vie de Marie-à-la Coque, composée par M. l'Archevêque de Sens. [1732].

Factum oder Vertheidigungs-Schrifft Marien Catharinen Cadiere, wider den Pater Johann Baptist Girard, einem Jesuiten . . . Aus dem Frantzösischen übersetzet, etc. Cologne, 1732.

Fielding, Henry. *The Debauchees: or, the Jesuit Caught. A Comedy as it is acted at the Theater-Royal in Drury Lane.* London: J. Watts, 1746.

Flammermont, Jules. *Remontrances du Parlement de Paris au XVIIIe siècle.* Vol. 60, pt. 1, of *Collection de documents inédits sur l'histoire de France.* Paris: Imprimerie Nationale, 1888.

La Foire de Beaucaire; Nouvelle historique et galante. Amsterdam: Paul Marret, 1708.

Gaufridy, Jean-François. *Histoire de Provence*. 2 vols. Aix: Charles David, 1694.

[Gissey de Bordelet]. *Histoire du père Jean-Baptiste Girard jésuite, et de la delle. Marie-Catherine Cadière, divisée en 32 planches*. Paris, 1730 [*sic*].

Historische print- en dicht-tafereelen van Jan Baptiste Girard, en juffrou Maria Catharina Cadiere. N.p., 1735.

Ignatius of Loyola. *Personal Writings: Reminiscences, Spiritual Diary, Select Letters Including the Text of The Spiritual Exercises*. Translated and edited by Joseph A. Munitz and Philip Endean. New York: Penguin Books, 1996.

Il est temps de parler, ou compte rendu au public des oeuvres légales de Mr. Ripert de Montclar, et des événemens passés en Provence, à Paris, etc. à l'occasion des jésuites. Nouvelle édition, corrigée et augmentée. Vol. 1 of 2. Arles: Pierre Le Franc, 1764.

Les Intrigues secrettes des Jésuites traduites du Monita Secreta où l'on a joint l'extrait de la faculté de Théologie de Paris de l'an 1554 et la prophétie de Sainte Hildegarde morte 1181. N.p., 1729.

Jaucourt, Louis, and Denis Diderot. "Jesuit." In *The Encyclopedia of Diderot and d'Alembert Collaborative Translation Project*. Translated by Jason T. Kuznicki. Ann Arbor, Mich.: MPublishing, University of Michigan Library, 2003. http://hdl.handle.net/2027/spo .did2222.0000.033.

Jingle, Jeremy. *Spiritual fornication. A burlesque poem. Wherein the case of Miss Cadière and Father Girard are merrily display'd. In three canto'*. London: H. Cooke, [1732].

[Jouin, Nicolas]. *Procès contre les jésuites pour servir de suite aux causes célèbres*. Brest, 1750.

Languet de Gergy, Jean-Joseph. *La Vie de la vénérable mère Marguerite-Marie, religieuse de la Visitation Sainte Marie du monastère de Paray-le Monial en Charolais. Morte en odeur de sainteté en 1690*. Paris: Mazieres and Garnier, 1729.

Lettres de messire Jean Soanen évêque de Senez. 2 vols. Cologne: Aux dépens de la Compagnie, 1750.

Lettres écrites d'Aix, pendant le procez du père Girard, et de la Cadière; contenant plusieurs anecdotes curieuses dont le Public n'est pas encore instruit. N.p., [1731].

The Life of St. Teresa of Jesus, of the Order of Our Lady of Carmel. Translated by David Lewis. http://www.guten-berg.org/dirs/etext05/8trsa10h. htm#prologue.

Madame de Sévigné, de sa famille et de ses amis, etc. Edited by M. Monmerqué. 12 vols. Paris: Hachette, 1862.

Marais, Mathieu. *Journal et mémoires de Mathieu Marais avocat au parlement de Paris sur la régence et le règne de Louis XV (1715–1737)*. Edited by Adolphe de Lescure. 4 vols. Paris: Firmin-Didot, 1868.

Maurice de Toulon. *Traité de la peste et des moyens de s'en preserver. Abregé et réimprimé avec d'autres remedes tirez d'ailleurs par les soins du père André François de Tournon, capuchin*. Lyon: Frères Bruyset, 1720.

Mémoires pour servir à l'histoire de la calotte. Nouvelle édition, augmentée des III et IV parties. Première partie. Aux états Calotins: De l'imprimerie calotine, 1752.

Motifs des juges du parlement de Provence, qui ont été d'avis de condamner le p. Jean-Baptiste Girard, envoyez à M. le Chancelier le 31 décembre 1731. Ensemble la lettre de ce magistratà Mr. le président de Maliverny: la réponse de ce juge, et celle des autres messieurs qui ont été de son opinion. N.p., 1733.

Narbonne, Pierre. *Journal de Police.* 2 vols. Paris: Éditions Paleo, 2002.

Nugent, Thomas. *The Grand Tour; or, A Journey through the Netherlands, Germany, Italy, and France.* 4 vols. London: J. Rivington and Sons, 1778.

Pascal, Blaise. *The Provincial Letters.* Translated by Thomas McCrie. New York: Modern Library, 1941.

Phélypeaux, Jean. *Relation de l'origine, du progrès et de la condamnation du quiétisme répandu en France avec plusieurs anecdotes curieuses.* N.p., 1732.

Pièces historiques sur la peste de Marseille et d'une partie de la Provence, en 1720, 1721 et 1722. 2 vols. Marseille: Chez les Principaux Libraires, 1820.

Plaidoyer de M. de Ripert de Monclar, procureur-général du roi au parlement de Provence, dans l'affaire des soi-disans jésuites, [1763].

Playstowe, Philip. *The gentleman's guide in his tour through France, with a correct map of all the post-roads, the experience of travelling in a post-chaise, stage coach, or inland water carriage.* 9th ed. London: G. Kearsley, 1777.

"Poèmes satiriques du XVIIIe siècle." Université Jean Monnet, Institut Claude Longeon. https://satires18.univ-st-etienne.fr/présentation.

Portrait au naturel des Jesuites et anciens ou modernes: ou image véritable du premier et du dernier siècle de la société de Jésus fin du parallèle de la doctrine des payens avec celle des Jesuites et de la Bulle Unigenitus. Amsterdam: Nicolas Potier, 1731.

Portrait des jésuites dont les traits sont tirez de la Constitution "Unigenitus", adressé à son Éminence Monseigneur le Cardinal de Fleury, premier ministre de France. [1734/35].

Procédure sur laquelle le père Jean-Baptiste Girard, jésuite, Catherine Cadière, le père Estienne-Thomas Cadière dominicain, Mre. François Cadière prêtre, et le père Nicholas de S. Joseph carme déchaussé ont été jugé par arrêt du parlement de Provence, du 10 octobre 1731. Aix: Joseph David, 1733.

Ravaisson, François, ed. *Archives de la Bastille. Documents inédits.* 19 vols. Paris: Durand et Pedone-Lauriei, 1866–1904.

Recueil Clairambault-Maurepas: Chansonnier historique du XVIIIe siècle. Edited by Emile Raunié. 10 vols. Paris: A. Quantin, 1880–84.

Recueil de lettres du p. Girard et de la demoiselle Cadière, dont les originaux ont été produits au procès. Réflexions générals sur ces lettres. N.p., [1731].

Recueil général des pièces concernant le procez entre la demoiselle Cadière, de la ville de Toulon; et le père Girard, jésuite. 8 vols. La Haye: Swart, 1731.

Recueil général des pièces concernant le procez entre la demoiselle Cadière de la ville de Toulon. Et le père Girard, jésuite, recteur du séminaire royal de la marine de ladite ville. 2 vols. N.p., 1731.

Recueil général des pièces contenues au procez du père Jean-Baptiste Girard, jésuite, recteur du séminaire de Toulon, et de demoiselle Catherine

Cadière, querellante. 5 vols. Aix:
Joseph David, 1731.

*Réflexions simples et naturelles sur
monsieur Pâris et sur le père Girard.*
Amsterdam: Nicolas Potier, 1733.

*Relation de ce qui s'est passé au parlement
d'Aix dans l'affaire des jésuites, depuis
le 6 mars 1762, 1763.*

*Relation de la mission faite à Aix en
Provence au mois de may 1733. Par
les pères jésuites.* [1733].

*Relation historique, très-curieuse et très
intéressante, de la vie et de la mort de
Messire Jean-André Audibert, curé de
la métropole Saint-Saveur de la ville
d'Aix en Provence.* France, 1780.

Richer, François. *Causes célèbres et
intéressantes avec les jugemens qui
les on décidées.* Amsterdam: Michel
Rhey, 1772.

Saint-Fonds, François Bottu de la
Barmond, and Laurent Dugas de
Bois Saint-Just. *Correspondance littéraire et anécdotique entre Monsieur
de Saint Fonds et le president Dugas,
membres de l'académie de Lyon, 1711-
1739.* Edited by William Podebard. 2
vols. Lyon: Mathieu Paquet, 1900.

Saint-Simon, Louis de Rouvroy, duc de.
*Memoirs of the Duc de Saint-Simon
on the Times of Louis XIV and the
Regency.* Translated by Katherine
Prescott Wormeley. 4 vols. Boston:
Hardy, Pratt, 1902.

Sales, Francis de. *An Introduction to a
Devout Life.* New York: Fredrick
Pustet, 1920.

Smollett, Tobias. *Travels through France
and Italy.* Evanston, Ill.: Marlboro
Press/Northwestern, 1997.

*Suite des procédures de Catherine Cadière,
contre le révérende père Girard,
contenant la réponse au mémoire
instructif de ce jésuite.* La Haye:
Henri Scheurleer, 1731.

*La Vie de la très honorée Soeur Anne-
Magdelaine Rémuzat, religieuse de
la Visitation Sainte-Marie, morte
en odeur de sainteté dans le premier
monastère de Marseille.* Marseille:
Brebion, 1760.

*Vie de la Vénérée soeur Anne-Madeleine
Rémuzat, décédée le 15 février 1730 au
premier monastère de la Visitation
Sainte-Marie.* Lyon and Paris: Félix
Girard, 1868.

Villeneuve, François de. *Lettre de
Monseigneur évêque de Viviers au p.
Girard.* 1731. *The Wanton Jesuit: or,
Innocence seduced. A New Ballad
Opera. As it is acted at the New
Theatre in the Hay-Market.* London:
J. Millan, 1731.

Young, Arthur. *Arthur Young's Travels
in France during the Years 1787,
1788, 1789.* Edited by Miss Betham-
Edwards. London: George Bell, 1906.

SECONDARY SOURCES

Agulhon, Maurice. *Histoire de Toulon.*
Toulouse: Privat, 1980.
———. *Pénitents et Francs-Maçons de
l'ancienne Provence.* Paris: Fayard,
1968.

Ardoin, Paul. *La Bulle "Unigenitus" dans
les diocèses d'Aix, Marseille, Fréjus,
Toulon.* 2 vols. Marseille: Imprimerie
Saint Lazare, 1936.

Armogathe, Jean-Robert. *Le Quiétisme.*
Paris: Presses Universitaires de
France, 1973.

Armstrong-Partida, Michelle. "Priestly
Wives: The Role and Acceptance of
Clerics' Concubines in the Parishes
of Late Medieval Catalunya."
Speculum 88, no. 1 (2013): 166–214.

Baecque, Antoine de. "Les Éclats du rire: Le Régiment de la calotte, ou les stratégies aristocratiques de la gaieté française (1702–1752)." *Annales: Histoire, Sciences Sociales* 52 (May–June 1997): 477–511.

Baker, Keith Michael. *Inventing the French Revolution: Essays on French Political Culture in the Eighteenth Century.* Cambridge: Cambridge University Press, 1990.

Balsama, George. "Madame Guyon, Heterodox. . . ." *Church History* 42 (September 1973): 350–65.

Beik, William. *A Social and Cultural History of Early Modern France.* Cambridge: Cambridge University Press, 2009.

Bell, David A. *Lawyers and Citizens: The Making of a Political Elite in Old Regime France.* New York: Oxford University Press, 1994.

Benimeli, J. A. Ferrer. "Le Procès fait aux jésuites en France et en Espagne." *Revue de l'histoire de l'Église de France* 90 (2004): 227–37.

Bergin, Joseph. *Church, Society, and Religious Change in France, 1580–1730.* New Haven: Yale University Press, 2009.

———. *The Politics of Religion in Early Modern France.* New Haven: Yale University Press, 2014.

Berlanstein, Lenard R. *Daughters of Eve: A Cultural History of French Theater Women from the Old Regime to the Fin de Siècle.* Cambridge, Mass.: Harvard University Press, 2001.

Bernos, Marcel. *Les Sacrements dans la France des XVIIe et XVIIIe siècles: Pastorale et vécu des fidèles.* Aix-en-Provence: Université de Provence, 2007.

———. "La Sexualité et les confesseurs à l'époque moderne." *Revue de l'histoire des religions* 209, no. 4 (1992): 413–26.

———. "Des Sources maltraitées pour l'époque moderne: Manuels de confession et recueils de cas de conscience." *Revue d'histoire de l'Église de France* 86 (2000): 479–92.

Bertrand, Régis. "La Peste en Provence aux temps modernes." *Provence historique* 189 (1997): 401–12.

Bever, Edward. "Witchcraft Prosecutions and the Decline of Magic." *Journal of Interdisciplinary History* 40 (Autumn 2009): 263–93.

Bien, David. *The Calas Affair: Persecution, Toleration, and Heresy in Eighteenth-Century Toulouse.* Princeton: Princeton University Press, 1960.

Bilinkoff, Jodi. *Related Lives: Confessors and Their Female Penitents, 1460–1750.* Ithaca: Cornell University Press, 2005.

Birn, Raymond. *Royal Censorship of Books in Eighteenth-Century France.* Stanford: Stanford University Press, 2012.

Black, Jeremy. "France in 1730: A Tourist's Account." *Francia. 2 Fruhe Neuzeit* 16, no. 2 (1989): 39–59.

Blaufarb, Rafe. *The Politics of Fiscal Privilege in Provence, 1530s–1830s.* Washington, D.C.: Catholic University of America Press, 2012.

Bohanan, Donna. *Old and New Nobility in Aix-en-Provence, 1600–1695: Portrait of an Urban Elite.* Baton Rouge: Louisiana State University Press, 1992.

Bonnefon, Paul. "Diderot prisonnier à Vincennes." *Revue d'histoire littéraire de la France* 6, no. 2 (1899): 200–224.

Bossy, John. "The Social History of Confession in the Age of Reformation." *Transactions of the Royal Historical Society*, 5th ser., 25 (1975): 21–38.

Briggs, Robin. *Communities of Belief: Cultural and Social Tension in Early Modern France*. Oxford: Clarendon Press, 1989.

———. *Witches and Neighbors: The Social and Cultural Context of European Witchcraft*. New York: Viking, 1996.

Broekhuysen, Arthur. "The Quietist Movement and Miguel de Molinos." *Journal of Religion and Psychical Research* 14, no. 3 (1991): 139–43.

Brown, Diane Berrett. "The Female *Philosophe* in the Closet: The *Cabinet* and the Senses in French Erotic Novels, 1740–1800." *Journal for Early Modern Cultural Studies* 9 (Fall/Winter 2009): 92–116.

Bruneau, Marie-Florine. *Women Mystics Confront the Modern World: Marie de l'Incarnation (1599–1672) and Madame Guyon (1648–1717)*. Albany: State University of New York Press, 1998.

Burke, Peter. *Popular Culture in Early Modern Europe*. New York: Harper and Row, 1978.

Cabasse, Prosper. *Essais historiques sur le parlement de Provence, depuis son origine jusqu'à sa suppression, 1501–1790*. 3 vols. Paris: A. Pihan Delaforest, 1826.

Caen-Lyon, Nicolas. *La Boîte à Perrette: Le jansénisme parisien au XVIIIe siècle*. Paris: Albin Michel, 2010.

Cagnac, Moïse. *De l'appel comme d'abus dans l'ancien droit français*. Paris: Libraire Poussielgue, 1906.

Calder, Andrew. "Molière, le Tartuffe and Anti-Jesuit Propaganda." *Zeitschrift für Religions- und Geistesgeschichte* 28, no. 3 (1976): 303–23.

Campbell, Peter R. *Power and Politics in Old Regime France, 1720–1745*. London: Routledge, 1996.

Campbell, Peter R., Thomas E. Kaiser, and Marisa Linton. *Conspiracy in the French Revolution*. Manchester: Manchester University Press, 2007.

Céard, Jean. "Démonologie et démonopathies au temps de Charcot." *Histoire des sciences médicales* 28, no. 4 (1994): 337–43.

Certeau, Michel de. *The Mystic Fable*. Translated by Michael B. Smith. Chicago: University of Chicago Press, 1992.

Chammas, Jacqueline. "Le Clergé et l'inceste spirituel dans trois romans du XVIIIe siècle: *Le Porter des Chartreux, Thérèse philosophe* et *Margot la ravaudeuse*." *Eighteenth-Century Fiction* 15, no. 3 (2003): 687–704.

Chase, Richard R., Jr. "Jules Michelet and the Nineteenth-Century Concept of Insanity: A Romantic's Reinterpretation." *French Historical Studies* 17 (Spring 1992): 725–46.

Chaunu, Pierre, Madeleine Foisil, and Françoise de Noirfontaine. *Le Basculement religieux de Paris au XVIIIe siècle*. Paris: Fayard, 1998.

Choudhury, Mita. "A Betrayal of Trust: The Jesuits and Quietism in Eighteenth-Century France." *Common Knowledge* 15, no. 2 (2009): 164–80.

———. "'Carnal Quietism': Embodying Anti-Jesuit Polemics in the Catherine Cadière Affair, 1731." *Eighteenth-Century Studies* 39, no. 2 (2006): 173–86.

————. *Convents and Nuns in French Politics and Culture.* Ithaca: Cornell University Press, 2004.

————. "Female Mysticism and the Public Sphere in Eighteenth-Century France." In *Under the Veil,* edited by Katherine Quinsey, 145–71. Newcastle: Cambridge Scholars Press, 2012.

————. "An Unlikely Pair: Satire and Jansenism in the *Sarcelades,* 1731–1764." *French Historical Studies* 36 (2013): 543–70.

Clapiers-Collongues, Balthasar de. *Chronologie des officiers des cours souveraines de Provence.* Aix-en-Provence: B. Niel, 1904.

Coleman, Charly J. *The Virtues of Abandon: An Anti-Individualist History of the French Enlightenment.* Stanford: Stanford University Press, 2014.

Collins, James B. *The State in Early Modern France.* Cambridge: Cambridge University Press, 1995.

Collomp, Alain. "Alliance et filiation en haute Provence au XVIIIe siècle." *Annales: Histoire, Sciences Sociales* 32, no. 3 (1977): 445–77.

————. *La Maison du père: Famille et village en Haute-Provence au XVIIe et XVIIIe siècles.* Paris: Presses Universitaires de France, 1983.

Constantin, Hervé. *Toulon, entre peste et cholera.* Toulon: Les Presses du Midi, 2003.

Cottret, Monique. *Jansénisme et Lumières: Pour un autre XVIIIe siècle.* Paris: Éditions Albin Michel, 1998.

Cousin, Bernard. "Images des saints et imaginaire de la sainteté en Provence (XVIIe–XIXe siècles)." *Provence historique* 195 (1999): 179–89.

Crook, Malcolm. *Toulon in War and Revolution: From the Ancien Régime to the Restoration, 1750–1820.* Manchester: Manchester University Press, 1991.

Cross, Wilbur L. *The History of Henry Fielding.* 3 vols. New Haven: Yale University Press, 1918.

Cubells, Monique. *La Provence des lumières: Les parlementaires d'Aix au XVIIIe siècle.* Paris: Maloine, 1984.

Cubitt, Geoffrey. *The Jesuit Myth: Conspiracy Theory and Politics in Nineteenth-Century France.* Oxford: Clarendon Press, 1993.

Curran, Andrew. "Rethinking Race History: The Role of the Albino in the French Enlightenment Life Sciences." *History and Theory* 48 (2009): 151–79.

Darnton, Robert. "Blogging Now and Then (250 Years Ago)." Lecture at the Annual Meeting for the Society for French Historical Studies, Cambridge, Mass., April 6 2013.

————. "An Early Information Society: News and the Media in Eighteenth-Century Paris." *American Historical Review* 105 (February 2000): 1–35.

————. *The Forbidden Best-Sellers of Pre-Revolutionary France.* New York: W. W. Norton, 1995.

————. *Poetry and the Police: Communication Networks in Eighteenth-Century Paris.* Cambridge, Mass.: Belknap Press of Harvard University Press, 2010.

Davis, Natalie Zemon. *Society and Culture in Early Modern France.* Stanford: Stanford University Press, 1975.

de Boer, Wietse. *The Conquest of the Soul: Confession, Discipline, and Public Order in Counter-Reformation Milan.* Boston: Brill, 2001.

Delayen, Gaston. *La Sainte de M. de Toulon: Le Procès de la Cadière et du père Girard et la grande querelle du parlement de Provence.* Paris: Collection Littéraire Justitita, 1928.

Desan, Suzanne, and Jeffrey Merrick. *Family, Gender, and Law in Early Modern France.* University Park: Penn State University Press, 2009.

DeToledo, J. C., D. Palmerola, and M. R. Lowe. "Sexual Molestation and Psychogenic Seizures: The 1731 Trial of Marie Catherine Cadière versus Father Jean-Baptiste Girard." *Epilepsy Behavior* 2, no. 6 (December 2001): 601–2.

Diefendorf, Barbara B. *From Penitence to Charity: Pious Women and the Catholic Reformation in Paris.* New York: Oxford University Press, 2004.

Domenech, Jacques. "L'Image du père Girard dans l'oeuvre du marquis d'Argens: Du fait divers—l'affaire jugée à Aix-en-Provence—à l'élaboration d'un personage présadien." In *Treize Études sur Aix et la Provence au XVIIIe siècle; Actes du colloque sur Aix et la Provence,* 41–53. Aix-en-Provence: Université de Provence, 1995.

Dompnier, Bernard. "Ordres, diffusion des dévotions et sensibilités religieuses: L'Exemple des capuchins en France (XVIIe–XVIIIe siècles)." *Dimensioni e problemi della ricerca storica: Rivista del Dipartimento di studi storici dell'Università La Sapienza di Roma* 2 (1994): 21–59.

Duccini, Hélène. "Regard sur la littérature pamphlétaire en France au XVIIe siècle." *Revue Historique* 260 (October–December 1978): 313–99.

Duprat, Annie. *Histoire de France par la caricature.* Paris: Larousse, 1999.

Emmanuelli, François-Xavier. "Le Monde du droit, clé de l'histoire politique dans la Provence d'Ancien Régime." *Revue historique de droit français et étranger* 55, no. 3 (1977): 403–11.

Fabre, Gérard. "La Peste on l'absence de Dieu? Images votives et représentations du mal lors de la peste provençale de 1720." *Archives de sciences sociales des religions* 36 (1991): 141–58.

Fabre, Pierre-Antoine, and Catherine Maire, eds. *Les Antijésuites: Discours, figures et lieux de l'antijésuitisme à l'époque moderne.* Rennes: Presses Universitaires de Rennes, 2010.

Fairchilds, Cissie C. *Poverty and Charity in Aix-en-Provence, 1640–1789.* Baltimore: Johns Hopkins University Press, 1976.

Farge, Arlette. *Subversive Words: Public Opinion in Eighteenth-Century France.* Translated by Rosemary Morris. University Park: Penn State University Press, 1995.

Farge, Arlette, and Jacques Revel. *The Vanishing Children of Paris: Rumor and Politics Before the French Revolution.* Translated by Claudia Miéville. Cambridge, Mass.: Harvard University Press, 1991.

Fauve-Chamoux, Antoinette. "To Remarry or Not: Well-Being, Female Property, and Widowhood in Early-Modern France." In *The Transmission of Well-Being: Gendered Marriage Strategies and Inheritance Systems in Europe (17th–20th Centuries),* edited by Margarida Durães, Antoinette Fauve-Chamoux, Llorenç Ferrer, and Jan Kok, 413–46. Bern: Peter Lang, 2009.

Ferber, Sarah. *Demonic Possession and Exorcism in Early Modern France.* London: Routledge, 2004.

Froeschlé-Chopard, Marie-Hélène. "La Bibliothèque des dominicains de Toulon au XVIIIe siècle." *Provence historique* 171 (1993): 16–24.

———. "La Dévotion au Sacré-Coeur: Confréries et livres de piété." *Revue de l'histoire des religions* 217, no. 3 (2000): 531–46.

———. "Les Dévotions des confréries, reflet de l'influence des ordres religieux?" *Dimensioni e problemi della ricerca storica: Rivista des dipartimento di studi storici dal medioevo all'età contemporanea dell'Università la Sapienza* 2 (January 1994): 104–26.

———. "Le Jansénisme dans les bibliothèques des couvents de Toulon au XVIIIe siècle." *Revue d'histoire de l'Église de France* 83, no. 210 (1997): 57–79.

Funck-Brentano, Frantz. *Les Nouvellistes, avec la collaboration de M. Paul d'Estrée*. Paris: Hachette, 1905.

Gaffarel, Paul. *La Peste de 1720 à Marseille et en France [Texte imprimé]: D'après des documents inédits*. Paris: Perrin, 1911.

Garrioch, David. *The Formation of the Parisian Bourgeoisie, 1690–1830*. Cambridge, Mass.: Harvard University Press, 1996.

Gasquet, Marie. *La Vénérable Anne-Madeleine Rémuzat*. Paris: Flammarion, 1935.

Gay, Jean-Pascal. *Morales en conflit: Théologie et polémique au Grand Siècle (1640–1700)*. Paris: Cerf, 2011.

Génestal, Robert. *Les Origines de l'appel comme d'abus*. Paris: Presses Universitaires de France, 1951.

Gibbs, Janet M. "The Perception of Sainthood in Seventeenth-Century France." *Essays in History* 31 (1988): 37–56.

Goldsmith, Elizabeth. *Publishing Women's Life Stories in France, 1647–1720: From Voice to Print*. Aldershot: Ashgate, 2001.

Goldstein, Jan. "The Hysteria Diagnosis and the Politics of Anticlericalism in Late Nineteenth-Century France." *Journal of Modern History* 54 (June 1982): 209–39.

Goodman, Dena. *The Republic of Letters: A Cultural History of the French Enlightenment*. Ithaca: Cornell University Press, 1994.

Goulemot, Jean-Marie. *Forbidden Texts: Erotic Literature and Its Readers in Eighteenth-Century France*. Translated by James Simpson. Philadelphia: University of Pennsylvania Press, 1995.

Gouzi, Christine. *L'Art et le jansénisme au XVIIIe siècle*. Paris: Nolin, 2007.

———. "L'Image du diacre Pâris: Portraits gravés et hagiographie." *Chrétiens et sociétés XVIe–XXIe siècles* 12 (2005): 29–58.

Graham, Lisa Jane. "Crimes of Opinion: Policing the Public in Eighteenth-Century Paris." In *Visions and Revisions of Eighteenth-Century France*, edited by Christine Adams, Jack R. Censer, and Lisa Jane Graham. University Park: Penn State University Press, 1997.

Grasland, Claude, and Annette Keilhauer. "'La Rage de collection': Conditions, enjeux et significations de la formation des grands chansonniers satiriques historiques à Paris au début du XVIIIe siècle (1710–1750)." *Revue d'histoire moderne et contemporaine* 47, no. 3 (2000): 458–86.

Guignard-Vanuxem, Cécile, and Paul-Henry Fleur. *L'Odeur du bûcher: L'Affaire de sorcellerie qui ébranla la Provence en 1731.* Coudray-Macouard: Cheminements, 2001.

Haas, Louis. "Boccaccio, Baptismal Kinship, and Spiritual Incest." *Renaissance and Reformation/ Renaissance et Réforme* 13 (1989): 343–56.

Hanley, Sarah. "Social Sites of Political Practice in France: Lawsuits, Civil Rights, and the Separation of Powers in Domestic and State Government, 1500–1800." *American Historical Review* 102 (February 1997): 27–52.

Hardwick, Julie. *Family Business: Litigation and the Political Economies of Daily Life in Early Modern France.* Oxford: Oxford University Press, 2009.

———. *The Practice of Patriarchy: Gender and the Politics of Household Authority in Early Modern France.* University Park: Penn State University Press, 1998.

Harris, Ruth. "The 'Unconscious' and Catholicism in France." *The Historical Journal* 47 (June 2004): 331–54.

Haydon, Colin. "Anti-Catholicism and Obscene Literature: *The Case of Mrs Mary Catharine Cadière* and Its Context." In *The Church and Literature*, edited by Peter Clarke and Charlotte Methuen, 202–18. Woodbridge, Suffolk, UK: Published for the Ecclesiastical Society by the Boydell Press, 2012.

Hennet, Léon. *Le Régiment de la calotte.* Paris: Librairie des Bibliophiles, 1886.

Hildesheimer, Françoise. *La Terreur et la pitié: L'Ancien Régime à l'épreuve de la peste.* Paris: Publisud, 1990.

Hill, Christopher. *The World Turned Upside Down: Radical Ideas During the English Revolution.* London: Temple Smith, 1973.

Hogue-Poullet, Marie-Françoise de la. "Oratoriens et Jésuites à Toulon." *Provence historique* (1976): 159–68.

Höpfl, Harro. *Jesuit Political Thought: The Society of Jesus and the State, c. 1540–1630.* Cambridge: Cambridge University Press, 2004.

Howarth, William D. "The Theme of Tartuffe in Eighteenth-Century Comedy." *French Studies* 4 (1950): 113–27.

Hsia, R. Po-Chia. *The World of Catholic Renewal, 1540–1770.* Cambridge: Cambridge University Press, 1998.

Hudson, Nicholas. "'From Nation to Race': The Origin of Racial Classification in Eighteenth-Century Thought." *Eighteenth-Century Studies* 29 (Spring 1996): 247–64.

Hurteau, Pierre. "Catholic Moral Discourse on Male Sodomy and Masturbation in the Seventeenth and Eighteenth Centuries." *Journal of the History of Sexuality* 4, no. 1 (1994): 1–26.

Jacobs, Margaret. "The Materialist World of Pornography." In *The Invention of Pornography: Obscenity and the Origins of Modernity, 1500–1800,* edited by Lynn Hunt, 157–202. New York: Zone Books, 1993.

Jonas, Raymond. *France and the Cult of the Sacred Heart: An Epic for Modern Times.* Berkeley: University of California Press, 2000.

Jones, Colin. *The Great Nation: France from Louis XV to Napoleon.* London: Penguin, 2002.

———. "Plague and Its Metaphors in Early Modern France." *Representations* 53 (Winter 1996): 97–127.

Jonsen, Albert R., and Stephen Toulmin. *The Abuse of Casuistry: A History of Moral Reasoning.* Berkeley: University of California Press, 1988.

Kaiser, Thomas E. "Money, Despotism, and Public Opinion in Early Eighteenth-Century France: John Law and the Debate on Royal Credit." *Journal of Modern History* 63 (1991): 1–28.

———. "The Public Sphere." In *The Oxford Handbook of the Ancien Régime,* edited by William Doyle, 409–28. Oxford: Oxford University Press, 2012.

Kettering, Sharon. *Judicial Politics and Urban Revolt in Seventeenth-Century France: The Parlement of Aix, 1629–1659.* Princeton: Princeton University Press, 1978.

Kostroun, Daniella. *Feminism, Absolutism, and Jansenism: Louis XIV and the Port-Royal Nuns.* Cambridge: Cambridge University Press, 2011.

Kreiser, B. Robert. "The Devils of Toulon: Demonic Possession and Religious Politics in Eighteenth-Century Provence." In *Church, State, and Society Under the Bourbon Kings of France,* edited by Richard M. Golden, 173–221. Lawrence, Kans.: Coronado Press, 1982.

———. *Miracles, Convulsions, and Ecclesiastical Politics in Early Eighteenth-Century Paris.* Princeton: Princeton University Press, 1978.

Kulik, Alexander. "How the Devil Got His Hooves and Horns: The Origin of the Motif and the Implied Demonology of *3 Baruch.*" *Numen* 60 (2013): 195–229.

Kuznicki, Jason T. "Sorcery and Publicity: The Cadière-Girard Scandal of 1730–1731." *French History* 21, no. 3 (2007): 289–312.

Lachiver, Marcel. *Les Années de misère: La Famine au temps du Grand Roi.* Paris: Fayard, 1991.

Laforêt, Claude. "L'Hiver 1709, petite ère glaciaire." *Histoire Magazine* 27 (March 1983): 72–77.

Lambert, Gustave. *Histoire de la peste de Toulon en 1721.* Toulon: Aurel, 1861.

Lamotte, Stéphane. "L'Affaire Girard-Cadière: Un Fait divers à l'épreuve du temps, de 1728 à nos jours." 2 vols. Ph.D. diss., Université de Montpellier, III, 2011.

———. "Du retentissement aux discours sur l'affaire du P. Girard et de la Cadière: Mémoires d'un scandale de la mémoire (de 1728 à nos jours)." M.A. thesis, Université de Montpellier, III, 2005.

———. "Le Fait divers dans la ville: Girard et la Cadière à Toulon." In *Villes et représentations urbaines dans l'Europe méditerranéenne (XVIe–XVIIIe siècles): Mélanges offerts à Henri Michel,* edited by Joël Fouilleron and Roland Andréani, 79–95. Montpellier: Université Paul-Valéry, Montpellier, III, 2011.

———. "L'Iconographie dans l'affaire Girard-Cadière." *Liame* 19 (2007): 79–109.

———. "Le P. Girard et la Cadière dans la tourmente des pieces satiriques." *Dix-Huitème Siècle* 39, no. 1 (2007): 431–53.

———. "Voltaire, le jésuite et la pénitente: L'Affaire Girard-Cadière." *Cahiers Voltaire* 7 (October 2008): 23–39.

Lanson, Gustave. *Voltaire.* Translated by Robert A. Wagoner. New York: John Wiley and Sons, 1960.

Lanza, Janine. *From Wives to Widows in Early Modern Paris: Gender, Economy, and Law*. Aldershot: Ashgate, 2007.

Lemaître, N. "Confession privée et confession publique dans les paroisses du XVIe siècle." *Revue d'histoire de l'Église de France* 69, no. 183 (1983): 189–208.

Le Roy Ladurie, Emmanuel. *Carnival in Romans*. Translated by Mary Feeney. New York: George Braziller, 1980.

Lough, John. *France on the Eve of Revolution: British Travellers' Observations, 1763–1788*. Chicago: Dorsey Press, 1987.

Loupès, Philippe. *La Vie religieuse en France au XVIIIe siècle*. Paris: SEDES, 1993.

Maher, Michael, S.J. "Confession and Consolation: The Society of Jesus and Its Promotion of the General Confession." In *Penitence in the Age of Reformations*, edited by Katharine Jackson Lualdi, and Anne T. Thayer, 184–200. Aldershot: Ashgate, 2000.

Maire, Catherine. *De la cause de Dieu à la cause de la nation: Le Jansénisme au XVIIIe siècle*. Paris: Gallimard, 1998.

———. *Les Convulsionnaires de Saint-Médard*. Paris: Gallimard/Julliard, 1985.

———. "Les Jansénistes face aux convulsionnaires (1732–1747)." In *Foi, croyances, superstitions dans l'Europe des Lumières*, edited by Clotilde Prunier, 131–44. Montpellier: Presses universitaires de la Méditerranée, 2002.

———. "La Legende noire des jésuites." *L'Histoire* 84 (December 1978): 38–45.

———. "Quelques mots piégés en histoire religieuse moderne: Jansénisme, jésuitisme, gallicanisme, ultramontanisme." *Annales de l'Est* 1 (2007): 13–43.

———. "Les Querelles jansénistes de la décennie 1730–1740." *Recherches du Diderot et sur l'Encyclopédie* 38 (April 2005): 71–92.

Manning, Ruth. "A Confessor and His Spiritual Child: François de Sales, Jeanne de Chantal, and the Foundation of the Order of the Visitation." *Past and Present*, supp. 1 (2006): 101–17.

Marshman, Michelle. "Exorcism as Empowerment: A New Idiom." *Journal of Religious History* 23 (1999): 265–81.

Martin, Lynn A. *The Jesuit Mind: The Mentality of an Elite in Early Modern France*. Ithaca: Cornell University Press, 1988.

Masse, Daniel. *Toulon pas à pas*. Le Couteau: Horvath, 1989.

Maza, Sarah. *Private Lives and Public Affairs: The Causes Célèbres of Prerevolutionary France*. Berkeley: University of California Press, 1993.

———. "Le Tribunal de la Nation: Les Mémoires judiciaires et l'opinion publique à la fin de l'Ancien Régime." *Annales: Economies, Sociétés, Civilisations* 42 (1987): 73–90.

McManners, John. *The Clerical Establishment and Its Social Ramifications*. Vol. 1 of *Church and Society in Eighteenth-Century France*. Oxford: Clarendon Press, 1998.

———. *The Religion of the People and the Politics of Religion*. Vol. 2 of *Church and Society in Eighteenth-Century France*. Oxford: Clarendon Press, 1998.

Mead, William Edward. *The Grand Tour in the Eighteenth Century*. New York: Benjamin Blom, 1972.

Méchin, Edouard. *L'Enseignement en Provence avant la revolution: Annales du college royal Bourbon d'Aix*. 3 vols. Marseille: Imprimerie de la Ruche, 1891.

Melton, James Van Horn, ed. *Cultures of Communication from Reformation to Enlightenment*. Aldershot: Ashgate, 2002.

———. *The Rise of the Public in Enlightenment Europe*. Cambridge: Cambridge University Press, 2001.

Merrick, Jeffrey W. *The Desacralization of the French Monarchy in the Eighteenth Century*. Baton Rouge: Louisiana State University Press, 1990.

———. "Patriarchalism and Constitutionalism in Eighteenth-Century Parlementary Discourse." *Studies in Eighteenth-Century Culture* 20 (1990): 317–30.

Michel, Marie-José. *Jansénisme et Paris 1640–1730*. Paris: Klincksieck, 2000.

Michelet, Jules. *La Sorcière*. 2 vols. Paris: Librairie Marcel Didier, 1956.

Mollenauer, Lynn Wood. *Strange Revelations: Magic, Poison, and Sacrilege in Louis XIV's France*. University Park: Penn State University Press, 2007.

Monahan, W. Gregory. *Year of Sorrows: The Great Famine of 1709 in Lyon*. Columbus: Ohio State University Press, 1993.

Moody, Joseph N. "French Anticlericalism: Image and Reality." *Catholic Historical Review* 56 (January 1971): 630–48.

Moureau, François. *De Bonne Main: La Communication manuscrite au XVIIIe siècle*. Paris: Universitas, 1993.

———. "Preface." In *Thérèse philosophe ou mémoires pour servir à l'histoire du père Dirrag et de mademoiselle Éradice*, 14–27. Saint-Étienne: Publications de l'Université de Saint-Étienne, 2000.

Mousnier, Roland E. *The Institutions of France Under the Absolute Monarchy, 1598–1789*. Translated by Arthur Goldhammer. 2 vols. Chicago: University of Chicago Press, 1984.

Muchembled, Robert. *Culture populaire et culture des élites dans la France moderne (XVe–XVIIIe siècles)*. Paris: Flammarion, 1978.

Nelson, Eric. *The Jesuits and the Monarch: Catholic Reform and Political Authority in France (1590–1615)*. Aldershot: Ashgate, 2005.

Paoletti, Ciro. "Prince Eugene of Savoi, the Toulon Expedition of 1707, and the English Historians: A Dissenting View." *Journal of Military History* 70 (October 2006): 939–62.

Parès, A-Jacques. *Le Procès Girard-Cadière (Toulon Aix . . . 1731)*. Marseilles: Institut Historique de Provence, 1928.

Le Parlement de Provence, 1501–1790: Actes du colloque d'Aix-en-Provence, 6 et 7 avril 2001. Aix-en-Provence: Publications de l'Université de Provence, 2002.

Paulson, Ronald, and Thomas Lockwood. *Henry Fielding: The Critical Heritage*. London: Routledge and K. Paul, 1969.

Pavone, Sabina. *The Wily Jesuits and the Monita Secreta: The Forged Secret Instructions of the Jesuits; A History* and a Translation of the "Monita." Translated by John P. Murphy. Saint Louis: Institute of Jesuit Sources, 2005.

Pensa, Henri. Sorcellerie et religion: Du désordre dans les esprits et dans les moeurs aux XVIIe et XVIIIe siècles. Paris: Librairie Félix Alcan, 1933.

Perovic, Sanja, ed. Sacred and Secular Agency in Early Modern France: Fragments of Religion. London: Continuum, 2012.

Phillips, Henry. Church and Culture in Seventeenth-Century France. Cambridge: Cambridge University Press, 1997.

Pillorget, René. "Le Complot papiste dans l'imaginaire anglais au XVIIe siècle." Storia della storiografia/Histoire de l'historiographie 14 (1988): 119–35.

Préclin, Edmond. Les Jansénistes du XVIIIe siècle et la constitution civile du clergé: Le développement du ri-chérisme; Sa propagation dans le bas clergé. Paris: Libraire Universitaire J. Gambier, 1929.

Quéniart, Jean. L'Imprimerie et la libraire à Rouen au XVIIIe siècle. Paris: Klincksieck, 1969.

Randall, Catharine. "'Loosening the Stays': Madame Guyon's Quietist Opposition to Absolutism." Mystics Quarterly 26, no. 1 (2000): 8–30.

Rapley, Elizabeth. The Dévotes: Women and Church in Seventeenth-Century France. Montreal: McGill-Queen's University Press, 1990.

Rapley, Robert. A Case of Witchcraft: The Trial of Urbain Grandier. Montreal: McGill-Queen's University Press, 1998.

Ravel, Jeffrey S. "Husband-Killer, Christian Heroine, Victim: The Execution of Madame Tiquet, 1699."

Seventeenth-Century French Studies 32 (2010): 120–36.

———. The Would-Be Commoner: A Tale of Deception, Murder, and Justice in Seventeenth-Century France. Boston: Houghton Mifflin, 2008.

Riddle, John M. Contraception and Abortion from the Ancient World to the Renaissance. Cambridge, Mass.: Harvard University Press, 1992.

Root, Hilton. Peasants and King in Burgundy: Agrarian Foundations of French Absolutism. Berkeley: University of California Press, 1987.

Schwartz, H. Stanley. "Jacques Autreau, a Forgotten Dramatist." PMLA 46, no. 2 (1931): 498–532.

Scott, Virginia. "The Actress and Utopian Theatre Reform in Eighteenth-Century France: Riccoboni, Rousseau, and Restif." Theatre Research International 37 (2002): 18–27.

Sedgwick, Alexander. Jansenism in Seventeenth-Century France: Voices in the Wilderness. Charlottesville: University of Virginia Press, 1975.

———. The Travails of Conscience: The Arnauld Family and the Ancien Regime. Cambridge, Mass.: Harvard University Press, 1998.

Sentuc, Anne. "Mysticisme hystérique ou hystérie mystique?" Historama 22 (1985): 83–85.

Sluhovsky, Moshe. Believe Not Every Spirit: Possession, Mysticism, and Discernment in Early Modern Catholicism. Chicago: University of Chicago Press, 2007.

———. "The Devil in the Convent." American Historical Review 107 (December 2002): 1379–1411.

———. "Discernment of Difference, the Introspective Subject, and the Birth of Modernity." *Journal of Medieval and Early Modern Studies* 36 (Winter 2006): 169–99.

———. "A Divine Apparition or Demonic Possession? Female Agency and Church Authority in Demonic Possession in Sixteenth-Century France." *Sixteenth Century Journal* 27 (Winter 1996): 1039–55.

Smith, Jay M. *Monsters of the Gévaudan: The Making of a Beast.* Cambridge, Mass.: Harvard University Press, 2011.

Storex, Isabelle. *Le Chancelier Henri François d'Aguesseau (1668–1751): Monarchiste et liberal.* Paris: Éditions Publisud, 1996.

Strayer, Brian E. *Suffering Saints: Jansenists and "Convulsionnaires" in France, 1640–1799.* Brighton: Sussex Academic Press, 2008.

Takeda, Junko Thérèse. *Between Crown and Commerce: Marseille and the Early Modern Mediterranean.* Baltimore: Johns Hopkins University Press, 2011.

Timmermans, Linda. *L'Accès des femmes à la culture (1598–1715): Un Débat d'idées de Saint François de Sales à la marquise de Lambert.* Paris: Honoré Champion, 1993.

Trumbach, Randolph. "The Transformation of Sodomy from the Renaissance to the Modern World and Its General Sexual Consequences." *Signs* 37, no. 4 (2012): 832–47.

Tuttle, Leslie. "Celebrating the *Père de Famille*: Pronatalism and Fatherhood in Eighteenth-Century France." *Journal of Family History* 29 (2004): 366–81.

Van Kley, Dale. *The Damiens Affair and the Unravelling of the Ancien Regime, 1750–1770.* Princeton: Princeton University Press, 1984.

———. "Jansenism and the International Suppression of the Jesuits." In *Enlightenment, Reawakening, and Revolution, 1660–1815*, edited by Stewart J. Brown and Timothy Tackett. Cambridge: Cambridge University Press, 2006.

———. *The Jansenists and the Expulsion of the Jesuits from France, 1757–1765.* New Haven: Yale University Press, 1975.

———. *The Religious Origins of the French Revolution: From Calvin to the Civil Constitution, 1560–1791.* New Haven: Yale University Press, 1996.

———. "The Religious Origins of the French Revolution, 1590–1791." In *From Deficit to Deluge: The Origins of the French Revolution*, edited by Thomas E. Kaiser and Dale K. Van Kley, 104–38. Stanford: Stanford University Press, 2011.

Vartanian, Aram. "Eroticism and Politics in *Lettres persanes*." *Romanic Review* 60 (1969): 23–33.

Vergé-Franceschi, Michel. *Toulon: Port Royal, 1481–1789.* Paris: Tallendier, 2002.

Vovelle, Michel. "La Découverte de la Provence, ou Les Primitifs de l'ethnographie provençale (1750–1850)." *Francia* 7 (1979): 219–49.

———. *Piété baroque et déchristianisation en Provence au XVIIIe siècle: Les Attitudes devant la mort d'après les clauses des testaments.* Paris: Plon, 1973.

Wachenheim, Pierre. "Art et politique, langage pictural et sédition dans l'estampe sous le règne de Louis XV."

2 vols. Diss., Université de Paris I (Panthéon-Sorbonne), 2004.

———. "Bernard Picart graveur des jansénistes: Propositions pour un corpus séditieux." In *Interkulturelle Kommunikation in der europäischen Druckgraphik im 18. und 19. Jahrhundert/The European Print and Cultural Transfer in the 18th and 19th Centuries/Gravure et communication interculturelle en Europe aux 18e et 19e siècles*, edited by Philippe Kaenel and Rolf Reichardt, 333–56. Hildesheim: Georg Olms Verlag, 2007.

———. "Le 'péril de séduction': Les Jésuites face aux gravures jansénistes au XVIIIe siècle." *Nouvelles de l'estampe* 201 (July–September 2005): 24–44.

Waddington, Raymond B. *Aretino's Satyr: Sexuality, Satire, and Self-Projection in Sixteenth-Century Literature and Art*. Toronto: University of Toronto Press, 2004.

Wadsworth, Philip. "The Art of Allegory in La Fontaine's Fables." *French Review* 45 (May 1972): 1125–35.

Walker, Anita M., and Edmund H. Dickerman. "A Notorious Woman: Possession, Witchcraft, and Sexuality in Seventeenth-Century Provence." *Historical Reflections/ Réflexions Historiques* 27, no. 1 (2001): 1–26.

Walton, Charles. *Policing Public Opinion in the French Revolution: The Culture of Calumny and the Problem of Free Speech*. Oxford: Oxford University Press, 2009.

Wells, Mitchell P. "Some Notes on the Early Eighteenth-Century Pantomime." *Studies in Philology* 32, no. 4 (1935): 598–607.

Wolff, Philippe. "Jefferson on Provence and Languedoc." *Proceedings of the Annual Meeting of the Western Society for French History* 3 (1975): 191–205.

Wright, Wendy M. "Inside My Body Is the Body of God: Margaret Mary Alacoque and the Tradition of Embodied Mysticism." In *The Mystical Gesture: Essays on Medieval and Early Modern Spiritual Culture in Honor of Mary E. Giles*, edited by Robert Boenig, 185–92. Aldershot: Ashgate, 2000.

Index